# THE NEW CAMBRIDGE HISTORY
# OF INDIA

*Bengal: The British Bridgehead*

# THE NEW CAMBRIDGE HISTORY OF INDIA

*General editor* GORDON JOHNSON

Director, Centre of South Asian Studies, University of
Cambridge, and Fellow of Selwyn College

*Associate editors* C. A. BAYLY

Smuts Reader in Commonwealth Studies, University of
Cambridge, and Fellow of St Catharine's College

*and* JOHN F. RICHARDS

Professor of History, Duke University

Although the original *Cambridge History of India*, published between 1922 and 1937, did much to formulate a chronology for Indian history and describe the administrative structures of government in India, it has inevitably been overtaken by the mass of new research published over the last fifty years.

Designed to take full account of recent scholarship and changing conceptions of South Asia's historical development, *The New Cambridge History of India* will be published as a series of short, self-contained volumes, each dealing with a separate theme and written by a single person. Within an overall four-part structure, thirty complementary volumes in uniform format will be published during the next five years. As before, each will conclude with a substantial bibliographical essay designed to lead non-specialists further into the literature.

The four parts planned are as follows:

I The Mughals and their Contemporaries.

II Indian States and the Transition to Colonialism.

III The Indian Empire and the Beginnings of Modern Society.

IV The Evolution of Contemporary South Asia.

A list of individual titles in preparation will be found at the end of the volume.

# THE NEW CAMBRIDGE HISTORY OF INDIA

## II · 2

*Bengal: The British Bridgehead*
Eastern India 1740–1828

P. J. MARSHALL

KING'S COLLEGE, LONDON

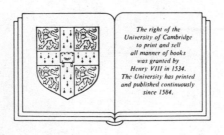

The right of the
University of Cambridge
to print and sell
all manner of books
was granted by
Henry VIII in 1534.
The University has printed
and published continuously
since 1584.

CAMBRIDGE UNIVERSITY PRESS

CAMBRIDGE

NEW YORK   PORT CHESTER

MELBOURNE   SYDNEY

Published by the Press Syndicate of the University of Cambridge
The Pitt Building, Trumpington Street, Cambridge CB2 1RP
40 West 20th Street, New York, NY 10011, USA
10 Stamford Road, Oakleigh, Melbourne 3166, Australia

First published 1987
Reprinted 1990

Printed in Great Britain by the University Press, Cambridge

*British Library cataloguing in publication data*
Marshall, P.J.
Bengal: the British bridgehead:
Eastern India 1740–1828.–
(The New Cambridge History of India)
1. I(ndia, Northeaster–History
I. Title
945'.1029    DS483

*Library of Congress cataloguing in publication data*
Marshall, P.J. (Peter James)
Bengal: the British bridgehead:
(The New Cambridge History of India)
1. Bengal (India)—History.
2. India—History 18th century.
3. India—History 19th century.
I. Title.  II. Series.
DS485.B48M36    1986    954'.14029    86-9719

ISBN 0 521 25330 6

*Frontispiece:* The East India Company's Resident
at the Court of the Nawabs of Bengal c. 1785.

BO

# CONTENTS

# GENERAL EDITOR'S PREFACE

*The New Cambridge History of India* covers the period from the beginning of the sixteenth century. In some respects it marks a radical change in the style of Cambridge Histories, but in others the editors feel that they are working firmly within an established academic tradition.

During the summer of 1896, F.W. Maitland and Lord Acton between them evolved the idea for a comprehensive modern history. By the end of the year the Syndics of the University Press had committed themselves to the *Cambridge Modern History*, and Lord Acton had been put in charge of it. It was hoped that publication would begin in 1899 and be completed by 1904, but the first volume in fact came out in 1902 and the last in 1910, with additional volumes of tables and maps in 1911 and 1912.

The *History* was a great success, and it was followed by a whole series of distinctive Cambridge Histories covering English Literature, the Ancient World, India, British Foreign Policy, Economic History, Medieval History, the British Empire, Africa, China and Latin America; and even now other new series are being prepared. Indeed, the various Histories have given the Press notable strength in the publication of general reference books in the arts and social sciences.

What has made the Cambridge Histories so distinctive is that they have never been simply dictionaries or encyclopedias. The Histories have, in H.A.L. Fisher's words, always been 'written by an army of specialists concentrating the latest results of special study'. Yet as Acton agreed with the Syndics in 1896, they have not been mere compilations of existing material but original works. Undoubtedly many of the Histories are uneven in quality, some have become out of date very rapidly, but their virtue has been that they have consistently done more than simply record an existing state of knowledge: they have tended to focus interest on research and they have provided a massive stimulus to further work. This has made their publication doubly worthwhile and has distinguished them intellectually from other sorts of reference book. The Editors of the *New Cambridge History of India* have acknowledged this in their work.

The original *Cambridge History of India* was published between 1922 and 1937. It was planned in six volumes, but of these, Volume 2 dealing with the period between the first century A.D. and the Muslim invasion of India never appeared. Some of the material is still of value, but in many respects it is now out of date. The last fifty years have seen a great deal of new research on India, and a striking feature of recent work has been to cast doubt on the validity of the quite arbitrary chronological and categorical way in which Indian history has been conventionally divided.

The Editors decided that it would not be academically desirable to prepare a new *History of India* using the traditional format. The selective nature of research on Indian history over the past half-century would doom such a project from the start and the whole of Indian history could not be covered in an even or comprehensive manner. They concluded that the best scheme would be to have a History divided into four overlapping chronological volumes, each containing about eight short books on individual themes or subjects. Although in extent the work will therefore be equivalent to a dozen massive tomes of the traditional sort, in form the *New Cambridge History of India* will appear as a shelf full of separate but complementary parts. Accordingly, the main divisions are between I *The Mughals and their Contemporaries*, II *Indian States and the Transition to Colonialism*, III *The Indian Empire and the Beginnings of Modern Society*, and IV *The Evolution of Contemporary South Asia*.

Just as the books within these volumes are complementary so too do they intersect with each other, both thematically and chronologically. As the books appear they are intended to give a view of the subject as it now stands and to act as a stimulus to further research. We do not expect the *New Cambridge History of India* to be the last word on the subject but an essential voice in the continuing discourse about it.

# PREFACE

British territorial empire in South Asia began in Bengal, Bihar and Orissa, the area chosen for this volume of the *New Cambridge History of India*. Over much of the area the British were in control by 1765, but to show something of the circumstances in which they gained power and of the inheritance which so powerfully shaped the early years of their rule, it seemed appropriate to include the reign of the last effective ruler of eastern India under the aegis of the Mughal empire. The starting point for this book is therefore 1740. The choice of 1828 as a closing date is a more or less arbitrary one. By the 1820s the new regime was firmly established in eastern India (except in the newly conquered Assam, which is excluded from this volume) and many of its enduring characteristics were becoming apparent. Certain developments towards the end of the decade – the founding of the Brahmo Samaj, the arrival of Lord William Bentinck, the failure of the great Agency Houses – do, however, suggest that within an established framework British–Indian relations were entering a new phase. For some of these developments, 1828 has some significance for marking off the old from the new.

Entrusting this volume to a British historian with serious deficiencies in his knowledge of the sub-continent inevitably means that its emphasis will be on the new colonial regime. I am, however, very conscious of the immense debt which I owe to the vigorous tradition of historical scholarship which flourishes in eastern India, especially in a now-divided Bengal. This has enabled me to mask some of my shortcomings by presenting the findings of others to those who have had neither the time nor the opportunity to seek them for themselves.

Other debts are more immediate. Dr Gordon Johnson and Dr C. A. Bayly have been indulgent and trusting editors. Dr Bayly's suggestions have been especially helpful. My colleague at King's College, London, Dr Friedhelm Hardy, has patiently answered questions. The British Academy gave me a grant to go to West Bengal and to

Bangladesh in 1982. I received much help on that trip from friends in the universities of Dhaka and Calcutta.

The Frontispiece to the book is a gouache by an Indian artist, presumed to be after an original painted 1785–8 by George Farington. The central figures are the Resident, Sir John D'Oyly, and the Nawab, Mubarak-ud-Daula. For permission to reproduce it, I am grateful to the India Office Library and Records, and the British Library Board.

P.J. MARSHALL

# NOTE

Generally accepted modern spellings of place names are used throughout, except in quotations.

*Abbreviations used:*

Add. MS   Additional Manuscript, British Library, London
IOL       India Office Library (British Library), London
IOR      India Office Records (British Library), London
*PP*       *Parliamentary Papers* (House of Commons), London

Unless otherwise indicated, the place of publication of all works cited is London.

Map 1 Eastern India, 1740–1828: places mentioned in the text

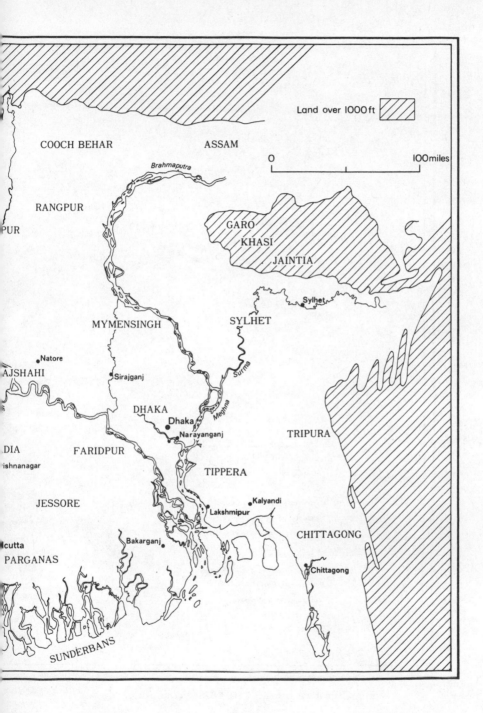

COOCH BEHAR        ASSAM

Land over 1000 ft

RANGPUR

PUR

Brahmaputra

0           100 miles

GARO

KHASI

JAINTIA

MYMENSINGH        Sylhet

SYLHET

Natore

AJSHAHI        Sirajganj

Surma

DHAKA

Dhaka      Meghna

Narayanganj

DIA        FARIDPUR        TRIPURA

ishnanagar

TIPPERA

JESSORE        Kalyandi

Lakshmipur

cutta        Bakarganj        CHITTAGONG

PARGANAS

Chittagong

SUNDERBANS

xiii

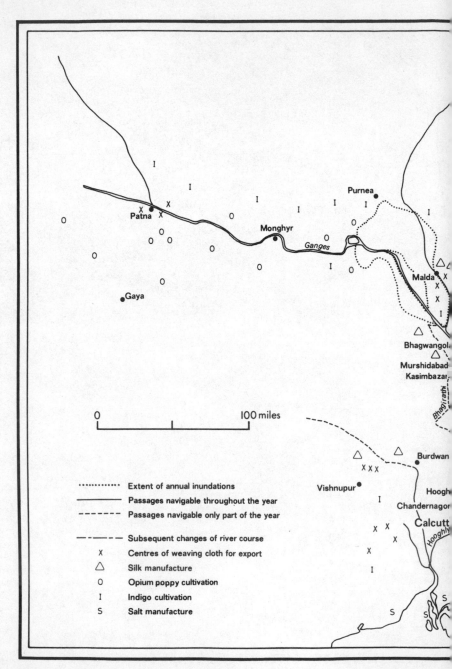

Map 2 Eastern India, 1740–1828: economic

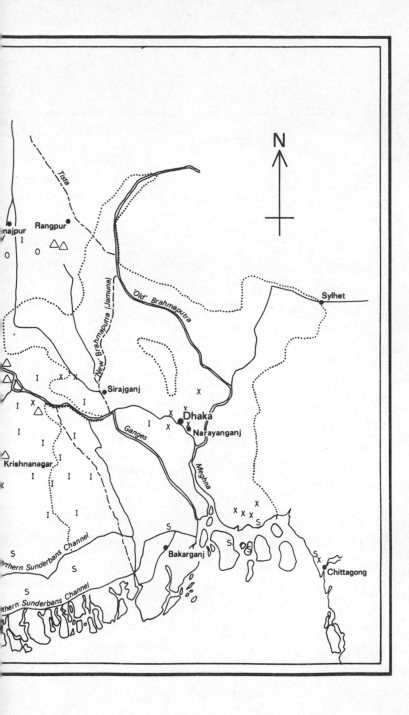

# CHAPTER 1

# THE SETTING FOR EMPIRE

Early in the eighteenth century the very diverse areas which now make up three states of contemporary India, West Bengal, Bihar and Orissa, together with present-day Bangladesh, were loosely welded together under a single Governor to form the eastern wing of the Mughal empire. In 1765 authority over the Mughal provinces of Bengal, Bihar and Orissa was formally transferred to the East India Company and by the 1820s these provinces had become the eastern wing of a vast new British empire in India. The chronological span of this volume of the *New Cambridge History of India* has thus been chosen to cover the replacement of Mughal rule by the first British regime in India.

Until fairly recently, such a choice of dates would require little explanation or defence. Contemporary Englishmen sometimes described the changes that took place in the middle of the eighteenth century in Bengal as a 'revolution', and later generations of historians tended to agree with them. The change from Mughal to British rule has commonly been seen as the beginning of a 'modern' era, not only for the peoples of eastern India but for the whole sub-continent. For very good reasons, what happened in Bengal during the early years of British rule has become one of the classic case studies for those concerned with assessing the impact of foreign rule on conquered societies.

In recent years, however, the revolutionary consequences of the establishment of colonial rule have been called into question for many different parts of the world. The ability of Europeans to transform non-European societies, for better or for worse, over relatively short periods of time seems dubious. Assumptions that non-European societies left to themselves generally proved inert or that they changed significantly only under outside impulses are generally discredited. Colonial rule, with its vast detritus of written records easily accessible to historians, and the growth of international trade which usually accompanied it, may look like the most formidable agents of change, but in many cases they can be shown to be only one part of a complex pattern of developments, other processes working at quite different speeds but often ultimately with much greater effect. A chronology which is determined by the rise and firm establishment of a colonial regime may thus prove to be a somewhat misleading one.

Such an approach to the modern history of eastern India has much to commend it. Whatever the ultimate significance of their rule, the British were by no means the only bringers of change. Even the configuration of the land was in flux in some areas. It has been said that 'Both geography and history were remade in Bengal as the eighteenth century drew to a close, and . . . not less than six new rivers appeared on the scene, moulding Bengal's economic history'.[1] The region's greatest river, the Ganges, could change its course suddenly, washing away settlements as it ate into its banks with a noise that 'might be compared to the distant rumbling of artillery, or thunder', but in return creating highly fertile new islands of silt.[2] A recent article has put forward a powerful case for arguing that the economy of India in general and especially of regions like Bengal was not an unchanging landscape either, but was undergoing 'important structural changes in the course of the seventeenth and eighteenth centuries', well before colonial rule.[3] A similar case could no doubt be established for the mental landscape of the peoples of eastern India. For some, mostly a limited elite in Calcutta, close contact with Europeans brought about a profound change after the establishment of British rule; but it does not necessarily follow that language, culture or beliefs were in general resistant to change. Long-term patterns of evolution, which have produced the modern cultural identities of the peoples of the region, clearly go far beyond the colonial period.

In the history of eastern India the fall of the Mughals and the coming of the British are only episodes in a much longer play whose principal actors inevitably remain anonymous: pioneers who settled new lands, merchants who organised handcrafts, Vaishnavite teachers, guardians of Muslim shrines and even the rivers and the *Anopheles* mosquito. Nevertheless, the easily identified actors, the last Nawabs and the British merchants and administrators had roles which are extremely important. The Nawabs, and to a much greater extent the British, had

[1] Radhakamal Mukerjee, *The Changing Face of Bengal* (Calcutta, 1938), p. 7.
[2] R.H. Colebrooke, 'On the Course of the Ganges through Bengal', *Asiatick Researches*, VII (1801), 15–16.
[3] F. Perlin, 'Proto-industrialization and Pre-colonial South Asia', *Past and Present*, XCVIII (1983), 56.

at their disposal instruments with a high potential for altering the societies over which they ruled. They operated a system of taxation which tried to extract a large proportion of the resources of the mass of the population and whose workings had a crucial effect on the distribution of local power throughout the provinces. Through British dominance eastern India's role in international trade was greatly developed, with important consequences for merchants, cultivators and artisans.

Later chapters of this book try to chart the effect of Mughal and British rule on the peoples of eastern India. At every point, however, the work of the agents of both the old and the new imperial regime was likely to be guided, modified or even stultified by the human and physical environment within which they had to operate. This chapter attempts to indicate something of that environment and of its own patterns of change, which evolved over a much longer period than the seventy-five years with which this volume is concerned.

An area whose western extremity is a segment of the Gangetic plain that extends across northern India, and whose eastern extremity is in the rain-forested hills along the Burmese border, contains many different physical and human environments. Most of Bengal receives a high level of rainfall and much of it is irrigated by the flooding of its great rivers. So it is primarily a land of rice cultivation. But there were marked differences in the eighteenth century between old areas of often highly concentrated settlement, predominantly in western and central Bengal, and those parts of the north and the east of the province which had been colonised relatively recently. Ecologically most of Bihar is very much part of the north Indian plain and its economic and cultural links were to the westward rather than with deltaic Bengal. It is a drier land than Bengal and its agricultural patterns were more varied, rice being supplemented by other food grains. It too had areas of old concentrated settlement, mostly to the south of the Ganges, and areas of expanding new settlements, mostly to the north. Orissa consisted of deltaic rice plains, fringed, as the whole area was, by uplands in which so-called 'tribal' peoples extracted a living from the forests or by cultivating clearings.

During the period covered by this volume a shift in the balance between western and eastern Bengal, which was to become very apparent by the mid nineteenth century, seems to have been well under way. Settlement was expanding in the east and agricultural output was increasing. In parts of the west growth seems to have stopped and decline may even have set in. These changes were a consequence of shifts in the river system. Over a long period the western half of the delta that constitutes much of Bengal was becoming 'moribund', while the eastern half remained 'active'. This difference was caused by the fact that the main volume of the water brought down by the Ganges no longer found its way to the sea down the western arms of the delta, which tended to silt up, but carved out channels ever further to the east, which carried most of the water. This process gathered speed in the later eighteenth century, when the chief sufferer was beginning to be the Hooghly, the river in western Bengal which had apparently become the main channel for the Ganges in the previous century and on which the region's major ports, Calcutta, Chandernagore and Hooghly itself, had been established. The advantages which the Hooghly ports had once enjoyed of easy access both to the sea and to the main course of the Ganges and therefore to upper India, were diminishing in the second half of the eighteenth century. Neither the Bhagirathi nor the Jalangi, the rivers which link the Hooghly to the Ganges, could be relied on to provide sufficient depth of water to enable river boats to use them all the year round. In 1824 Bishop Heber reflected with astonishment that only fifty years before a great warship had been able to get up to Chandernagore, a little above Calcutta; that this was now inconceivable was striking 'proof of the alterations which have taken place in this branch of the Ganges'.[4]

The declining volume of water in its rivers was to have other malign effects on western Bengal. It was 'a well known fact' by 1833 that lands flooded every rainy season by the Hooghly 'preserve their original fertility' because of the silt spread on them, and can be cropped every year. The 'higher soils', however, which were not flooded, are 'gradually and rapidly impoverishing' and certain crops could be raised on them only 'at intervals of three or four years'.[5] The proportion of land in western Bengal which is regularly flooded has diminished in modern times, and it seems likely that the productivity of agriculture was beginning to be adversely affected in the period covered by this volume. Another consequence of the declining flows through the

    [4] R. Heber, *Narrative of a Journey through the Upper Provinces of India* (2 vols., 1849 edn), I, 63.
    [5] H. Piddington, 'On the Fertilising Principle of the Inundations of the Hugli', *Asiatic Researches*, XVIII (1833), 224–5.

western arms of the Ganges delta also seems to have been making itself felt. As the rivers became more stagnant, malaria-bearing mosquitoes bred more freely. The district of Murshidabad, taking its name from the Nawab's capital on the Bhagirathi river, was once regarded as healthy, but 'a sad reverse' took place early in the nineteenth century; 'almost everywhere there is in that part of the country a severe autumnal epidemic' of 'fever'.[6] However, although the area which they regularly irrigated was declining, the rivers of western Bengal were still capable of sudden flooding, breaking the thousand miles of embankments which the British were thought to have inherited,[7] and inundating vast areas, as in 1801, with catastrophic effects on cultivation and heavy loss of life.[8]

Bengal's agriculture was dominated by rice growing. A good water supply was crucial for the success and quality of the crop. In low-lying areas assured of abundant flood water the main crop in western Bengal, as elsewhere, was the high yielding *aman* rice which was harvested in the winter to produce fine quality rice. Poorer cultivator grew *aman* rice not for their own consumption but for sale. In higher areas, where prolonged immersion could not be guaranteed, the autumn *aus* rice was the staple. This produced a lower yield of poorer quality grain, which was eaten by 'the lower classes of the inhabitants'. Dry areas, like the northern part of the district of Nadia, were largely dependent on *aus* rice.[9] In favourable conditions the *aus* autumn harvest could often be followed by another crop of winter rice transplanted as seedlings. Good quality land used for *aus* rice would be clear for the winter sowings of crops like cotton and oil seeds, especially mustard, whose oil was used in all cooking, for lighting and for anointing the body. Pulses, such as lentils and peas, an almost universal item of diet, and the coarse grains like millet, the food of the poor and of animals, were either grown interspersed with rice or as another winter-sown crop. Sugar cane took up ground for the best part of the year. Mulberry cuttings could be expected to produce leaves for feeding to silk worms for up to seven years. Those who cultivated mulberry usually reared silk worms as well. Sugar cane and mulberry, like cotton

[6] F. Buchanan, cited in B.B. Chaudhuri, 'Agricultural Growth in Bengal and Bihar, 1770–1860', *Bengal Past and Present*, XCV (1976), 328.

[7] J. Rennell, 'An Account of the Ganges and Burrampooter Rivers', *Memoir of a Map of Hindoostan* (3rd edn, 1793), p. 350.

[8] There is much historical material on floods in H.L. Harrison, *The Bengal Embankment Manual* (Calcutta, 1875).

[9] IOR, Bengal Board of Revenue: Grain, 3 Nov. 1794, Range 89, vol. 27.

and the higher quality pulses and oil seeds, needed to be grown on land above the flood level and required laborious cultivation with much watering and manuring; rice was not usually manured at all. A wide variety of vegetables were grown in small garden plots. Ploughing by bullocks was the basic method of cultivation for every crop. The number of bullocks, together with cows and buffaloes kept for their milk, seemed prodigious to the Europeans; one was prepared to guess that there might be 200 million head of cattle in Bengal in the 1790s. [10] The quality of the stock was, however, thought by English observers to be very poor.

Rural society in western Bengal, and indeed in the whole area covered by this volume, can be analysed from two points of view: who was engaged in cultivating the land and who appropriated the portion of the produce of the land that the cultivator was obliged to surrender in the name of the state's taxation. The vast majority of the population cultivated the land and paid tax but most of the wealth and power in rural society came not from direct cultivation but from rights to participate in the taxation system (the 'revenue', as the British called it). These rights gave their holders both a proportion of what was collected and some degree of authority over the cultivators. Holders of revenue rights constituted a very complex hierarchy. At one extreme were great *zamindar*s, who were responsible for levying taxation from hundreds of thousands of cultivators; at the other extreme were village *malik*s in Bihar, who were lords of a small part of a village. The nature of revenue and of the right to collect it are examined in relation to late Mughal and early British rule in Chapters 2 and 4. This chapter is concerned with agriculture and with the people who cultivated the land and made the payments on which the revenue-collecting hierarchy and the empires of the Mughals and the British ultimately depended.

By virtually any definition, those who cultivated the land in eastern India in this period were peasants. The family was the basic unit of production. There is, however, much evidence to suggest that there were many gradations within peasant society from deep poverty to relative affluence. Almost all such evidence comes from the British period and much of it is derived from certain districts of northern Bengal, which may not have been typical. Nevertheless, there are indications which

[10] [H.T. Colebrooke and A. Lambert], *Remarks on the Present State of the Husbandry and Commerce of Bengal* (Calcutta, 1795), p. 141.

suggest that these divisions between richer and poorer peasants were fairly general throughout Bengal, if less marked in the east, and that they were of long standing, predating British conquest.

At the lowest level were men without any land at all, who made their living by working on the land of others for wages. Such men certainly existed in some numbers: in a district in northern Bengal, called Dinajpur, 18 per cent of the rural population were classed as *krishan*s, or labourers, early in the nineteenth century.[11] But the great majority of the rural population seem to have been cultivators in some degree; the totally landless were the exception. Even in Dinajpur, 'the inhabitants in general' were described as 'settled cultivators and householders'.[12] The main division in rural society was not between the landed and the landless, but between those who were able to cultivate enough land for a living and those who were not.

That very many of the rural population of Bengal were not able to cultivate enough land to support themselves does not seem to have been due either to any absolute shortage of land or to an excessive pressure of numbers on the land. In 1753 Robert Orme wrote that every part of Bengal, 'if duly cultivated, would produce exceedingly more than its occasions', but he thought that 'no part of the province is cultivated in proportion to the wants of the inhabitants who reside on it'.[13] Francis Buchanan, by far the most persistent and perceptive of early inquirers, reported some sixty years later that, even in heavily populated districts with many very small holdings, 'a very large portion of excellent land is unoccupied'.[14] What seems to have determined the size of a man's holding was not the availability of land but his ability to command the wherewithal to clear and cultivate it, that is the extent of what Europeans called his 'stock'. Bullocks for ploughing were the main item of stock. A pair of oxen could normally keep between three and six acres under cultivation.[15] A poor cultivator, able to command only one or two pairs of bullocks, would thus be most unlikely to be able to grow enough to sustain his family and pay

[11] S. Taniguchi, 'The Structure of Agrarian Society in Northern Bengal', Unpublished Ph.D. thesis, Calcutta University, 1977, p. 249.

[12] Cited in Taniguchi, 'Agrarian Society', pp. 220–1.

[13] R. Orme, *Historical Fragments of the Mogul Empire* (1805), pp. 404–5.

[14] On Rangpur, in M. Martin, *History, Antiquities, Topography and Statistics of Eastern India* (3 vols., 1838), III, 482.

[15] See estimates by Buchanan, ibid., by G. Harris, Evidence, 21 May 1830, *PP*, 1830, VI, 307; and by W. Ward, *Account of the Writings, Religion and Manners of the Hindoos* (4 vols., Serampore, 1811), IV, 81.

his taxes. He and his family would almost certainly have to supplement their income by working for wages. He might be able to work for a share of the crop on the land of others (sharecropping seems to have been very widely practised) or to work for wages in cash or kind, especially at harvest time. His wife might earn wages from spinning cotton or husking rice. In addition the poorer cultivator would almost certainly have to borrow. Borrowing could take the form of cash advances, for the purpose of purchasing oxen or paying tax demands, or, very commonly, of receiving grain either for seed corn or for feeding one's family between harvests. For making repayments the poorer cultivator had no assets except his future labour or his future crops. Both might be mortgaged almost permanently.[16] It was commonly said that for each measure of grain borrowed at sowing or before the harvest, a measure-and-a-half would have to be paid back after the harvest. In Nadia repayment of loans of seed corn was said to be 'generally double the amount of the advance'.[17] A well-documented case near Calcutta in 1770 showed that those who advanced money to cultivators to be repaid at harvest expected a return of 100 to 150 per cent.[18] Once cultivators had got into debt they were likely to become 'the mere servants of the corn-merchants', surrendering their crop to them every harvest time in return for enough to keep their families alive and to pay their taxes.[19]

By the beginning of the nineteenth century it was thought that 'the great body of the Bengal farmers' had been reduced to the state of being 'servants' of grain dealers. More precise estimates, based on surveys of parts of northern Bengal by Buchanan and others, suggest that 'more than half of the peasantry' were 'lacking in sufficient agricultural stocks to cultivate the minimum size of agricultural holding'. The earliest survey, one for a village in Rangpur in 1770, showed 70 per cent to be below self-sufficiency.[20]

The 'middling farmer', at least in northern Bengal, was said to be one who could keep three, four or five ploughs at work, presumably with his own family and some hired labour.[21] 'Rich and respectable

---

[16] Buchanan described how a cultivator who borrowed Rs. 6 in Rangpur would be required to work for a year to pay off the principal and to do additional months for the interest (Survey of 'Ronggopur', IOL, MS Eur.D.75, book IV, p. 112).

[17] IOR, Bengal Board of Revenue: Grain, 3 Nov. 1794, Range 89, vol. 27.

[18] Calcutta High Court Records, Mayor's Court, Young v. Gopaul Sircar.

[19] Ward, Account of the Hindoos, IV, 80.

[20] Taniguchi, 'Agrarian Society', pp. 241–50.

[21] Buchanan in Martin, Eastern India, II, 904.

husbandmen' in the twenty-four Parganas near Calcutta 'employ from four to ten servants or labourers from time to time as necessary, and cultivate the land in the proper season'.[22] The poor were largely limited to growing rice or coarse grains, since they could not afford the outlay on potentially profitable crops. Only the more affluent could afford to plant cash crops. In Burdwan in the west, those who grew sugar cane 'being rich, can generally afford to bestow proper labour and manure on their cane grounds, so as to return them constantly an abundant crop'.[23] Above the 'respectable' farmers were the positively rich who might cultivate a hundred acres or more. The interests of such men were likely to extend far beyond the profits which they derived from their own farming to include profits from lending out stock and money to many poorer cultivators who virtually worked for them, either as formal sharecroppers or by handing over the greater part of their harvest as repayment for loans. Many large farmers were also money lenders and dealers in grain. Their power was often bolstered by holding offices such as that of *mandal*, or headman of the village, and they often crossed the line between cultivators of the land and those who profited from the collection of the revenue, becoming under-collectors for their villages.

At least in the west and the north then, Bengal society seems to have been divided between a broad base consisting of some landless labourers and a very large number of poor cultivators, most of whom were probably also engaged in sharecropping or wage labour, and a narrower apex of clearly self-sufficient or prosperous peasants. The extent to which caste reinforced economic divisions in Bengal at this period is uncertain. 'Dominant' cultivating castes have been identified for parts of western Bengal as being the Kaivartas, the Sadgops or the Aguris.[24] Low caste Hindus or 'tribal' peoples from the western hills occupied the lowest rungs of the hierarchy of the cultivators or the landless in the same areas.[25]

The rural population of western Bengal in this period also included many artisans: men who processed sugar cane or oil seeds, potters, smiths and metal workers, spinners of cotton yarn and silk winders,

[22] Radha Kanta Deva, 'An Account of the Agriculture of the 24 Parganas', *Transactions of the Agricultural and Horticultural Society of India*, I (1829), 50.
[23] [J. Prinsep], *Bengal Sugar* (1794), p. 82.
[24] R. Ray, *Change in Bengal Agrarian Society, c. 1760–1850* (New Delhi, 1979), pp. 52–3.
[25] R.K. Gupta, *Economic Life of a Bengal District: Birbhum 1770–1856* (Burdwan, 1984), pp. 282–4, 288–90.

weavers and those engaged in other crafts associated with making cloth. For instance, in one large village near Calcutta, a survey of the inhabitants according to caste for 1788–9 produced the following figures for artisan castes and their families: out of 3,018 Hindu men, women and children, there were 19 coppersmiths, 66 carpenters, 40 silversmiths, 41 oilmen and 180 weavers.[26] A large proportion of what many rural artisans made must have been intended for strictly local consumption. For instance, smiths are described as being scattered throughout the villages of Bengal in ones or twos, making the agricultural implements or fish hooks required by their neighbours.[27] The extent to which artisans in Bengal were tied to the service of cultivators in return for rewards in kind or allocations of land, a system which has come to be known as *jajmani*, is unclear. Some village craftsmen were said to give 'without reward a portion of their labour for the benefit of the public or the service of their superiors'.[28]

In parts of the countryside of western Bengal, however, artisans were concentrated in numbers far beyond any strictly local needs. They were working for distant markets, either in Bengal itself, or in other parts of India, or overseas. They dealt not with local patrons but with the representatives of merchants from the towns or with professional brokers. Iron ore deposits, for instance, in the western district of Birbhum had led to a concentration there of mining operations and small forges.[29] The production of salt took place on a very large scale on the coastal belt from the mouth of the Hooghly to the border of Orissa and also in the Sundarbans area. During the salt-making season several thousand boilers were employed either by merchants or by local *zamindar*s in an elaborate process of evaporating sea water. The manufacture of silk was concentrated in certain areas where mulberries were grown. Silk worms of the highest quality were thought to be available around Kasimbazar, close to Murshidabad, and they were also reared in other parts of western Bengal. The cultivators of mulberry either reeled silk from their own cocoons or sold the cocoons to be reeled by professional silk winders called *nacaud*s, who worked in their own houses but increasingly by the end of the period in large workshops.

[26] 'Enumeration of the Inhabitants of the Village of Seebpore', IOL, MS Eur.F.95, fo. 64.   [27] Ward, *Account of the Hindoos*, IV, 107–8.
[28] [Colebrooke and Lambert], *Remarks on Bengal*, pp. 46–7.
[29] R.K. Gupta, 'Iron Manufacturing Industry of Birbhum', *Journal of Indian History*, LVIII (1980), 93–108.

Weaving of relatively coarse cheap cloth for local needs was carried on in most Bengal villages, but colonies of weavers were also grouped in certain areas where they specialised in making particular types of high quality cloth for export, either overland to northern India or by sea from the Hooghly ports. In western Bengal the cloth for export was usually woven in villages close to the Hooghly or to the Ganges, the obvious route to northern India. The weavers needed a supply of cotton, and this was partly grown locally and partly imported by sea from western India or overland from the Deccan. Raw cotton was spun by an army of women working in their homes. Once the cloth had been woven, it required 'finishing' by other craftsmen, such as bleachers, dyers and embroiderers. Although certain areas specialised in particular types of cloth, concentration of production into large units, like the silk reeling workshops, was rarely attained. Weavers had some organisation of their own, based on caste councils or *panchayats*, but essentially they seem to have worked as individual households.[30]

The extent to which artisans formed a 'manufacturing' or even an 'industrial' sector separate from agriculture is a matter for dispute.[31] The general view of Europeans was that what they had come to recognise as the 'division of labour' hardly existed: artisans cultivated land and agriculturalists were also employed part of the time in other pursuits, the implication being that inefficiency was the inevitable consequence of lack of specialisation. That relatively few people were completely separated from agriculture in this period seems to be irrefutable. There seems to have been a kind of continuum: poor cultivators, seeking means of eking out their meagre earnings from the land by their own occasional labour as coolies or by their wives' spinning, were at one end; the highly skilled weaver working virtually full time on cloth for export, while his plot of land was cultivated by hired labour, was at the other end.[32] However, the fact that nearly all artisans had some connection with the land does not necessarily imply

[30] D.B. Mitra, *The Cotton Weavers of Bengal* (Calcutta, 1979); H. Hossain, 'The East India Company and the Textile Producers of Bengal, 1750–1813', Unpublished D.Phil thesis, Oxford University, 1982.

[31] If an 'industrial' sector can be shown to have existed, the concept of 'deindustrialisation' in the nineteenth century becomes more plausible. For a recent statement, see M. Vicziany, 'The Deindustrialisation of India in the Nineteenth Century', and A.K. Bagchi, 'A Reply' in *Indian Economic and Social History Review*, XVI (1979), 105–61.

[32] This was noted by Buchanan, see Martin, *Eastern India*, II, 978; G. Harris described weavers in east Bengal as 'little landlords' (Evidence, 21 May 1830, *PP*, 1830, VI, 307).

that artisan production was inefficient or that there could not be major shifts of emphasis as men were encouraged either to spend much more time on the craft side of their employment or, conversely, to spend much less time on it, as the demand for their skills diminished.

The divisions of wealth and status which marked those who cultivated the land were in part reproduced among those who also worked off the land. At the bottom of the pile were the coolies and porters who laboured in the towns or who did such work as embanking, together with the great armies of boatmen, whose physically debilitating work seems to have been very ill rewarded, and the very industrious 'poor and illiterate' fishing people.[33] Those village craftsmen who were tied to the service of the cultivators were presumably also in a weak position. Some other groups, such as the *mulangi* salt boilers, were tied to their employment by rigorous conditions. The situation of the skilled artisan, working in a more or less specialised way for a wider market than his village could provide, is less clear. There were no doubt some individuals who worked at their own inclination, eventually taking their finished articles to the local market, where they could bargain for what they thought an appropriate price. But the evidence, at least from the British period, strongly suggests that most skilled artisans were in fact working to the orders either of the agents of merchants or of brokers who earned a commission on what they resold to merchants. Such artisans usually received 'advances' before beginning work, that is they were given their raw materials, such as cotton thread, silk cocoons or other equivalents of the peasant's seed corn, or they were paid cash, deducted from the final price of the finished goods. It has recently been argued that the system of advance payments to the artisans does not necessarily imply that they were in a state of dependence or had lost their power of bargaining.[34] On the other hand, there is much to suggest that advances often accumulated into debts which could not be paid off, so that the artisan, like the poorer cultivators, mortgaged his labour in return for what his creditor was prepared to allow him to maintain his family and pay his taxes. The tendency for some artisans to become virtually paid employees of particular merchants, above all

[33] Ward's phrase, *Account of the Hindoos*, IV, 115–17.
[34] K.N. Chaudhuri, *The Trading World of Asia and the English East India Company 1660–1760* (Cambridge, 1978), pp. 256–7.

of the British East India Company, was marked by the beginning of the nineteenth century.

Suggestions that 'pre-colonial' India was a society of largely self-sufficient villages living in isolation from one another have long been dismissed by historians. Such a description would be totally inappropriate for Bengal well before the coming of the British. Many artisans worked for far distant markets. Peasant cultivators too worked for money. Crops such as cotton, sugar cane, mulberry, and oil seeds were obviously for the most part 'cash crops'. So too was a considerable part of the rice crop, especially the *aman* winter rice. Revenue payments, except in parts of Bihar, were made in cash, which circulated very widely, the mass of the poor using cowries.[35] Credit, if on very stringent terms for the poor, was available to most levels of society. Credits could be transferred and bills of exchange were widely issued and discounted. The vigour of the indigenous banking and credit system is suggested by the fact that in the early nineteenth century, far from displacing it, British banking came to some extent to depend on it.

By the mid eighteenth century Bengal had to a degree developed an integrated economy with marked regional specialisations, some areas producing grain surpluses, others concentrating on certain cash crops or on particular lines of textiles. There was a network of markets throughout the province. Great wholesale markets had been established at strategic points on the rivers, such as that at Bhagwangola, on the Ganges near Murshidabad,[36] or Narayanganj near Dhaka. The numerous large local markets were usually called *ganj*s. Small-scale transactions took place at village *hat*s, normally held on certain days of each week. One documented village market of the 1770s, for instance, significantly had three stalls dealing in cowries and two money-changers' booths among its thirteen shops.[37]

Integration was aided by a system of communications of reasonable quality by any pre-industrial standard. Water was of course the basis of Bengal's transport. With the exception of certain districts west of the Hooghly, wrote the geographer James Rennell, 'we may safely pronounce, that every part of the country, has, even in the dry season, some navigable stream within 25 miles at farthest; and more com-

[35] The importance of cowries has recently been stressed by Perlin, 'Proto-industrialization', pp. 75–6.
[36] K.M. Mohsin, *A Bengal District in Transition: Murshidabad 1765–93* (Dacca, 1973), pp. 14–15.   [37] Ibid., p. 20.

monly, within a third part of that distance.'[38] The unreliability of the rivers during the dry months, especially in western Bengal, seriously limited navigation between February and June, but at other times of the year boats were a cheap and effective system of transport. Land transport was another matter. Such roads as Bengal possessed were thought to be deteriorating by the eighteenth century, and neither the Nawabs nor at first the East India Company were inclined to remedy this situation. As a result, the use of carts was impractical in many areas, so there was little alternative to using pack animals, especially bullocks. It was generally agreed that goods on bullocks could not be expected to move more than eight or ten miles a day, even in good conditions.[39]

A rough uniformity of prices in major centres throughout Bengal, at least by the end of the eighteenth century, seems to be the clearest evidence of economic integration. There are indications of the existence of what has been called 'a regional grain market' for Bengal.[40] Early in the nineteenth century the relative stability of grain prices 'in the neighbourhood of the navigable rivers' and in the 'vicinity of large towns' was noted.[41] Uniformity of prices was, however, limited to such areas. In the remoter countryside very wide fluctuations in grain prices were frequently recorded from district to district, even over quite short distances, from year to year, and from month to month in any one year.[42]

The extent to which agriculture and handcrafts had become commercialised by the middle of the eighteenth century is some indication of the extent of the networks operated by merchants throughout eastern India. Before the rise of British power, the very richest Bengal merchants, like those in other parts of India, seem to have been involved in a wide range of enterprises. They were bankers and shipowners, and dealers in commodities such as fine quality textiles

[38] Rennell, *Memoir of a Map of Hindoostan*, p. 335.
[39] [Colebrooke and Lambert], *Remarks on Bengal*, p. 126; O. Feldbaek, 'Cloth Production and Trade in Late Eighteenth-century Bengal', *Bengal Past and Present*, LXXXVI (1967), 138.
[40] D.L. Curley, 'Rulers and Merchants in Late Eighteenth-century Bengal', Unpublished Ph.D. thesis, Chicago University, 1980, p. 49. See also the valuable price statistics in A.S.M. Akhtar Hussain, 'A Quantitative Study of Price Movements in Bengal during the Eighteenth and Nineteenth Centuries', Unpublished Ph.D. thesis, London University, 1978.
[41] W.B. Bayley, 'Statistical View of the Population of Burdwan', *Asiatick Researches*, XII (1816), 553.
[42] [Colebrooke and Lambert], *Remarks on Bengal*, p. 75; Akhtar Hussain, 'Quantitative Study'.

which had a potentially high markup. They maintained *kuthi*s or branches in different parts of Bengal and agents and connections all over India. The lesser merchants tended to specialise in the trade of particular areas or in single commodities such as grain, salt, sugar or textiles. They too might have branches of their business separate from the main one and were likely to employ many agents, or *gumashta*s, who bought and sold on their behalf. Although there were many specialist bankers and money changers, usually called shroffs by the English, most merchants had to be financiers as well as traders in goods. Most goods were obtained by advance payments, which often amounted to money lending, and most deals involved currency manipulation. The term *mahajan* was used both for a merchant and for a banker.

The merchant communities of Bengal were very diverse in origin. Some of them were native Bengalis, typically the Subanabaniks, the goldsmith caste, many of whom specialised in banking, or the Setts and Basaks, weaving castes who had become textile dealers. But specialist merchant groups, the equivalent of Bania or Vaisha castes in other parts of India, were not a notable feature in Bengal. Lists of merchants, such as those of merchants dealing with the East India Company, show names from a wide variety of castes, including Brahmins. Bengal also attracted many non-Bengali merchants. It was the eastern end of the great networks of trade by land and river that crossed northern India to the Punjab and Rajasthan. Thus those merchant groups which dominated trade all over northern India also settled in Bengal.[43] Gujaratis and Rajasthanis were particularly prominent. Gujaratis were the largest traders in silk. They were naturally attracted to Murshidabad and Kasimbazar, at the centre of Bengal's high quality silk belt. They set up their Jain temples at both places. Manik Chand, an Oswal from Rajasthan, came to Murshidabad early in the eighteenth century, where he established what became the greatest of all the merchant operations, the house of Jagat Seth, bankers to the Nawabs. A considerable community of Oswals grew up at Murshidabad. Khatris from northern India were also important in the Bengal towns, as were so-called 'Mughal' merchants, Muslims from Iran and central Asia. Gosains and Sannyasis, trading members of Hindu religious orders, also did a large business in Bengal. Armenians were another group from Iran who settled in Bengal to trade.

The residence in Bengal of merchant communities who were not of

[43] Discussed in C. A. Bayly, *Rulers, Townsmen and Bazaars: North Indian Society in the Age of British Expansion 1770–1870* (Cambridge, 1983), pp. 160–2.

Bengali origin indicates the importance of the province in trade with other parts of Asia. A very large volume of exports, especially of textiles, went to the cities of northern India by boat up the Ganges or by bullock caravan. Smaller overland trades were plied with Nepal, Tibet and Assam. By sea Bengal was closely linked with the rich province of Gujarat in western India, supplying it with raw silk and sugar. Bengal textiles were much in demand in the countries of the Middle East, being shipped to ports on the Red Sea and the Persian Gulf. Exports to southeast Asia mostly consisted of cotton piece goods and opium.

Many European merchants also lived in Bengal, participating in its inter-Asian trade and shipping its textiles and saltpetre to Europe. The Portuguese, settled in Bengal since the sixteenth century, still carried on trade, but by the eighteenth century European enterprise was dominated by the East India Companies of Britain, the Netherlands and France. Until the British military victories, these companies were very similar. Directors in the European capitals stationed 'servants' of the companies throughout Asia in trading 'factories'. In Bengal the major factories were sited on the Hooghly river in the west. By the middle of the eighteenth century factory settlements had expanded to become considerable towns, virtually under the rule of the company's Governor and his Council. In these settlements Europeans carried on much private business as well as organising the trade of their companies. Many Indian merchants and artisans also moved there. The companies' Bengal trade had grown enormously in the late seventeenth and early eighteenth centuries, as sales of Bengal cotton cloth in Europe rose spectacularly. Until the emergence of European manufacturing industry at the very end of the eighteenth century, Bengal's trade with Europe was set in a pattern which consisted essentially of the exchange of piece goods and silk for silver, rather than for manufactured European exports. The Europeans also greatly stimulated Bengal's trade to the east, especially to Batavia and Canton.

Some towns grew up round the centres of the Nawabs' government. Others were the creation of the powerful *zamindars*, Burdwan, Natore, seat of the Rani of Rajshahi, and Krishnanagar in Nadia, described in 1763 as 'a well peopled town with good buildings',[44] being obvious examples. But the major towns were the creation of merchants. The most important towns of western Bengal were strung along the

[44] Account by Warren Hastings, IOL, Orme MSS, OV, 67, p. 143.

Hooghly and the Bhagirathi rivers, between the Nawab's capital of Murshidabad and British Calcutta. The European settlements developed some of the characteristics of European towns anywhere, while Murshidabad was graced by the palaces, mosques and gardens of the Nawabs. Yet all the Hooghly towns remained essentially the towns of Indian merchants and Indian artisans, dominated by their great bazaars, or central markets, and strings of smaller *ganj*s. By the middle of the eighteenth century very large numbers of people, sometimes estimated at well over 100,000 in each, were living at Murshidabad and Calcutta. Within both towns merchant communities tended to live apart round their own mosques, temples or churches. Artisans also had their own distinct quarters, *tola*s, *para*s or *mohalla*s. Those in Murshidabad were called after jewellers, potters, milkmen, dealers in timber and sugar sellers.[45] By the 1750s Calcutta had 'weavers, carpenters, bricklayers, smiths, tailors, braziers' employed within its bounds.[46] For all the vigour of the enterprise within them, the Hooghly towns struck visitors as being overgrown villages, or rather as disorganised clusters of villages. Such an impression was not misleading. Town merged easily into country in eighteenth-century Bengal, and the country tended to dominate. But this was not the domination of bucolic backwardness; rather it was the domination of a countryside, at least near the Hooghly, where much of agriculture was commercialised and handcrafts were being produced in villages on a large scale. Parts of western Bengal had become 'rurban', that is, by a recent definition, marked by 'a scattering within country villages and small rural towns of many of those functions normally considered to be primarily urban in kind'.[47] In other words, the relative lack of urban development does not necessarily imply an underdeveloped economy.

And yet sophisticated as western Bengal's economy undoubtedly was by the middle of the eighteenth century, merchants and artisans still rested on an agrarian base. If that gave way, serious disruption would follow. Whether the agrarian base held up depended in the last resort on the monsoon. By comparison with northern India, western

---

[45] K.M. Mohsin, 'Murshidabad in the Eighteenth Century', in *The City in South Asia: Pre-modern and Modern*, ed. K. Ballhatchet and J. Harrison (1980), p. 79; see also G. Bhadra, 'Social Groups and Relations in the Town of Murshidabad 1765–93', *Indian Historical Review*, II (1975–6), 312–38.
[46] J. Long, *Selections from Unpublished Records of Government* (reprint, Calcutta, 1973), p. 122. [47] Perlin, 'Proto-industrialization', p. 78.

Bengal usually enjoyed an assured and abundant rainfall. On occasions, however, it was seriously deficient. Food shortages and ultimately famine could then ensue. The worst shortages for sixty years occurred in 1752. The price of rice at Murshidabad rose to six times its previous level.[48] 'Multitudes' of 'dead and dying' and 'many thousands of walking skeletons' appeared in the streets of Calcutta.[49] 1761 was a year of 'great scarcity of grain' around Calcutta, leading to very high prices. In 1769 the rains failed over most of Bihar and Bengal. By the early months of 1770 mortality in western Bengal was very high. People died of starvation or in a debilitated state were mowed down by diseases which spread especially where the starving congregated to be fed.[50] The proportion of the population who perished can never be known. One-third of the inhabitants of Bengal were sometimes said to have died. Other conjectures were one-fifth.[51] What seems to be certain is that the core areas of western and central Bengal were devastated: these included the districts of Murshidabad, Rajshahi, Birbhum, Hooghly, Nadia and parts of Burdwan. One indication of the scale of mortality in the worst areas is an estimate that one-third of those who raised silk worms in the famous silk area around Murshidabad were dead.[52] The low-lying delta areas, even in the west, suffered rather less.[53] Everywhere the most vulnerable seem to have been 'the workmen, manufacturers and people employed in the river, who were without the same means of laying by stores of grain as the husbandmen'.[54]

The terrible *chalisa*, the famine which ravaged northern India in 1783, caused alarm in Bengal, but seems to have produced no more than limited scarcities in some western districts. Bengal was in fact entering a long period of relative immunity. In the 1820s it was being

[48] Orme, *Historical Fragments*, p. 405.
[49] J.Z. Holwell, *India Tracts* (2nd edn, 1764), p. 165.
[50] This was noted by R. Kyd, 'Memorandum for Forming a Memoir or Report of the State of the Provinces', IOL, MS Eur.F.95, fo. 168.
[51] Shore, minute of June 1789, *PP*, 1812, VII, 182.
[52] West Bengal Archives, Controlling Committee of Commerce, 18 Nov. 1772, vol. 1, p. 576.
[53] Reports by G. Vansittart and P. Dacres, 20 Jan., 10 Feb., 1775, IOR, Home Miscellaneous, vol. 206, pp. 147–8, 186, 192–3.
[54] Memoir by Sir G. Campbell, in J.C. Geddes, *Administrative Experience Recorded in Former Famines* (Calcutta, 1874), p. 421. The same groups suffered again in the great 1943 famine. Recent studies of the 1943 disaster suggest interpretations of 1770 which unfortunately cannot be tested for lack of evidence (P.R. Greenhough, *Prosperity and Misery in Modern Bengal: The Famine of 1943–4* (New York, 1982); A.K. Sen, *Poverty and Famines* (Oxford, 1981)).

said that 'famine and even scarcity have been unknown' for nearly forty years.[55]

Even without famine the death rate in Bengal in this period seems to have been very high, especially among young chidren. Buchanan noted that the villages of Dinajpur swarmed with children, 'but', he grimly added, 'fever annually sweeps away immense numbers'.[56] The missionary William Ward supposed that one-fifth of the children born in Bengal never reached the end of their first year.[57] A survey of Calcutta births for 1837–8 found that he was indeed right, 585 out of 2,781 children were dead within their first twelve months.[58] 'Fevers', usually divided into 'intermittent' and 'remittent', presumably different forms of the as yet undiagnosed malaria, were thought to be the main cause of infantile death and of the debilitation of adults. 'Intermittent fever prevails all over the valley of the Ganges to a greater or lesser extent at all seasons of the year', wrote one authority. 'Fevers' were noted to be most prevalent in marshes, flooded rice fields and near stagnant water.[59] Great fever epidemics were recalled, for example that of 1762, which allegedly carried off 50,000 'blacks' and 800 Europeans at Calcutta.[60]

Other epidemic diseases made their appearance. Smallpox was thought always to be present in Bengal in a mild form, but to 'rage' every seventh year.[61] Variolation was widely practised and may have significantly reduced mortality. Europeans took little note of cholera until an outbreak began in 1817. Six thousand people were believed to have died in Jessore that year, while the cholera spread both west to Calcutta and into eastern Bengal, accounting for many thousands more victims.[62] Thereafter cholera was regarded as 'an endemic in the whole of British India', making its appearance 'each hot season' in Bengal.[63] By 1839 cholera was nearly matching 'fever' among listed causes of deaths in Calcutta.

[55] W. Hamilton, *The East-India Gazetteer* (2 vols., 1828), I, 189.
[56] Martin, *Eastern India*, II, 690.    [57] Ward, *Account of the Hindoos*, II, 344.
[58] D. Stewart, 'Explanatory Note' to 'Statistical Report of the Duration of Diseases', *Journal of the Asiatic Society of Bengal*, VIII (1839), 708.
[59] K. Mackinnon, *A Treatise on the Public Health, Climate, Hygiene and Prevailing Diseases of Bengal and the North West Provinces* (Cawnpore, 1848), pp. 117, 199.
[60] J.R. Martin, *Notes on the Medical Topography of Calcutta* (Calcutta, 1837), p. 120.
[61] J.Z. Holwell, *An Account of the Manner of Inoculating for the Small Pox in the East Indies* (1767), pp. 3–4.
[62] J. Jameson, *Report on the Epidermick Cholera Morbus . . . in the years 1817, 1818 and 1819* (Calcutta, 1820).    [63] Mackinnon, *A Treatise*, pp. 79–80.

Spectacular as the epidemics appeared to be, Europeans came to appreciate that eastern India need not otherwise be lethal to those who were well housed and ate appropriately. Much of the high death rate among its peoples was therefore due to poor living conditions and undernourishment. Women died in large numbers in childbirth. Children were 'subject to swellings in the belly', said to 'proceed from a bad diet'.[64] 'Were the natives better provided with food, clothing and lodging', concluded Buchanan, they would live longer and withstand 'fever' better.[65]

The very high death rate in normal times was presumably more than matched by a high birth rate, since there is clear evidence that the population of Bengal was increasing during the famine-free early nineteenth century. Yet Buchanan's observations in the district of Rangpur suggest that the birth rate cannot have been very high. Women in Rangpur were married very early, but their first child was usually not born until they were seventeen or eighteen and the intervals between subsequent births were often five years and 'seldom less than three'. Most women did not bear more than four children. Buchanan had, however, heard that child-bearing in Calcutta began rather earlier, at fifteen or sixteen.[66]

Eastern Bengal was less affected than the western half by such problems as occasional rainfall failure leading to famine, declining rivers or malaria. The rainfall of the east was virtually guaranteed, while the main volume of Ganges water was increasingly passing to the sea through eastern outlets. For instance, at the beginning of the nineteenth century a new channel was carved out between the eastern districts of Jessore and Faridpur. As well as getting a major share of the Ganges water, eastern Bengal received the entire outflow of the gigantic Brahmaputra and of other great rivers like the Tista and the Meghna. The flooding of these rivers fertilised large areas. By 'the latter end of July, all the lower parts of Bengal, contiguous to the Ganges and the Burrampooter are overflowed and form an inundation of more than a hundred miles in width'.[67] Silt was not only deposited on the land but formed new land, or *chars*, of great fertility. The vigour of the annual floods seems to have prevented the formation of suitable habitats for the malaria-bearing mosquitoes, which flourished in the more stagnant western delta.

---

[64] R. Kyd, 'Some Remarks on the Soil and Cultivation on the Western Side of the River Hooghly', IOL, MS Eur.F.95, fo. 71.   [65] Martin, *Eastern India*, III, 483.
[66] Ibid., III, 482.   [67] Rennell, *Memoir of a Map of Hindoostan*, p. 349.

Unlike those of the west, the main eastern rivers were open to boats throughout the year. Thus the farmers of the east had easy access to the urban markets in the west. Two routes linked the Hooghly with eastern Bengal through the Sundarbans, and 'during the season when the western branch of the Ganges is almost dried up, the whole trade of Bengal (the western provinces excepted)' passed through them.[68] Sylhet, a district in the far eastern corner of Bengal, could export its produce to the west all the year round, either up the Ganges to Bhagwangola, the market for Murshidabad, or to Calcutta by the Sundarbans routes.[69]

Settlement of the lands around the eastern delta seems to have occurred rapidly in the seventeenth and eighteenth centuries. New migrants were no doubt partly being attracted to the area by the opportunities which the shifting course of the rivers were offering for profitable cultivation, but they were also attracted by the success of the newly established Mughal regime in creating stability. For much of the seventeenth century eastern coastal and river areas had been raided by Portuguese from Chittagong and by Maghs from the Arakan coast. In 1665, however, the Mughals took Chittagong and established a military regime in the far east of Bengal, 'the inhabitants afterwards greatly increasing and the lands being improved by cultivation'.[70] A Mughal fleet was stationed at Dhaka to keep at bay raids from the Maghs, which continued intermittently into the East India Company period. There are indications that the process of opening up eastern Bengal was going ahead at speed in the later eighteenth century. Some notes on 'The Geography of Bengal', evidently written about 1765, observe that at Jessore 'by far the greatest part of the lands are either woods or morass' and that Tippera 'contains only a narrow strip of land' fringed by hills and jungles.[71] Seven-eighths of Jessore and seven-ninths of Tippera were said to be under cultivation in 1801.[72] After travelling through Tippera in 1798 Buchanan wrote:

No country which is dead level, and unadorned by elegant arts can be more beautiful than that through which I have today come. It is one continuous field yielding the richest crops, free from all the stiffness of regular fences, and

[68] Ibid., pp. 363–4.
[69] IOR, Bengal Board of Revenue: Grain, 31 Oct. 1794, Range 89, vol. 27.
[70] Evidence of H. Verelst, 4th Report, Secret Committee, 1773, *Reports from Committees of the House of Commons* (12 vols., 1803–6), IV, 97.
[71] Notes by G. Ironside, IOL, Orme MSS, 'India', XVII, 4950.
[72] *PP*, 1812–13, IX, 337, 416.

only interrupted by the natives' cottages concealed in groves of fruit trees, that are variegated with all the irregularity of luxuriant nature.[73]

Buchanan provided further evidence of recent development in the eastern delta when he described Sirajganj, a town in Mymensingh which had not been mentioned in Rennell's survey of the 1760s, as 'the chief place of trade' in Bengal by 1809.[74] Yet well into the nineteenth century European observers continued to believe that the pressure of people on the land was much less in the east than in the west.

With vast tracts of low-lying land annually irrigated and fertilised by the floodings of the great rivers, eastern Bengal was the natural home for the *aman* winter rice. It was capable of producing very large rice harvests. In 1753 Robert Orme noted that 'the country about Dacca... is alone sufficient to supply the whole province of Bengal with rice'.[75] Dhaka, Sylhet and Bakarganj were described in 1790 as 'the granaries of this part of Bengal'.[76] Bakarganj, on the estuary of the Padma, became the great collecting point for rice surpluses throughout eastern Bengal and seems to have been the largest grain market in the whole province. From Bakarganj grain boats could reach Calcutta in about five days' sailing.[77] As early as 1754 it was thought that Calcutta would be reduced to 'the greatest necessity and misery' if the rice market at Bakarganj were to be closed.[78]

In addition to its abundant rice harvests, cash crops were grown in eastern Bengal on land above the flood line. Oil seeds, sugar cane and pulses were very widely raised, as in western Bengal. The east also specialised in tobacco and betel nut in certain areas and in very high grade cotton, or *kopas*, which was grown especially in a belt along the Meghna river for supplying the weavers of Dhaka.

Those who investigated Bengal's rural society in the late nineteenth or early twentieth centuries generally believed that the peasantry were less stratified and that the very poor and landless were less numerous in the east than in the west. Evidence for the delta areas for earlier

[73] F. Buchanan, 'Account of a Journey through the Provinces of Chittagong and Tiperah', Add. MS 19286, fo. 3.
[74] Survey of 'Ronggopur', IOL, MS Eur.D.75, book V, pp. 82–3.
[75] Orme, *Historical Fragments*, p. 404.
[76] Kyd, 'Remarks', IOL, MS Eur.F.95, fo. 44a.
[77] West Bengal Archives, Committee of Grain, 6 Nov. 1783, bundle 1.
[78] *Fort William–India House Correspondence*, (New Delhi, 1949–), I, *1748–56*, ed. K.K. Datta (1958), p. 736.

periods is scanty. Land was no doubt abundant, but lack of resources with which to clear new land and to begin cultivation was again the limitation. Poor cultivators were thus forced to seek other earnings, as in the west. In Tippera Buchanan found many holdings of only ten acres and came to the conclusion that there was 'hardly such a thing as a farmer'. Men fed their families from the produce of the land, but they bought clothing, paid their taxes and made religious offerings from what they earned from crafts, labouring or working on boats.[79] In Sylhet at a rather later period it was said that men did not undertake cultivation of more land than they needed for growing food for their families, but chose rather to earn money in 'pursuits which do not require a capital', acting as boatmen or coolies.[80] There is no evidence about the extent of debt, but the indications would seem to be of a peasant society under fewer pressures than that in the west. Allegations were already being made, as they were frequently to be in the future, that the east Bengal peasant was able to be idle for parts of the year.[81] If caste subordination reinforced a hierarchy of poverty in the west, this too was likely to be less prevalent in the east. Many of the rural population were Muslims and many others were from a single Hindu caste, Namasudras. In newly settled areas caste structures seem to have had little time to evolve.

It should be stressed, however, that these tentative conclusions apply only to the belt of country across the lower courses of the rivers. Conditions in the northern areas of eastern Bengal seem to have been very similar to those in the west. Two districts in this area, Dinajpur and Rangpur, were surveyed by Buchanan. He described a society sharply divided between rich and poor. The rich (*jotedars*, as they were increasingly to be called) cultivated large farms with hired labour or sharecroppers, lent money and stock to their poorer neighbours, and traded in grain. The poor were often very poor indeed and heavily in debt. William Carey, the missionary, who lived in Dinajpur for many years, agreed that the population was 'in general extremely poor'.[82]

Artisans were spread through the villages of eastern Bengal as in the west, and again artisans were concentrated in certain areas working for

[79] Buchanan, 'Journey through Chittagong and Tiperah', Add. MS 19286, fo. 4.
[80] Captain Fisher, 'Memoir of Sylhet, Kachar and the Adjacent Districts', *Journal of the Asiatic Society of Bengal*, IX (1840), 820–2.
[81] Report by Magistrate of Tippera, 1802, *PP*, 1812–13, VIII, 416–17.
[82] W. Carey, 'Remarks on the State of Agriculture in the District of Dinajpoor', *Asiatick Researches*, X (1808), 3.

distant markets. Salt boiling took place in Noakhali and Chittagong districts. Silk was made in Rangpur. Large concentrations of weavers making cotton cloth for export had developed at Kalyandi, Lakhshmipur and above all around Dhaka. The weavers at Dhaka were the most famous in India. During the seventeenth century royal workshops had been set up to supervise the manufacture of 'Jamdanees' and other muslins of legendary fineness intended for the court of the Mughal emperor. Cloth of many other varieties was also produced. In the later eighteenth century some 8,000 looms were said to be worked around Dhaka.[83] Weavers varied from the Tantis, a specialised weaving caste, who made the most prestigious cloth and maintained rituals of parades and festivals far into the nineteenth century, to lower caste Hindus and Muslims, who worked on the coarser qualities. Spinning was again done on a part-time basis by very large numbers of women.

Dhaka, capital of Bengal in the seventeenth century, was by far the largest town in eastern Bengal. Chittagong, its nearest competitor, was described at the end of the eighteenth century as being 'very populous', but it consisted of little more than huts of grass thatch and bamboo. It was really a number of 'scattered villages, occupying the narrow vallies which separate the south end of the low hills'.[84] Parts of Dhaka were at least built of brick, even though such buildings appeared 'very mean' and 'mostly of one storey only' to a visitor of 1765, who thought it a city in decline.[85] In 1801, out of some 44,000 dwellings, only 3,000 or so were of brick, but the population was thought to be still some 200,000.[86] Descendants of the Nawabs' officials continued to live at Dhaka in some state and merchants took up their residence there: Europeans, Armenians, Mughals, Pathans, north Indian Hindus and Muslims, as well as Bengalis. Painters, carpenters, weavers, fishermen, gold- and silversmiths, milkmen, shell workers, blacksmiths and potters all had quarters named after them.

Famine caused by drought rarely affected the delta areas of east

---

[83] See figures in Chaudhuri, *Trading World*, p. 263; Anisuzzaman, *Factory Correspondence and other Bengali Documents in the India Office Library and Records* (1981), p. 6.

[84] Buchanan, 'Journey through Chittagong and Tiperah', Add. MS 19286, fo. 76.

[85] J. Rennell to G. Burrington, 31 Aug. 1765, IOR, Home Miscellaneous, vol. 815.

[86] A. Karim, 'An Account of the District of Dacca', *Journal of the Asiatic Society of Pakistan*, VII (1962), 340.

Bengal, although weavers and spinners around Dhaka died in 1770.[87] Famines could, however, be caused by sudden and excessive flooding. Normally the growth of the winter rice matched the rising flood level, so that it kept 'its top above the water', even at a depth of ten or twelve feet; but if the rice was 'overtopped' and died off, the result could be calamitous.[88] Such a calamity occurred in 1784, when the rice was 'buried many feet under water' and there was heavy mortality at Sylhet.[89] In 1787 there was continuous rain from March to July. The growing rice was again drowned and destroyed. Floods caused by excessive rain and the rising of the rivers were followed by floods caused by inundations of the sea, whipped up by a cyclone. This was a perennial hazard in eastern Bengal, especially for the settlers on the highly fertile islands of largely new land in the estuaries of the rivers. In 1787 the sea also broke through an elaborate system of dykes in the western district of Midnapur, which reminded Englishmen of Holland, since 'a great proportion' of it was 'only made habitable by the sea dyke'.[90] The mortality from flood and famine in eastern Bengal was very high in 1787. Sixty thousand were thought to have died in Dhaka district alone.[91]

Foreigners who concerned themselves at all with the cultural life of Bengal in the eighteenth century were virtually unanimous in their diagnosis of it. They believed that they were seeing a culture or cultures in an advanced state of degeneration. In their view there was an ancient 'Hindu' body of learning and precepts (for which they came to have some sympathy) and a less ancient Muslim body of learning and precepts (for which they had rather less sympathy in most cases). Contemporary Hindus and Muslims were thought to be almost universally ignorant of their canonical learning and extremely lax in the following of canonical precepts. Meaningless superstition and morally corrupt practices prevailed everywhere. The theory of degeneration has been extremely influential, and not only with foreigners. During the nineteenth century Hindu and Muslim reformers frequently saw

[87] West Bengal Archives, Controlling Committee of Commerce, 26 May 1773, vol. III, p. 710.    [88] Kyd, 'Remarks', IOL, MS Eur.F.95, fo. 42.
[89] *Bangladesh District Records: Dacca Records*, I (1784–7), ed. S. Islam (Dacca, 1981), p. 78.    [90] Harrison, *Bengal Embankment Manual*, p. 29.
[91] J. Taylor, *A Sketch of the Topography and Statistics of Dacca* (Calcutta, 1840), p. 304.

themselves as rescuing pure ancient tradition from the deplorable accretions of later centuries, including the eighteenth.

Modern scholarship, however, is less inclined to accept without question either theories of ancient purity and recent regeneration, with a long period of decay in between, or the confident judgements about entities such as 'Hinduism' which underlie such theories. An alternative point of view has emerged, according to which the eighteenth century appears not necessarily as a period of backsliding from supposedly classical canons but as a phase in a much longer process of the evolution of the local traditions which have given Bengal a distinctive cultural identity in modern times.

Some learned and pious Hindus certainly lived up to foreigners' expectations that they should be immersed in the study of what was taken to be the universal wisdom of Hindus in general. Sanskrit, the universal language of Hindu learning, was being studied by pandits in eighteenth-century Bengal. These sometimes derided men were able to provide the first British 'Orientalist' scholars, such as Charles Wilkins, Sir William Jones and Henry Thomas Colebrooke, both with texts and with the linguistic capacity and insights which enabled them to translate and interpret the texts. Teachers of Sanskrit remained throughout the period covered by this volume 'a highly venerated and influential portion of native society'.[92] A survey for the 1830s suggested that there might be some 1,800 pandits teaching 10,800 pupils.[93] For most, the instruction went no further than a rudimentary capacity to read and a little knowledge of grammar. A Christian missionary commented that Brahmins who took their duties as family priests at all seriously would have some capacity to read Sanskrit and that a knowledge of its grammar was quite widely diffused among them.[94]

In a few centres Sanskrit learning that went beyond basic grammar was cultivated. The most notable of such centres were in the district of Nadia. During the second half of the eighteenth century the zamindars of Nadia were well-known patrons of scholarship. In the 1780s William Jones, who spent some time at Nadia, referred to it as 'the celebrated university of Brahmans'.[95] The main subject studied at Nadia and at other centres of advanced learning in Bengal was the

[92] W. Adam, *Reports on the State of Education in Bengal*, ed. A. Basu (Calcutta, 1941), pp. 274–5.
[93] A. Mukherjee, *Reform and Regeneration in Bengal 1774–1823* (Calcutta, 1968), p. 4.
[94] Ward, *Account of the Hindoos*, I, 194.
[95] *Letters of Sir William Jones*, ed. G. Cannon (2 vols., Oxford, 1970), II, 754.

Nyaya system of logic. What have been called 'able products of Nadia' had also kept alive 'a flourishing, but not assertive or brilliant tradition of sastric learning' in the law.[96] It was from this source that Englishmen were given their first introduction to Hindu law. Pandits were still teaching Nyaya, law and grammar at some twenty-five *tol*s, or individual schools, in Nadia in 1829. Up to sixty students attended each *tol*.[97]

More characteristic of the mass of Bengali Brahmins than study of Nyaya was their commitment to the cult of Sakta, of divine energy, usually in the female form of Devi, Kali or Durga. English observers believed that the majority of high caste Bengalis were followers of Sakta by the early nineteenth century. For instance, the missionary William Ward reported that 'Kalee is the guardian deity of very many of the Bengalees, especially the Brahmuns'.[98] Bengal had a number of places of pilgrimage that were sacred to the Goddess, including the great shrine at Kalighat within the bounds of Calcutta, which flourished during the eighteenth century. During this period, Tantric treatises were composed, temples with Sakta dedications were built, and Sakta themes dominated much of eighteenth-century poetry. Veneration of Kali as the loving divine mother gained immense popularity through the lyrics of the mid eighteenth-century poet Ramprasad Sen. The great festival of modern Bengal, the Durga Puja, had an important place in Calcutta's life in the later eighteenth century.[99] By the beginning of the nineteenth century, 'immense sums' were being spent at the festival and 'all business throughout the country is laid aside for several days'.[100]

The cults pertaining to the Goddess appear to have deep roots in the local folk culture of Bengal. By the eighteenth century they had gained a kind of respectability: recognition by Brahmins and incorporation into what was to become accepted as the mainstream of 'Hinduism' in eastern India. Very many other local cults appear to have flourished throughout the villages of Bengal without being incorporated.

The other great institutionalised cult in Bengal by the eighteenth century was what is called Vaishnavism, although it took the form of

[96] See J.D.M. Derrett, *Religion, Law and the State in India* (1968), p. 231.
[97] *PP*, 1831–2, IX, 438.     [98] Ward, *Account of the Hindoos*, III, 192.
[99] Its observance is clearly described in the novel *Hartly House* (Anon., 2 vols., 1789), II, 78.     [100] Ward, *Account of the Hindoos*, III, 121.

devotion to the Lord Krishna. It had a massive following, especially among those of lower caste status. Ward believed that 'eight parts out of ten of the whole Hindoo population are the disciples of this god [Krishna]. The far greater part of them, however, are of the lower orders'.[101] Bengali Vaishnavism had been profoundly influenced since the sixteenth century by the reformer, saint and, to many, incarnation of God, Chaitanya. In theory it was organised by Gosains, who were descended from Chaitanya's followers. There were numerous houses of Vaishnavite orders and many types of wandering mendicants. The Vaishnavites also had their great places of pilgrimage, such as those in Nadia, associated with Chaitanya. They too produced much devotional literature and their themes, above all the love of Krishna and Radha, inspired a huge body of poetry.

Both Sakta and Vaishnavite Hinduism provided opportunities for the great Rajas and *zamindars* of eighteenth-century Bengal to act as patrons of festivals, builders of temples and promoters of literature and learning. The *zamindars* of Nadia were especially munificent. They attracted distinguished pandits to their schools, where they subsidised students, built great temples, celebrated the worship of Kali on a massive scale, and were the patrons of Bharatchandra, the most highly esteemed of eighteenth-century poets. Bharatchandra gave an idealised description of the court of a Hindu Raja, who was attended by 'story tellers, poets, Brahmana; teachers, scholars'.[102] Bharatchandra apparently used Burdwan, another major centre of patronage, as his model. The saintly Rani Bhawani, *zamindar* of Rajshahi for a long period, also endowed learning and temples, and the Rajas of Vishnupur were patrons of Vaishnavites. They built at least eighteen temples after 1656.[103]

From the second half of the eighteenth century religious patronage began to shift away from Rajas and *zamindars*. This was especially marked in temple-building. 'An immense proliferation of temple-building' took place. Those who endowed temples are said increasingly to have been 'new aspirants for social leadership' from 'lower castes of the traders, artisans and cultivators'.[104] New temples in small

---

[101] Ibid., III, 241.

[102] R. Inden, 'The Hindu Chieftain in Middle Bengali Literature', *Bengal: Literature and History*, ed. E.C. Dimock (E. Lansing, 1967), p. 26.

[103] H. Sanyal, 'Temple-building in Bengal from the Fifteenth to the Nineteenth Century', in *Perspectives in Social Sciences*, (Calcutta, 1977–), I, ed. B. De (1977), pp. 161, 165.    [104] Ibid., I, 134.

towns and villages provided an outlet for the development of architectural styles that were characteristic of Bengal, the so-called *chala* and *ratna*; they were reproductions of forms used for ordinary village huts.[105] Such temples were an outlet too for a decorative medium, again highly characteristic of Bengal, the use of terracotta.[106] Lower caste patronage also extended to poetry, especially *kabi* songs, in preference to the long *mangala* narrative poems commissioned by *zamindar*s, and to religious ceremonies, lavish celebrations of *sradha*s for the deceased and of *sati*s, the ritual burning of widows, which so horrified Europeans and was therefore so frequently described by them. Most recorded *sati*s were committed by Sudra castes.[107]

The widening diffusion of religious patronage in eighteenth-century Bengal has been seen by some commentators as symptomatic of a society that remained conservative in its values but which was undergoing considerable social mobility. The ideals to which men aspired have been described as the unchanging ideals deemed appropriate to high caste Hindus: 'righteousness, humility, self-respect, love of scholarship, knowledge of the scriptures, and respect for the gods, Brahmins and the guru'.[108] Worldly success was left to the basely born. Yet in reality many high-caste Bengalis were seeking success in the world, and many Sudras were aspiring to live according to righteousness. Englishmen often noted how many Brahmins were involved in trade, in government office or in the service of Europeans. On the other hand, Sudras who had won wealth and power in the world were forming sub-groups within their castes and seeking higher ritual ranking for these new sub-groups.[109] Temple-building was a means of turning wealth into recognition. 'Collective contributions towards temple-building by a caste group . . . enhanced the social prestige of the group and helped them to acquire greater respectability in terms of the local hierarchy of caste.'[110]

*Chala* temples with their terracotta decorations were one manifestation of a distinctly Bengali culture. The continuation in the eighteenth century of a long tradition of poetry written in Bengali was

---

[105] In addition to Sanyal, 'Temple-building', pp. 161, 165; see D.J. McCutchion, *Late Medieval Temples of Bengal* (Calcutta, 1970).

[106] See Z. Haque, *Terracotta Decorations of Late Medieval Bengal* (Dacca, 1980).

[107] Mukherjee, *Reform and Regeneration*, pp. 248–9.

[108] T. Raychaudhuri, *Bengal under Akbar and Jahangir* (2nd edn, New Delhi, 1969), p. 24. [109] H. Sanyal, *Social Mobility in Bengal* (Calcutta, 1981).

[110] Sanyal, 'Temple-building', p. 134.

another. The beginnings of a new tradition, prose in Bengali, was yet another. Assumptions that Bengali prose had no standing by comparison with Sanskrit or even Persian in the eighteenth century and that it emerged only in the nineteenth century have been questioned. What have been perceived as significant developments had occurred before the British introduced the printing press or missionaries and the East India Company tried to convey written information through Bengali. In the first place, a more standardised form of speech, at least among the formally educated, was apparently developing in the later eighteenth century. This was to provide 'the standard language for prose'. As in so many other respects, the influence of the Hooghly towns prevailed: 'the educated colloquial' of Calcutta and Nadia 'became the standard one for Bengal'.[111] Early prose writings have been described as 'the priest's handbook, the pundit's first book of logic and the physician's *vade mecum*, all in abridged form and in Bengali'.[112] Persian influences, however, are very pronounced in much written Bengali surviving from the eighteenth century.

Bengali was the medium used in village schools. Such schools were quite widely available. A famous survey conducted in the 1830s concluded that there was probably a school of some sort in two-thirds of the estimated 150,000 villages in Bengal. A child that attended such a school would in theory be taught to form the letters of the Bengali alphabet and to keep the kind of accounts that would enable a cultivator to compete on more than totally unequal terms with merchant and tax assessor. Modest as these aims seemed to many English contemporaries, it is clear that very few children attained such skills. The great mass of children simply did not go to school: virtually no female children did, and out of 22,637 male children in the Rajshahi district, 19,993 were described in 1835 as 'wholly uninstructed'.[113] Those who did attend schools rarely did so with the consistency or for the length of time needed to acquire any basic skills. Estimates of the proportion of the adult population who were literate varied for the 1830s between 9 per cent and 2.3 per cent for different districts.[114] Six per cent literacy among all adult males was suggested for the northern district of Dinajpur in the early nineteenth century.[115] Some

[111] S.K. Chatterjee, *Origin and Development of the Bengal Language* (2 vols., new edn, Calcutta, 1975), I, 134–9.
[112] S. Sen, *History of Bengali Literature* (new edn, Delhi, 1979), p. 148.
[113] Adam, *Reports*, pp. 190–1.    [114] Mukherjee, *Reform and Regeneration*, p. 13.
[115] Martin, *Eastern India*, II, 706.

Englishmen were not, however, unimpressed by what they saw. George Harris, an indigo planter, believed that the schools offered 'merely a little writing, and reading Bengali, and keeping accounts', but he found children 'all eager to learn; the boys went with the greatest pleasure to it'.[116] In his old age Warren Hastings even attributed to Indians in general 'superior endowments in reading, writing and arithmetic than the common people of any nation in Europe (if Scotland be not an exception)'.[117] Be that as it may, it seems to be the case that long before British rule Hindu Bengal possessed a highly literate elite that was confined to a limited number drawn largely from the higher castes. The gap between this elite and the great mass of the population seems to have been very wide indeed. William Carey thought that the 'common people' had difficulty in understanding what an educated Bengali was saying.[118]

Theories of degeneration were thought to apply to Muslims as well as to Hindus in Bengal. The arguments usually put forward are that although the Nawabs nominally maintained a Muslim temporal order, their presence was too weak and in any case soon to be too thoroughly subverted by the British to prevent the mass of indigenous Bengali converts from relapsing into heterodoxy. Whether the greater part of Bengali Muslims had ever added more than a thin Islamic veneer to a much older set of beliefs and practices is, however, open to question.

The effectiveness of the Nawabs as a force for Islamic orthodoxy is hard to assess. They were Shi'ites in a largely Sunni community and they showed some tendency to be accommodating towards their Hindu subjects. Nevertheless, they tried to enforce the law of the *Sharia* through a regular hierarchy of courts. Men from Islamic countries outside India, especially Shi'ites from Iran, were attracted to Bengal to work in the Nawabs' service. Two government-supported *madrassa*s propagated Islamic learning.[119] Law seems to have been studied widely. The East India Company found no shortage of scholars who could provide them with texts and aid in making translations for

[116] Harris, Evidence, *PP*, 1830, VI, 304.
[117] Comment added to letter of C. Wilkins to J. Sulivan, 25 Aug. 1813, Add. MS 29234, fo. 211.
[118] Cited by D. Kopf, 'The Dimensions of Literature... for the Study of Bengal 1800–30', *Bengal: Literature and History*, ed. E.C. Dimock, p. 105.
[119] Petition, 21 Sept. 1781, *Calendar of Persian Correspondence* (9 vols., Calcutta, 1919–49), VI, 89.

the use of European judges. Arabic was of course the language prized most by learned Muslims. It was taught wherever *madrassa*s or other Muslim colleges and schools existed, although the evidence, mostly from late in the period, suggests that only a small number of students were taught. Persian was on an entirely different footing. It was the language of Mughal government and of law. It was said that all papers submitted to officials of the Nawabs' government had to be in Persian; they would 'seldom or never condescend to receive petitions and letters in the Bengal language'. [120] Persian kept its official status under the British until the 1830s. It was therefore a language that was studied by educated Muslims and by many educated Hindus, especially those groups who specialised in government service. Even in the 1830s, 'The Persian language . . . must be pronounced to have a strong hold on native society.' Educated men:

acquire it in their earliest years at school, in after-life they continue to read the works it contains for instruction or amusement; they can converse in it, although it is not so employed in general society; and they employ it as the means of communication in the private correspondence of friendship and in the written transaction of business. [121]

Thus the institutions of Muslim government and those involved in the propagation of Muslim education were certainly present in eighteenth-century Bengal. It would seem, however, that their impact was largely confined to certain centres: Murshidabad, the capital; the port of Hooghly, the resort of merchants from outside Bengal, where there was a *madrassa* and an *imambara*; and Dhaka. What form the institutions of Islam took elsewhere is less certain. Muslims were numerous in the countryside. The consensus of British opinion by the early nineteenth century was that Muslims constituted about half the population of eastern Bengal, about a quarter in the central districts and a smaller proportion in the west. [122] Most Muslims were thought to be poor. In east Bengal they were chiefly artisans and small cultivators. In Rajshahi they were described as people 'beyond the reach of the simplest forms of literary instruction', 'cultivators of the ground, day-labourers, fishermen'. [123] Near Calcutta Muslims were 'fishermen, mariners, watermen, water carriers, bricklayers, military and domestic servants, and in some instances cultivators of the land'. [124] The

---

[120] Cited in A.K. Nazmal Karim, *The Dynamics of Bangladesh Society* (Delhi, 1980), p. 174.  [121] Adam, *Reports*, p. 291.
[122] Hamilton, *East-India Gazetteer*, I, 208.  [123] Adam, *Reports*, p. 158.
[124] Kyd, 'Remarks', IOL, MS Eur.F.95, fo. 70.

leadership available to the rural Muslims was not very powerful. Only the Pathan Rajas of Birbhum in the far west were of a comparable standing to the great Hindu *zamindar*s. In eastern Bengal descendants of officers in the Mughal army or from earlier waves of Muslim penetration were living on grants of revenue. Otherwise, the most powerful Muslims in the countryside were likely to be the Nawabs' *faujdar*s, or local military governors. The jurisdiction of these men was, however, largely confined to frontier areas, and their influence collapsed with the establishment of British rule.

The British believed that over most of Bengal, whether under Nawab or Company, the main burden of sustaining a Muslim order fell on local law officers, the *kadi*s, and on men of education whom they called 'mullas'. 'The Mulla . . . superintends the practice and punishes the breach of religious duties, the Cadi holds courts in which are tried all disputes of property', wrote Robert Orme of pre-British Bengal.[125] Most subdivisions of revenue administration had a *kadi* attached to them under the Mughals, and the *kadi*s continued to discharge their duties under the East India Company. It was said that they were required to pass examinations when under the Nawabs. Englishmen generally described them as men of respectable character and some learning. In northern Bengal, Buchanan encountered 'mollas', 'priests' of 'parishes' to him, whom he thought generally very ignorant,[126] as did William Adam those in other districts. Adam pointed out that there was no provision of specifically Muslim education at an elementary level apart from a relatively small number of schools offering Arabic and Persian. 'In Bengal the rural Mussalman population speak Bengali; attend indiscriminately with Hindus, Bengali schools; and read, write, correspond and keep accounts in that language.'[127] Presumably the great mass of Muslim children stood no more chance than the great mass of their Hindu counterparts of gaining any very high level of skills or knowledge from the village schools.

Buchanan reported very little observance of public prayer among Muslims in the districts he surveyed, but he noted characteristics of their religious life which others were to observe in many parts of Bengal. He believed that ascetics whom he called fakirs were the most influential leaders of the Muslim people. Especially influential were

---

[125] R. Orme, *History of the Military Transaction of the British Nation in Indostan*, (2 vols., 1763, 1778), I, 26.

[126] Martin, *Eastern India*, II, 724; III, 513.     [127] Adam, *Reports*, p. 440.

those fakirs who were the guardians of the shrines of revered persons, or *pir*s. Memorials commemorating the Sufis who had converted east Bengal seemed to him to be the real centres of Muslim devotion and in some cases attracted very large numbers of pilgrims. William Ward also found that 'all over the country small places, called durgahs [*dargah*s], are raised' at which Muslims prayed for intercession by saints.[128] Buchanan further reported that Hindu deities and shrines were openly honoured or had been only very thinly Islamicised. In Chittagong he found that Muslims had 'adapted some fable to almost every place esteemed holy by the Gentoos'.[129] Finally, Buchanan gave some indication of the very rich crop of syncretic Hindu–Muslim cults that had grown up in Bengal. In Rangpur he found an object of common worship to both Hindus and Muslims, called Satya Narayan by the one and Satya Pir by the other.[130] Later inquirers were to describe other exotic cults, such as that of Kwajah Khizr, a personage who protected mariners. Even the Murshidabad Nawabs and their deputies at Dhaka took part in celebrations in his honour.[131]

To Muslim reformers of the nineteenth century such cults and the apparent ignorance of most Muslims were wholly deplorable. Yet it is perhaps hardly surprising that the descendants of converts, whose contact with the main stream of Islam was at best thin and intermittent, should have retained much from their past together with the Bengali language. The way in which Islam developed in Bengal seems to have been yet another expression of Bengal's regional identity.[132]

As they travelled up the Ganges, Europeans looked out for signs to tell them that they were leaving Bengal for Bihar and thus entering what they regarded as 'Hindoostan'. At some point in the border districts of Bhagalpur and Purnea they crossed a language line between Bengali and Bihari, although the two languages shaded into one another and intermixed in these districts. Englishmen prided themselves on being able to distinguish physical characteristics that marked out Biharis from Bengalis. They noted that the sprawl of separate clusters of huts that characterised the Bengali village gave way to the more concentrated village settlements of Bihar. Above all, the further away from

[128] Ward, *Account of the Hindoos*, I, 138–9.
[129] Buchanan, 'Journey through Chittagong and Tiperah', Add. MS 19286, fo. 57.
[130] Martin, *Eastern India*, III, 512.
[131] J. Wise, *Notes on the Races, Castes and Trades of Eastern Bengal* (1883), p. 12.
[132] A. Roy, *The Islamic Syncretistic Tradition in Bengal* (Princeton, 1983).

the delta the traveller moved, the dryer the environment became.

Physically, the plains of Bihar can be divided into two regions, one to the north, the other to the south of the Ganges. To the north of the Ganges the plains are crossed by powerful rivers, such as the Gandaks and the Kosi, which flow out of the Himalayas into the Ganges. The rivers deposited much fertile alluvial soil but, as in western Bengal, they were capricious: on their best behaviour they flooded predictably and fertilised large areas with their silt; at their worst they changed course without warning and created devastation by immoderate flooding. The Great Gandak regularly created havoc until it was in some degree restrained by embankments early in the nineteenth century. The normal flooding of the Kosi helped to make the south-western districts of Purnea admirably fertile,[133] but it was also a river given to destroying crops, stock and habitation over wide areas. With lower rainfall than most of Bengal, Bihar north of the Ganges was prone to periodic droughts as well as to flooding. The district of Purnea was especially hard hit by the 1770 famine. In Darbhanga 'during the early years of British administration, hardly a year passed without the record of some natural calamity: in one year it was drought, in the next inundation'.[134]

In spite of natural hazards, however, northern Bihar was considered to be a fertile tract. Where it was effectively settled, heavy crops could be produced. Saran, for instance, was described as being a highly productive district in the early years of British rule. 'I do not think the present state of the cultivation . . . can be well exceeded; there are few or no waste lands', wrote the Collector in 1788.[135] Purnea was another district of dense population and high cultivation. Other areas remained thinly populated until much later. By the beginning of the nineteenth century, however, the spread of settlement throughout northern Bihar appeared to be general, rapid increases being noted in previously under-populated districts.[136] Like eastern Bengal, northern Bihar had a frontier of expanding settlement. The crops were very much those of the western portion of Bengal. Rice was the staple food

---

[133] C.U. Blake, 'An Agricultural Memoir of the Poornea District', *Transactions of the Agricultural and Horticultural Society of India*, I (1829), 153.

[134] L.S.S. O'Malley, *Bengal District Gazetteers: Darbhanga* (Calcutta, 1907), p. 70.

[135] IOR, Bengal Revenue Consultations, 18 Sept. 1789, Range 51, vol. 46, p. 210.

[136] H.R. Ghosal, 'Tirhut at the End of the Eighteenth and the Beginning of the Nineteenth Century', *Journal of the Bihar Research Society*, XXXIX (1953), 366–9; O'Malley, *Darbhanga Gazetteer*, p. 60.

grain and sugar and oil seeds were the main cash crops. Wheat and barley, however, were grown on a much greater scale than in Bengal. In Purnea wheat was 'generally very cheap and moderate' and was 'much sought after by all classes of people'.[137]

Bihar south of the Ganges was a land which neither had the northern tract's natural fertility nor suffered from its periodic disasters. South of the Ganges 'the alluvial filling' on the plain 'is shallow, a mere veneer'. The rivers flowing out of the Chota Nagpur plateau inundate the land less, both for good and for ill, than the rivers fed by the snows of the Himalayas.[138] Largely spared flooding, the peoples of southern Bihar have learnt how to protect themselves from drought. Although the area was devastated in 1770 after the rains failed in 1768 and 1769, in the early twentieth century it was said that 'famine has never been severe in modern times'.[139] If the lack of rain was less than total, artificial irrigation provided a life-line. Water was stored in ponds, called *ahar*s, which were created by building dams to catch rainwater. The ponds were also fed by diverting river water into artificial channels. The result of this ingenuity was to make it possible to grow rice crops in a country which, from the quality of its soil and the relative lack of water, seemed to be unsuited to it. Buchanan, touring the districts south of the Ganges, reported that rice was the main crop in all of them. The rice was harvested mainly in the winter. As was the case north of the Ganges, wheat and barley were grown extensively as *rabi*, spring crops. 'When rice is cheap it forms the principal article of subsistence of the natives here; but a scarcity of that article is supplied by barley' and coarse grains.[140] *Rabi* crops again included oil seeds and sugar as well as the opium poppy, cultivated on high quality land with much watering and manuring by a specialist gardener caste, called Koeris. In a thirsty land wells provided the water for the high value crops.

As in Bengal, those who cultivated the land in Bihar seem to have varied from the relatively comfortable to the large mass of the poor. Rural poverty seems to have been most acute in those areas north of the Ganges where settlement was dense. Buchanan found that this was so in Purnea. Sharecroppers and labourers for wages were numerous.

---

[137] IOR, Bengal Board of Revenue: Grain, 31 Oct. 1794, Range 89, vol. 27.
[138] O.H.K. Spate *et al.*, *India, Pakistan and Ceylon: the Regions* (3rd edn, 1967), p. 565. [139] Report of Irrigation Commission, *PP*, 1904, LXVI, part ii, p. 156.
[140] West Bengal Archives, Committee of Grain, 21 Nov. 1783, bundle 1.

Most of them were bound to their employers by debt at an 'enormous usery'.[141] In Saran many holdings were said to be miniscule; those who occupied them had to place their 'labour in seed time and harvest at the disposal' of their richer neighbours.[142] South of the Ganges Buchanan found few sharecroppers and believed that the incidence of debt among cultivators around Patna and Gaya was less than in other districts. But 'day labourers are numerous' and by labouring 'many small farmers gain a part of their subsistence'.[143]

Stratification of the rural population seems to have been more influenced by caste in Bihar than in Bengal. In Bengal members of the 'gentry' castes, most obviously Brahmins and Kayasthas, held rights to collect revenue from cultivators but, outside certain areas, seem rarely to have engaged directly in cultivation.[144] Peasant society tended therefore to be divided between 'respectable' agricultural castes and those lower down the scale. In Bihar 'gentry' were very numerous, especially in the western districts. Saran to the north of the Ganges, and Shahabad to the south of it, were great strongholds of Rajputs. In the area round Patna and Gaya Buchanan found that 'the greatest part of the land' was occupied by 'an immense number (80,000 families) of Brahmans, who . . . have betaken themselves entirely to agriculture and arms'.[145] These were the famous Bhumihar or 'military' Brahmins, who were found all over Bihar, like the Rajputs, but who also, like them, rarely occurred in Bengal. There were also far more Muslims in the countryside of Bihar than in that of Bengal who claimed *ashraf*, that is genteel status. As in Bengal, many of the Bihar 'gentry' regarded themselves as receivers of revenue rather than as farmers of the land. But they were so numerous that the revenue rights that many of them enjoyed as *malik*s were quite inadequate to support them. Most of them 'could not live decently without cultivating the land on their own account'.[146] The great mass of the Bihar 'gentry' seem indeed to have been indistinguishable from other cultivators. According to Buchanan, they usually denied that they held the plough, but many did.[147] Buchanan described them as a truculent and turbulent group, claiming privileges of paying taxes at reduced rates. They evidently

[141] Martin, *Eastern India*, III, 289.
[142] R. Rankine, *Notes on the Medical Topography of the District of Sarun* (Calcutta, 1839), pp. 36–7.     [143] Martin, *Eastern India*, I, 309.
[144] Ray, *Bengal Agrarian Society*, pp. 30–1.     [145] Martin, *Eastern India*, I, 157.
[146] Ibid., I, 312.     [147] Ibid., I, 157.

kept their distance from the cultivating castes, Kurmis, Koeris and Yadavs, who equally kept their distance from low caste groups and those deemed impure. In Purnea 'the best land is occupied by the highest castes, and pays the lowest rent'.[148]

Like Bengal, Bihar had artisans both scattered through villages and clustered in towns. It seems likely that most of them worked for strictly local markets; by the time Buchanan did his surveys this was certainly true of the weavers, the majority of whom wove coarse cloth for consumption in their immediate neighbourhood. But the Ganges linked Bihar easily with the great cities of northern India upstream and with Murshidabad, Calcutta and Europe downstream. In the area around Patna weaving communities specialising in cotton cloth for European markets existed from the mid seventeenth century. Patna was still a centre for exporting cloth to Indian and European markets in the early nineteenth century. By then Monghyr, further down the Ganges, had become a considerable centre for metal working, producing 'kettles, tea trays, guns, pistols, toasting-forks, cutlery' and other items appropriate to a 'tiny Birmingham'.[149] From the seventeenth century very large quantities of saltpetre, an essential raw material for gunpowder, were also exported from Bihar; suitably impregnated earth was gathered in most of the districts north of the Ganges and sold to European 'factories' for further processing and export.

Town life seems to have been significantly more developed in Bihar than in Bengal. In this, as in some other respects, Bihar seems to have had more in common with northern India further to the west than with the 'rurban' conditions which prevailed in parts of deltaic Bengal. In the winter of 1763–4 an East India Company military officer kept a journal of his march across what were later to be the districts of Patna and Gaya. He noted 'a whole chain of large towns and mud forts'. The town of Bihar with its 'famous dirgah' was 'very large and well supplied with provisions'. Tikari was 'a large town and fort . . . walled round with a stout wall and bastions, and an extream good wet ditch, both deep and broad'. Daudnagar was 'a remarkable handsome town and large . . . 'tis very populous and carrys on a considerable trade, especially in carpets'. Sasaram 'has been a famous place formerly as appears by its ruins'.[150] Three years later another officer visited Gaya, already one of the great pilgrimage cities of India. He found it

[148] Ibid., III, 284.   [149] Heber, *Narrative of a Journey*, I, 132.
[150] Captain Maclean's Journal, IOL, Orme MS 'India', XVII.

'spacious with many good buildings, the generality of brick and stone' and possessing a 'plentifully supplied bazaar'.[151] This list of towns in southern Bihar suggests that some were seats of important local potentates, like the Rajas of Tikari, some were places of trade, and some had grown up round Hindu and Muslim shrines.

Patna, the major city of Bihar, was concerned with government, trade and religion. As seat of the Mughal governor of the Bihar *Suba*, it attracted poets, painters and scholars, as well as men of business. In the mid eighteenth century it was said to be full of those 'who loved sciences and learning and employed themselves in teaching and being taught'.[152] Fifty years later, Buchanan (for whom Indian towns were something of a blind spot) thought it 'disagreeable and disgusting'.[153] But he recognised that it was an important centre of trade and finance, containing twenty-four banking houses of 'extensive credit'.[154]

By the mid eighteenth century Bihar was developing into a linguistic and cultural region in its own right. It too had centres of Sanskrit scholarship, the most notable being in the Tirhut district north of the Ganges, the ancient Mithila. Learning at Mithila was the monopoly of a group of Brahmins who were regarded as being extremely strict in their orthodoxy by comparison with most Brahmins in Bengal. In the 1830s there were still some fifty Sanskrit schools in the Tirhut district.[155] The Mithila region had developed one of the three main branches of the Bihari language, Maithili, which was spoken over a large belt north of the Ganges. It had a literature of considerable vitality in the eighteenth century. As in Bengal, the great *zamindari* families provided patronage for religion and learning. The Brahmins and poets of Mithila were sustained by the Rajas of Darbhanga at whose court in the mid eighteenth century both pandits 'singing the essence of the Vedas' and munshis 'elated with Persian knowledge' were said to be employed.[156]

As in Bengal, there were schools, at least in the larger villages, teaching elementary arithmetic and the rudiments of reading and writing.[157] William Adam, who investigated indigenous schools in parts of western Bengal in the 1830s, also inquired into schools in southern dis-

---

[151] Captain de Gloss's Survey, ibid., XVII, p. 4879.
[152] [Ghulam Husain Khan], *A Translation of the Seir Mutaqherin* (3 vols., Calcutta, 1789), II, 175.    [153] Martin, *Eastern India*, I, 39.
[154] Ibid., I, 380–1.    [155] Adam, *Reports*, p. 271.
[156] J.S. Jha, 'History of Darbhanga Raj', *Journal of Bihar Research Society*, XLVIII (1962), 42.    [157] J.S. Jha, *Education in Bihar 1813–59* (Patna, 1979), p. 20.

tricts of Bihar and in Tirhut. He concluded that: 'Vernacular instruction prevails to a greater extent in the Bengal than in the Behar districts visited' and that caste restrictions on education were more rigid. [158]

The Muslim communities in Bihar were smaller than those in the eastern half of Bengal; Buchanan estimated them to be about one-quarter of the population of the districts which he visited. In some towns the Muslim presence was pronounced, most obviously so in centres of Mughal government like Patna, the seat of the Governors of Bihar, or Purnea, where a very powerful *faujdar* had once had his court and one hundred Shi'ite families from Persia, people of 'high birth and decent education' were still living early in the nineteenth century. [159] Some towns were also dominated by notable Muslim shrines. In the countryside the Muslim population had more claims to social eminence than in many parts of Bengal. Considerable numbers called themselves Mughals, Syeds or Pathans, that is descendants of immigrants to India, and lived as 'a kind of gentry'. [160] But there were also many poorer cultivators and artisans, especially weavers.

Patna became a centre of learning in the eighteenth century. As conditions in Delhi deteriorated, Patna, as well as the cities of Awadh to the west, attracted displaced scholars, poets and painters. Arabic was studied there and a considerable corpus of Persian and Urdu poetry was written, not only under the patronage of Muslim noblemen but also under that of the Hindu Kayasthas who served the Nawabs' government. Patna played a part in the development of Urdu as a literary language in northern India. [161] The study of Persian, however, maintained its hold. Persian schools were still 'numerous' in southern Bihar in the 1830s. [162] Early in the nineteenth century Buchanan found that public Friday prayers were being celebrated at only two or three mosques in Patna, the largest congregation having only forty or fifty attenders. [163]

Bihar had a network of *kadi*s attached to revenue divisions, as in Bengal, and these also survived into the British period. Buchanan again identified 'mullas', but he believed that the real leadership for

---

[158] Adam, *Reports*, pp. 249–50.
[159] Martin, *Eastern India*, III, 150.    [160] Ibid., II, 111.
[161] These themes are discussed in F.L. Lehmann, 'The Eighteenth-century Transition in India: Responses of some Bihar Intellectuals', Unpublished Ph.D. thesis, University of Wisconsin, 1967.    [162] Adam, *Reports*, p. 440.    [163] Martin, *Eastern India*, I, 143.

rural Muslims in Bihar was, as in eastern Bengal, provided by mendicant fakirs, and by Sufi *pirzadas*. Tombs, shrines and pilgrimages again seem to have been important. Among the poorer Muslims Hindu cults and practices appeared to be still observed. A number of syncretic movements developed, such as that of Dariya in Shahabad.[164] On the other hand, Buchanan also provided evidence of increasing strictness among some Bihar Muslims by the beginning of the nineteenth century.

Eighteenth-century Orissa consisted of mostly wooded and hilly tracts in the west, where Rajput princelings ruled over a relatively thin population of tribal peoples, and more thickly populated alluvial plains in the east. The Orissa plains, like those of lower Bengal, were the deltas of great rivers, the Mahanadi and the Brahmani being the most important. The low land, or Mughalbandi as it was called, was inevitably almost entirely a rice-growing area. Salt was also produced along the coast, as in Bengal. Although it was much more highly developed than the hill tracts, in the eighteenth century Englishmen still thought that the Mughalbandi of Orissa was a poor area. The population density was low and much of the population was apparently highly migratory. Most areas produced only a single crop of rice. Famine, following drought or flood, was frequent. Orissa suffered in 1770 and again in 1775, 1780 and 1792–3.[165]

Few cash crops seem to have been grown, but there was a weaving industry. In the seventeenth century and for much of the eighteenth century, cotton cloth was exported from Balasore, the main port of Orissa, where the English East India Company maintained a factory. Gosains of Vaishnavite religious orders were important traders in Balasore cloth. They imported raw cotton from the Deccan and took away finished cloth and Orissa salt. Gosains and merchants from Gujarat not only organised Orissa's trade but also advanced money to the government and farmed the collection of taxes, especially during the period when Orissa was occupied by the Marathas from 1751 to 1803.[166] Gosains even held high office during the Maratha regime. Cuttack, the administrative centre, said to have a population of 40,000 in the early nineteenth century, contained 'several fine mansions of

---

[164] Described in Lehmann, 'Responses of Some Bihar Intellectuals'.
[165] B.S. Das, *Studies in the Economic History of Orissa* (Calcutta, 1979) pp. 105–6; B.C. Ray, *Orissa under the Marathas* (Allahabad, 1961), p. 135.　　[166] Das, *Studies*, pp. 242–6.

stone that belonged formerly to the Gossain and Parwar merchants, who engrossed all the trade and principal official employments of the province under the Mahrattas'.[167] South of Cuttack, on the sea at Puri, was the great temple complex dedicated to Jagannath. This attracted pilgrims from all over India, but especially from Bengal, on a scale comparable to the numbers that went to Gaya. By the beginning of the nineteenth century over 100,000 pilgrims a year made their way to the Jagannath temples.

The temples provided the main focus for a cultural identity that was specific to Orissa.[168] The Brahmins of Puri studied Sanskrit, but most of the abundant Vaishnavite literature produced at the temples and at the court of the Rajas of Khurda, the temples' patrons, was in Oriya.[169] Although close to Bengali, Oriya had developed into a regional language whose boundary in fact extended over the political frontier between Orissa and Bengal into parts of Midnapur on the Bengal side.

In the mid eighteenth century by far the largest part of the population of Bengal, Bihar and Orissa lived in the alluvial plains. On the edges of the plains a quite different world began: the world of the hills and of the 'tribals', the *adivasi*s or first settlers, most of whom had not been assimilated into Hindu or Muslim society. But although the hills remained a separate world, it was one into which the plains increasingly intruded, both under the Nawabs and under the East India Company.

To the west, the plains of southern Bihar, of western Bengal and of Orissa were fringed by hills: the Chota Nagpur plateau and its outliers, the Orissa and Bastar Hills and the northern spurs of the Eastern Ghats. All these highland areas had their 'tribal' inhabitants, although population and cultivation were rarely dense. Kharwars and Cheros lived on the eastern part of Chota Nagpur; Oraons, Mundas and Bhumijs on the central plateau; Bhuiyas and Paharias to the west; and Hos further south. The migratory Santhals were slowly moving the area which they occupied, extending their dominance westward towards the plains of Bengal. In the hills south of Orissa lived the Khonds and the Savara.

[167] A. Stirling, *Orissa: Its Geography, History, Religion and Antiquities* (1846), p. 34.
[168] See essays in A. Eschmann, H. Kulke and G.C. Tripathi, *The Cult of Jagannath and the Regional Tradition of Orissa* (Delhi, 1978).
[169] M. Mansinha, *History of Oriya Literature* (Delhi, 1978).

Over a long period the peoples of the plains had been increasingly extending their influence into the western hills. Would-be leaders of the tribes were often the first to be so influenced. There was a tendency for them to try to consolidate their authority by adopting a Hindu way of life, often styling themselves Rajputs, calling in Brahmin priests and Rajput soldiers from the plains and seeking recognition from the rulers of the plains, be they Mughal or British. New values and new settlers spread through the influence of tribal leaders, but the position of both the new 'Rajas' and their supporters could be precarious. Resentment could lead their tribal subjects to revolt. Under the East India Company both the Raja of Ramgarh and the Raja of Singhbhum faced such revolts.

Incursions into the hills were also organised by the Rajas and *zamindar*s of the plains who sought to extend their authority and at the same time to create a barrier protecting their territories by settling their followers along the frontier. Frontier settlements were usually created by giving land to people called *ghatwal*s, who held their lands on condition that they maintained the peace and protected the plains. *Ghatwal*s in their turn settled a militia on their lands, usually known as *paik*s. In the view of both the Nawabs' officials and their British successors, these frontier military colonies had a pronounced tendency to become centres of raiding and disorder, rather than of stability. Instability was indeed characteristic of the whole length of the western hills, as plainsmen pressed into them and encountered sporadic resistance.[170]

To the east, the plains of Bengal were also flanked by hills: the Garo, Khasi and Jaintia hills to the north of Mymensingh and Sylhet; and the Lushai hills and the Chittagong Hill Tracts in the ranges separating eastern Bengal from Burma. Again, a variety of peoples who were ethnically distinct from the Bengalis of the plains lived in these hills: Kochs in the far north; Garos, Khasis and Kacharis in the spur north of Sylhet; and Tripuras, Reangs, Chakmas and Kukis to the south. As with the western hills, there was a long history of penetration of the hills by ideas, settlers and trade. There were, however, marked differences between east and west. In the first place, the Bengalis and their rulers pushing east were likely to encounter strong powers com-

---

[170] Recent accounts can be found in J.C. Jha, *The Kol Insurrection of Chota-Nagpur* (Calcutta, 1964); C.P. Singh, *The Ho Tribe of Singhbhum* (New Delhi, 1978); F.G. Bailey, *Tribe, Caste and Nation* (Manchester, 1960).

ing from other directions, the Ahoms from the Assam valley and the formidable Burmese from the other side of the mountains. Secondly, the formation of states by chieftains in the hills seems to have gone further in the east than it had done in the west. Cooch Behar, the state of the Koch kings, had a long tradition of independence, while the Rajas of the states of Tripura, Jaintia, Manipur and Kachar all struck Buchanan as being 'pretty considerable chiefs'.[171] All five states were thoroughly Hinduised. During the eighteenth century some of these frontier states were incorporated into Bengal, as was the case with Tripura in 1761 and Cooch Behar in 1774, while the others maintained a more or less stable independence. Where state organisation was weaker, piecemeal penetration, often leading to conflict and resistance from the tribal peoples, occurred in a manner not unlike that in the western hills. Both the Garos and the Chakmas attracted traders seeking their cotton, settlers seeking their lands and the attentions of rulers claiming tribute from them. Affrays took place in both areas.[172]

The northern frontiers of Bengal and Bihar were formed by the forests and grasslands which fringed the foot-hills of the Himalayas. This was a country of small hill chiefs, most of whom were being subjugated during the second half of the eighteenth century by the new Gurkha rulers of Nepal. Pilgrims, traders and timber cutters crossed the frontiers, while the northern *zamindar*s of Bihar nursed claims to territory which was being absorbed by Nepal. The power of the Gurkhas, shown when they rebuffed intervention in the 1760s both from the Nawab of Bengal and from the East India Company, prevented these claims being pressed very vigorously. They were, however, to be the pretext for a major war between the British and Nepal in 1814.[173]

The shifting nature of the three provinces' frontiers, with a long-term tendency towards expansion, is yet another illustration of a proposition argued at the beginning of this chapter. The setting for the

[171] Martin, *Eastern India*, III, 682.

[172] For recent treatment of these areas see A.C. Banerjee, *The Eastern Frontier of British India 1784–1826* (3rd edn, Calcutta, 1964); N.K. Barooah, *David Scott in North-East India* (Delhi, 1970); R.L. Chakraborty, 'Chakma Resistance to early British Rule', *Bangladesh Historical Studies*, II, (1977), 133–56.

[173] For material on the northern frontier see K.C. Chaudhuri, *Anglo-Nepalese Relations: From the Earliest Times of the British Rule till the Gurkha War* (Calcutta, 1960).

empire of the late Nawabs and the early East India Company was not a static one. Terrain, economy, social order, beliefs and language were all undergoing change, which needs to be measured over a longer time span than the seventy-five years of this volume. What this period brought was a sudden political revolution with very important social and economic consequences. The regimes which the conquerors of eastern India established were to a considerable degree shaped by what the region already had to offer. As this chapter has tried to indicate, Bengal in particular offered its conquerors a great deal. It is not difficult to see why Bengal was so valuable a prop for the late Mughal empire. It could guarantee very large remittances, either in cash or in easily realisable bills, to the imperial centre at Delhi. Bengal's ability to generate surpluses which could be easily turned into cash was equally attractive to the British. Bengal financed a large part of British naval and military operations and important parts of British trade beyond its own frontiers.

The capacity to provide its rulers with easily accessible wealth depended on Bengal's system of taxation, which is described in Chapters 2 and 4. The taxation system depended, of course, on the capacity of agriculture to produce surpluses which could be taxed. It also depended on a market for agricultural products which enabled them to be sold for cash, and flows of trade which enabled cash collected in the countryside to be transferred to those areas where the government needed it. Agricultural markets, trade and taxation were all underpinned by the availability of credit at many levels throughout Bengal.

From the mid seventeenth century, if not earlier, its productive agriculture, the high level of the skills of its artisans and its financial and communications networks had procured Bengal an important place in international trade. Long before the British conquest, Bengal had become the most important area in Asia for the East India Company's trade. It was a very rich prize to be incorporated into a British empire based on commerce.

Finally, the human assets which eastern India offered to its conquerors went beyond the industry of its peasants and the skill of its artisans. From this area, and especially from Bengal, the Mughals and the British were able to attract to their service a group of mostly high caste Hindus who were able to become literate in Persian and English and to acquire the skills needed to staff the conquerors' bureaucracies.

Such men would seem to have been the products of some of the trends tentatively suggested in this chapter: a system of caste ranking with some flexibility in it rather than a rigid application to prescribed occupations, and an intellectual tradition capable of assimilating new influences. Without such men willing to act as its servants and intermediaries with the mass of the population the establishment of an alien regime would have been much more costly and difficult than it proved to be.

If Bengal had obvious assets to offer to its conquerors, closer acquaintance revealed, at least to the British, constraints on what they could expect to derive from their new provinces. Some of these constraints have been indicated in this chapter. Early British rule in Bengal can be seen from some points of view as a struggle to adjust expectations to what seemed to be stark reality. The adjustment was completed in 1793 by the famous Permanent Settlement, by which the British voluntarily renounced for ever any increase from taxation to be raised from the land. In retrospect the level of the 1793 settlement may seem to have represented a tolerable bargain from the conqueror's point of view by the end of the eighteenth century, but to many Englishmen of the time it signified an acceptance that a high yield of taxation so eagerly anticipated at the time of the conquest was not to be attained.

In part the failure to extract more may have been due, as one school of opinion believed, to a newly established and ignorant regime's inability to prevent the hierarchy of Indian intermediaries syphoning off a huge proportion of the tax yield. But there was another school, headed by the greatest of the early 'revenue' experts, John Shore, who doubted whether any 'man of experience' could believe that Bengal possessed 'prodigious wealth'.[174] There must be a ceiling on what could be taken from a peasantry, many of whom were too poor to extend their cultivation, even though there was as yet little pressure on land, many of whom were deeply in debt and the majority of whom would be plunged into destitution and death if the rains failed or a harvest was flooded. Contemporaries of Shore's believed that 'the peasantry at large' lived 'crowded in narrow huts, which are neither secured from intrusion nor from the weather, and are formed from materials which a wealthier class would refuse even for fuel', that they

---

[174] Minute of June 1789, *PP*, 1812, VII, 184.

ate 'unnutritive grains and pulse', and that they dressed in 'sack cloth and blanket'.[175] Such men were a fragile support for over-ambitious empires, and were not likely to be very susceptible to new cultural influences brought by their foreign rulers.

Contemporary Europeans believed that the soil of Bengal was extremely fertile. Empires were likely to take root there easily. Whether the roots would go deep or the harvest be abundant was less certain.

[175] [Colebrooke and Lambert], *Remarks*, pp. 64–5.

# CHAPTER 2

# LATE MUGHAL BENGAL

Even in the eighteenth century, provinces of the Mughal empire were in theory part of a fully integrated imperial system. The provincial government was manned by men who were loyal to the empire, not to the province where they happened to serve. Senior office holders owed their appointments to the Emperor and lost them at his pleasure, when they were dismissed or transferred to other provinces. A large part of the financial resources of any province was either allocated to support imperial service through the system of *jagirs*, grants of revenue for the upkeep of troops or distinguished individuals, or remitted to the imperial treasury.

When Alivardi Khan became Governor of Bengal, Bihar and Orissa in 1740, these areas were still provinces of the Mughal empire, but the way in which they were governed bore little resemblance to the system outlined above. Alivardi Khan ruled a virtually autonomous state. He seized his position by force, subsequently gaining imperial endorsement, and he filled offices at his own discretion, even if he sought imperial ratification for most of them later. The resources of Bengal itself were no longer allocated in imperial *jagirs*, although these survived in Bihar and Orissa. Earlier in the eighteenth century, money had gone from Bengal to the imperial treasury in great quantities; in Alivardi Khan's 'reign' the flow of tribute became very irregular. The links binding the three provinces to the imperial centre, itself seriously weakened, had become very tenuous. An independent state was in the making.

What kind of state might eventually have emerged in eastern India is an intriguing question. It is suggested in Chapter 1 that distinct cultural entities existed in Bengal and Orissa and, perhaps in a more diffused form, in Bihar. To assume that these identities could have been embodied in the course of time into some sort of 'national' state is to assume a great deal. There was of course a plurality of identities to be reconciled between the three provinces and within them. Moreover, the aristocracy who dominated the eighteenth-century state machinery for the most part identified themselves with the empire as a whole and not with the region. Nevertheless, given a long period of effective autonomy, some drawing together of state and subjects might perhaps have occurred. Such a development was taking place in other parts of India in the eighteenth century. Late Mughal Bengal was not, however, to be granted a long period of effective autonomy.

In addition to the Governor, or *Nazim*, Mughal provinces were ruled by a *Diwan*, who was separately appointed by the Emperor as a check on the *Nazim*. The *Nazim* was responsible for defence and law and order; the *Diwan* was responsible for finance and some aspects of justice. Alivardi Khan, however, succeeded in 1740 as a Nawab who combined the offices of both *Nazim* and *Diwan*. In so doing he was the heir of Murshid Kuli Khan, the architect of an autonomous Bengal, who had held the office of *Nazim*, together with his post as *Diwan*, from about 1716 until his death in 1727.[1]

Murshid Kuli Khan had in effect founded a dynasty. His successors would seek imperial confirmation, but it seems to have been fully accepted that it was the hereditary right of the family of Murshid Kuli Khan to be the Nawabs of Bengal. Unfortunately, however, an incontrovertibly legitimate succession had not been established. Each time a Nawab died, the succession was contested. In 1727 the conflict was resolved relatively easily. Murshid Kuli Khan's preference had been for his son-in-law, Sarfaraz Khan, but he was quickly deposed in a bloodless coup by his own father, Shuja Khan. On Shuja Khan's death in 1739, the contender this time was unconnected with the family of Murshid Kuli Khan. Alivardi Khan came from a family which had served in various parts of Mughal India. He and his brother were highly valued as soldier–administrators by Shuja Khan, and this led to his appointment as the Nawab's Deputy in Bihar. Bihar was the base from which Alivardi Khan launched his bid for the three provinces when Shuja Khan died in 1739. Sarfaraz Khan, the late Nawab's son, succeeded for the second time, but in 1740 Alivardi Khan invaded Bengal from Bihar and took the throne by force. Very large sums were sent to Delhi to obtain imperial confirmation, which was duly given, although the Emperor, Muhammad Shah, had no compunction in encouraging other claimants when the flow of tribute from Alivardi Khan began to dry up.[2]

[1] A. Karim, *Murshid Quli Khan and his Times* (Dacca, 1963).
[2] Z.U. Malik, *The Reign of Muhammad Shah* (New Delhi, 1977), pp. 240–8.

The practical power of the Nawabs of Bengal was such that Alivardi Khan was able to dispose of offices throughout the provinces with virtually no regard to Delhi. The major appointments were those of the *Naib*s, or Deputies, to the Nawab, appointed to Patna for Bihar, Cuttack for Orissa and Dhaka for eastern Bengal, which was virtually administered as a separate entity. As had become customary, Alivardi Khan tended to appoint his immediate relatives to these great commands, giving them able Hindu *diwan*s who did most of the administrative work. A Mughal province was in theory divided into smaller units, or *sarkar*s, whose defence and good order were the immediate responsibility of a *faujdar*. When imperial authority was fully enforced, *faujdar*s were appointed directly from Delhi. They should be 'men of great distinction and note', who were in 'the immediate service of the Emperor'.[3] Most of them were in fact the appointees of the Nawab. The *faujdar*s of Purnea were a notable exception. They had quarried out a virtually autonomous jurisdiction for themselves and permitted no intervention by the Nawabs.[4] At Hooghly the *faujdar* collected dues on Bengal's foreign trade and managed the Nawab's relations with merchants, including the Europeans. In other internal districts in Bengal *faujdari* jurisdiction had lapsed, the surviving *faujdar*s being concentrated along the frontier districts on both the western and the eastern borders of the province. The main office of the central administration under the immediate control of the Nawabs was the *Khalsa*, or Treasury, at Murshidabad. This was staffed by largely Hindu revenue administrators, who were known as *mutaseddi*s. Murshid Kuli Khan was said to have 'employed none but Bengally Hindus in the collection of the revenues, because they are most easily compelled by punishment to discover their malpractices'.[5] Whatever the truth of that, the profession of *mutaseddi* was in fact a well-established one, skills being passed on through families. The leading *mutaseddi* was the *Rairayan*, or Treasurer, of Bengal. As well as serving in the central *Khalsa*, *mutaseddi*s were deputed into the districts to manage the Nawabs' revenues as *amil*s or local *diwan*s.

By 1740 the three provinces had acquired an administrative system that was almost entirely separate from that of the rest of the empire.

---

[3] [Ghulam Husain Khan], *A Translation of the Seir Mutaqherin* (3 vols., Calcutta, 1789), II, 569–72.

[4] *Riyaz us Salatin*, translated by Abdus Salam (Calcutta, 1904), p. 261.

[5] *A Narrative of Transactions in Bengal*, translated by F. Gladwin (Calcutta, 1788), p. 61.

The Nawabs had also developed their own military forces. When he was employed in Bihar, Alivardi Khan had raised troops from among the Pathans settled in north India. He brought them with him to Bengal, where he kept a force of Pathans 'always on duty near his person'.[6] They were the nucleus of a considerable standing army of up-country sepoys and cavalry.

The taxation levied from Bengal was one of the major props of the Mughal Empire. By the middle of the eighteenth century, however, the flow of funds was much diminished. As the result of a deal concluded by Murshid Kuli Khan with the imperial administration, Bengal no longer supported troops or Mughal dignitaries by allocations of revenue from land as *jagir*s. The Nawab took the *jagir* lands in Bengal under his own direct management on the assumption that he would be able to extract, and remit to Delhi, larger sums than the *jagir* assignments. The *jagir*s granted for Bengal were transferred to Orissa, a much less promising field, where their holders would have to struggle to raise an adequate revenue.[7] About one-quarter of Bengal's revenue remained technically assigned to *jagir*s, but the allocations were for the costs of Bengal's government and defence and for the personal expenses of the Nawabs.[8] In Bihar and Orissa a considerable proportion of the total revenue was still committed to *jagir*s. In Bihar most of the revenue was thought to be so assigned by the middle of the century.[9] It seems, however, that only a few of the Bihar *jagir*s were at the disposal of the Emperor, while those in Orissa were to be totally lost to him within a few years.

Whether Bengal continued to support the Mughal Empire depended almost entirely on whether the Nawabs dispatched an adequate tribute to Delhi from the revenue which they collected from their provinces. Murshid Kuli Khan and Shuja Khan were said to have paid an annual tribute of Rs. 10,000,000.[10] In part the remittance was made by bills of exchange drawn by the great Murshidabad bankers, the Jagat Seths, on their house in Delhi. It was presumably possible for the bankers to dispose of bills for such large sums because of the great volume of Bengal textile exports to the cities of northern India. But it

[6] J.Z. Holwell, *Interesting Historical Events, Relative to the Province of Bengal*, 2nd edn (2 vols., 1766, 1771), I, 100.    [7] *Narrative*, trans. Gladwin, pp. 32–3.
[8] These are listed in J. Grant, 'Analysis of the Finances of Bengal', *PP*, 1812, VII, 272–3.    [9] Ibid., pp. 418–19.
[10] J.N. Sarkar (ed.), *The Bengal Nawabs* (Calcutta, 1952), p. 14; Malik, *Muhammad Shah*, p. 235.

seems that bullion was also shipped away from Bengal. An English observer noted that every year 'almost all the silver, coined or un-coined, which comes into Bengal' was sent off to Delhi, so that 'there is hardly currency enough left in Bengal to carry on any trade or even go to market for provisions and necessaries of life, till the next shipping arrives to bring a fresh supply of silver'.[11] While he was trying to obtain recognition of his usurpation, Alivardi Khan made very substantial extra payments of tribute to Delhi, as well as the Rs. 10,000,000.[12] Thereafter, payments seem to have been scaled down. An account drawn up in 1758 estimated that payments totalling Rs. 4,000,000 to Rs. 5,000,000 had been made over the previous fifteen years.[13] Other contemporary sources suggested that payments may have stopped altogether.[14] It seems unlikely that much was sent during the years 1742–51, when Alivardi Khan was fighting the Marathas.

The Emperors' inability to enforce a full and regular tribute was, as far as they were concerned, conclusive evidence that the provinces of eastern India were lost to the empire. There is, however, nothing to suggest that Alivardi Khan had consciously aimed at establishing a separate regional kingdom. He had nullified all practical imperial intervention in Bengal, but he had not thrown off his allegiance to the ideal of a Mughal empire. Nevertheless, whatever the Nawabs had intended, the reality was that Bengal, Bihar and Orissa were emerging as a separate entity. Whether this process would continue or be checked depended partly on the strength of pressures from outside the provinces and partly on the ability of the Nawabs to survive pressures against them from within. In the event, both kinds of pressure coincided to end the autonomy of the Nawabs and bring the provinces into an empire organised not from Delhi but from London.

The threats to the Nawabs from outside are described in Chapter 3. The internal stability of the provinces rested on the ability of the Nawabs to secure the obedience, and if possible, the positive loyalty of groups whose opposition to their government could be extremely dangerous. The Nawabs might have been able to erode the customary checks which the Emperors tried to enforce on provincial Governors, but this did not necessarily give them a monopoly of power within the

---

[11] Cited in J. Steuart, *The Principles of Money Applied to the Present State of the Coin of Bengal* (1772), pp. 62–3.    [12] Malik, *Muhammad Shah*, p. 241.
[13] IOL, Orme MSS, 'India', IV, fo. 875.
[14] C. Stewart, *The History of Bengal* (1813), p. 491.

provinces. Authority in Bengal rested on acquiescence as well as on coercion. Among those whose acquiescence the Nawabs had to seek were the Mughal aristocracy, who were their virtual peers, the officials who ran the administrative machine, the major revenue-paying zamindars and even the merchants and bankers.

By filling the major offices within the provinces with men of his own choosing, Alivardi Khan may have restricted imperial influence, but he had not necessarily assured himself of docile support. He recognised an obligation to choose from an aristocracy who were either recent migrants from Iran or central Asia or were from families established in India. Such men might treat him as he had treated Murshid Kuli Khan's family. They were highly factional, much given to conspiracy and very inclined to carve out autonomous jurisdictions for themselves. The armed forces that the Nawab had built up were a two-edged weapon, likely to turn against their master, as did the Afghans in Bihar in spectacular fashion in 1745 and again in 1748, when they sacked Patna and killed the Nawab's brother.

Hindu officials were perhaps less given to violent resistance, but their loyalty could not be taken for granted either. Their skills were indispensable. Without them, as the British were to learn in the early years of their rule, the revenue which made Bengal so attractive to its conquerors would not flow.

Most of the revenue came to the government from zamindars. Zamindar was a term which in Bengal, let alone in Bihar and Orissa, covered a wide variety of people. From 1793 onwards the status of a zamindar became legally defined with specific rights attached, as a result of a series of British enactments. In the eighteenth century this was certainly not the case. Contemporary Englishmen, who were obsessed with concepts of 'an ancient constitution' for Mughal India, spent much time and effort in trying to define what they regarded as the 'true' rights and duties of zamindars. Such efforts had only a limited value, however, as those people who were being referred to as zamindars by the middle of the eighteenth century had evolved from several different starting points. What they had in common was the right to collect taxation and the duty to pass part of it on to the government. The collection of taxation had also generally come to involve the exercise of some degree of authority over those who paid it. These rights had acquired a clear element of property. It was accepted that those who held them should not be deprived without due cause and that, in cases where they were dispossessed, they were entitled to an allowance as compensation. *Zamindari* rights had become heritable and could be bought and sold. Eighteenth-century Englishmen saw them as existing somewhere between what they understood as outright ownership of land on the one hand, and appointment to the office of tax collector at the pleasure of the ruler on the other. At least before 1793, *zamindars* appeared not to be land-lords owning estates; only a small part of the lands from which they collected tax usually seemed to belong to them. But the fact that the right to collect tax could be inherited, bought and sold implied that they were not simply government officials.[15]

Throughout most of India *zamindari* rights were divided into small units, and were exercised over a village or part of a village by those who claimed descent from members of a conquering force of the past or from the organisers of new settlements. Over parts of Bengal and much of Bihar small *zamindaris* were still flourishing in the eighteenth century; but in Bengal very large tracts had come to be incorporated under the control of a small number of *zamindaris*. The existence of large *zamindaris* is a very distinctive feature of Bengal's recent history. They constituted a layer of power which largely insulated the government, be it Mughal or British, from direct contact with large numbers of its subjects. Instead of endeavouring to assess and extract revenue from a mass of small payers, the government made contracts with a few large ones. In the process it inevitably devolved on the major *zamindars* considerable administrative and judicial responsibilities. The main concentration of large *zamindaris* was in western and central Bengal. Here the early Mughal regime was willing to make bargains with some chieftains who already enjoyed virtually autonomous status, while it also encouraged revenue administrators of proven competence to enter into ever larger contracts with the government. Its successors carried the process further. The Rajas of Vishnupur and Birbhum were obvious examples of old-established chieftains on the western frontier who retained their autonomy for a fixed tribute. Other large *zamindaris* were more recent creations, growing under

[15] N. Siddiqi, *Land Revenue Administration under the Mughals 1700–50* (1970); Chapter 2 is an analysis of *zamindars* throughout India. For Bengal, see W.K. Firminger, *Historical Introduction to the Bengal Portion of the 'Fifth Report'* (Calcutta, 1917); Chapter 2 remains a standard account. Recent accounts are: N.K. Sinha, *Economic History of Bengal from Plassey to the Permanent Settlement* (2 vols., Calcutta, 1956, 1962), II, Chapter 2; R. Ray, *Change in Bengal Agrarian Society c. 1760–1850* (New Delhi, 1979), Chapter 2.

Mughal rule as successful contractors or officials gained approval. The rise of Nadia began in the mid seventeenth century. Burdwan accumulated huge and immensely valuable holdings in western Bengal from the end of the seventeenth century. In the early eighteenth century Rajshahi and Dinajpur absorbed large numbers of smaller *zamindari*s. The growth of the great *zamindar*s is especially associated with Murshid Kuli Khan; by 1728 over a quarter of the nominal revenue of Bengal depended on the *zamindar*s of Burdwan and Rajshahi alone.[16] By the end of the Nawabs' rule 60 per cent of the revenue came from fifteen *zamindar*s. From the Nawabs' point of view, this concentration of resources into a few hands no doubt greatly simplified the problems of realising the revenue effectively. On the other hand, it created potentially formidable power blocs within Bengal, whose loyalty could not necessarily be guaranteed at all times.

A large *zamindari* was a complex administrative concern; it endeavoured to raise millions of Rupees in taxation from a huge area which was often scattered very widely rather than being in a consolidated unit. The *zamindari* of Rajshahi, for instance, was thought to extend over nearly 13,000 square miles.[17] The tax collections were managed by a hierarchy of *zamindari* officials reaching down to the level of the villages, or in many cases by contracts made with revenue 'farmers', who undertook to raise a certain sum from a certain area. But the administrative functions of a big *zamindari* went far beyond the narrowly defined levying of taxation. Taxation would flow only in conditions of order and stability in which agriculture and trade flourished. It was both in the *zamindar*'s interest and his duty to try to ensure order and stability. In theory the *faujdar*s were responsible for peace and security, but only a part of Bengal was covered by *faujdari* jurisdiction. Outside towns and the areas under the direct control of the *faujdar*s, the *zamindar*s were considered to be the only effective dispensers of justice and organisers of police. In order to enforce his revenue collections and preserve order a great *zamindar* maintained powerful forces. Militia and police were supported by lands allocated to them in the villages, while the *zamindar* often had a military establishment under his own immediate command. The Burdwan *zamindari* was served by over 30,000 militia and a force of household troops.[18] If a great *zamindar* withheld his revenue or defied the Nawab

[16] Grant, 'Analysis', *PP*, 1812, VII, 267–74.
[17] Sinha, *Economic History*, II, 17.    [18] Ray, *Bengal Agrarian Society*, pp. 96–7.

in some other way, it would take a major military operation to force him into submission.

The effectiveness of the Nawabs' government thus depended in large measure on an implied compact between them and fifteen or so major *zamindar*s. They relied on the *zamindar*s for much of their public revenue and for maintaining a stable order over wide areas. In return, the *zamindar*s evidently expected to be allowed a considerable margin of profit on their collections and a free hand in administering what was virtually their territory. Alivardi Khan seems to have accepted some such compact. He did not have to face serious *zamindari* rebellions in Bengal, while it was said that 'the zemindars were so well pleased with his conduct' that they made large extra contributions to his war expenses.[19] A Nawab who lost the confidence of the *zamindar*s would, as events were to show, be extremely vulnerable.

In the first half of the eighteenth century, although there had been a spectacular growth of large *zamindari*s, incorporating many smaller ones in the process, some parts of Bengal had been relatively unaffected by this development, and it seems probable that by the last years of the Nawabs the process of amalgamation had passed its peak and subdivision was starting. The areas where lesser *zamindar*s survived in greatest numbers were usually frontier ones, especially in the east. There *faujdar*s were able to exercise authority and organise collections from many revenue payers. In Chittagong there were thought to be 1,500 small *zamindar*s with over 3,000 in Midnapur on the southwest frontier.[20] Merely listing the holders of rights who could be called *zamindar*s greatly understates the number of people possessing revenue rights in certain districts. In Dhaka, for instance, *zamindar*s, even though they were relatively numerous, have been described as only 'at the apex of a pyramid of revenue-collecting rights'.[21] Below them were hundreds of small tenure holders, usually called *talukdar*s. Sometimes *talukdar*s paid directly to the government; more often they did so through the *zamindar*s. Some eighteenth-century *taluk*s originated from older revenue rights which had been incorporated into a new *zamindari*, but most appear to have been recent creations, granted to those who had settled new lands, or sold by existing *zamindar*s who wished to raise money.[22] Even in the great *zamindari*s in the last years of

[19] Stewart, *History of Bengal*, p. 491.  [20] Sinha, *Economic History*, II, 17.
[21] Ray, *Bengal Agrarian Society*, pp. 211–20.
[22] R. Datta, 'Aspects of the Agrarian System of Bengal during the second half of the Eighteenth Century', Unpublished M. Phil. thesis, J. Nehru University, 1980, pp. 68 ff.

the Nawabs, men who wished to invest in revenue rights seem to have been able to purchase *taluk*s.[23] Mounting pressure by the Nawabs' government for higher revenue from the *zamindar*s was evidently forcing them to make sales. The carving up of the great *zamindari*s, so marked under the British, seems to have begun under the Nawabs.

*Zamindar* was a term that also meant many different things in Bihar. Over large areas, what the British came to call 'village *zamindars*' when they encountered them in other parts of northern India were firmly established. Many Rajputs, Bhumihars or *ashraf* Muslims exercised rights to collect revenue from cultivators, even though in some cases they themselves cultivated the land. Such men were commonly called *malik*s. They were held to be entitled to be paid a *malikana* allowance whether they collected revenue for the government or not. They were often extremely numerous. In Tirhut district, north of the Ganges, the British Collector later found them to be 'numberless, few considerable, but many insignificant and those divided and subdivided into shares, that it would be endless to enumerate them'. One village in Saran district, which only paid a total revenue of Rs. 600, still had fifty-two 'proprietors' with rights in the revenue.[24]

The Mughal government had inevitably to employ intermediary collectors to handle the payments from this multitude of small *zamindar*s. Some of these men were *amil*s, that is other officials appointed by the government; others were chieftains of the leading clans of Rajputs and Bhumihars. In both cases there was a powerful trend towards turning their duties to collect for the government into property for themselves. In a manner probably not unlike that in the earlier eighteenth century in Bengal, government collectors tried to win acceptance as great *zamindar*s with permanent rights. In Bihar, however, the process had not gone so far as in Bengal and in many cases its outcome still depended on the use of force. North of the Ganges the Rajas of Darbhanga had successfully enlarged a grant made to them by the Emperor Aurangzeb and had 'for all practical purposes come to be regarded as the masters of the whole Sarkar of Tirhut'.[25] But further west, the Bettiah Raj of Champaran was still

---

[23] For an example in Rajshahi, see S.C. Nandy, *The Life and Times of Cantoo Baboo* (2 vols., Calcutta, 1978, 1981), I, 18–19.

[24] IOR, Bengal Revenue Consultations, 18 Sept. 1789, Range 51, vol. 46, pp. 92, 129.

[25] J.S. Jha, 'History of the Darbhanga Raj', *Journal of the Bihar Research Society*, XLVIII (1962), 61.

locked in conflict with the Nawab's government, which launched periodic forays against it. South of the river, the Rajput chiefs of Bhojpur had built up a large and powerful holding. Further to the east, the area around Patna and Gaya was the battle ground of Kamgar Khan of Hasua and Sundar Singh of Tikari, with interventions from the Rajput *zamindar* of Siris and Kutumba. Sundar Singh was said to live 'much in the same manner as his adversary Kamgar, seizing on all lands within his reach, plundering those who would not join his standard, and paying nothing to government without being compelled by an army'.[26] Although Bihar was potentially a valuable province, with a high target figure for the government revenue, early British inquiries showed that the Nawabs of Bengal had been able to extract virtually nothing from it until 1748 and only small amounts thereafter.[27] The British believed that 'the dependant rajahs and zemindars were continually in arms, and tho' these countries were rated very high, they generally compounded for the payment of half or one third, according to the situation of their possessions and their own strength'.[28]

Those who rendered revenue to the rulers of Orissa were also very diverse. The hilly areas were occupied by chiefs who paid a fixed tribute. A portion of the plains was under the direct control of the Rajas of Khurda, the old Orissa royal house, who also paid a fixed tribute. Elsewhere, the so-called Mughalbandi was divided into a mass of small revenue tenures under the direct administration of the government. Only a few of those who possessed revenue-collecting rights did so on a scale large enough to classify them as *zamindars*. The mass were normally referred to as *talukdars*.[29]

Thus the revenue paid to the Nawabs of Bengal, or in some cases to the holders of *jagir*s, came from many different intermediaries. The chiefs of autonomous states on the frontiers rendered tribute. On the plains of western and central Bengal powerful *zamindar*s, often recently risen to eminence, were responsible for huge payments from very extensive areas. In Bihar eminent *zamindar*s in the making paid what could be extracted from them by the threat of force. Throughout the three provinces a mass of village *malik*s, *talukdar*s and minor *zamindar*s

---

[26] F. Buchanan, *An Account of the Districts of Bihar and Patna* (2 vols., Patna, nd), II, 594.
[27] Figures in IOR, Bengal Select Committee Proceedings, 6 March 1769, Range A, vol. 9, pp. 126–7.    [28] Ibid., 9 Feb. 1769, Range A, vol. 9, p. 67.
[29] B.S. Das, *Studies in the Economic History of Orissa* (Calcutta, 1978), pp. 68–73.

were assessed and compelled to pay by the officials of the government.

How much these intermediaries eventually handed over to the government rarely depended on any accurate assessment of the resources in the territory for which they were responsible. Payments were fixed on the basis of some historic standard, usually with later adjustments. All such arrangements were, however, in the last resort the outcome of an implied trial of strength between the power of the government to compel and the capacity of the revenue payer to evade. The historic basis on which bargaining began in Bengal was the standard laid down by Murshid Kuli Khan in 1722. This was the first attempt to provide a new assessment of Bengal's revenue since 1582. It was, however, only partially based on measurement or detailed inquiry.[30] When subsequent Nawabs thought that a suitable pretext had presented itself, or that their will could prevail, they levied an *abwab*, or extra payment, on the 1722 assessment. Shuja Khan and Alivardi Khan both imposed *abwab*s on the 1722 assessment, increasing it by about 30 per cent.[31] When the principal revenue payers' shares had been fixed, some 400 of them appeared at a great annual ceremony at the Nawab's capital at Murshidabad, called the *Punyah*. At the *Punyah* the revenue payers were invested with insigniae of honour and in return delivered obligations to pay the following year's revenue. These obligations were usually honoured in the first instance by bankers, who were reimbursed as the collections were made.

Englishmen came to have a lively contempt for the Nawabs' methods of assessing revenue. They believed that they were based on 'conjectural estimates, so liable to error and deception'.[32] No doubt they were. But the government's problems were extremely intractable, as Englishmen themselves were to discover in due course. Even if they had possessed the coercive power to compel accurate assessment of the resources of the great tributary Rajas and *zamindar*s, they lacked the resources of skilled and trustworthy manpower to conduct such surveys. Neither the Nawabs nor the British could contemplate direct collection from millions of peasant cultivators. They had to strike bargains with intermediaries. In these bargains they would no doubt be deceived, even when they had the power to enforce an

---

[30] *Narrative*, trans. Gladwin, pp. 45–7.  [31] Grant, 'Analysis', *PP*, 1812, VII, 279–86.
[32] *Proceedings of the Controlling Committee of Revenue at Murshidabad* (12 vols., Calcutta, 1919–24), V, 147.

apparently advantageous assessment. The commonest form of deception was said to be the removal of land from payment of revenue to the government because it had been allocated to charitable purposes, such as the support of Brahmins and pious Muslims, of temples or of the tombs of saints. The British became obsessed with what they called 'rent-free land', believing that the loss of revenue was enormous and that the majority of such grants were fraudulent, merely enabling *zamindar*s to increase their profits rather than endowing piety. Although many estimates were no doubt exaggerated, rent-free land was very extensive under the British. It was commonly supposed that most grants had been made when the Nawabs' regime collapsed and before the new order was established. It is likely, though, that significant quantities of revenue had also escaped the Nawabs on such dubious charitable pretexts. The British certainly found much evidence of this when they took over land near Calcutta in 1757.[33] A contemporary Persian treatise assumed that most *zamindar*s held rent-free land on fictitious grounds.[34]

The formal rent roll of Murshid Kuli Khan for Bengal assessed the revenue to be raised from the province at Rs. 14,288,186. The additional *abwab*s brought the assessment to Rs. 18,684,067 by the time of Alivardi Khan's death.[35] In contemporary terms this was a public revenue of somewhat more than £2,000,000. How far the formal assessment was strictly applied at the annual *Punyah*s is unclear. Failure of major revenue payers to realise stipulated totals was said to be uncommon. On the other hand, Alivardi Khan at times of emergency, as when he had to buy support at Delhi after his accession,[36] or during his wars with the Marathas, appears to have levied very large extra contributions. However imperfect his revenue operations may have seemed in retrospect, they still allowed him to accumulate considerable reserves, at least in time of peace when he was not sending large sums to Delhi.[37]

If the Nawab was able to accumulate reserves, the evidence does not suggest that he did this by reducing to penury those who handled his revenue. Although pressures on them might be increasing, Englishmen believed that the major *zamindar*s were in general still very wealthy.

---

[33] Firminger, *Historical Introduction*, p. xcix.
[34] Translation in IOR, Home Miscellaneous, vol. 68, p. 737.
[35] *PP*, 1812, VII, 262–4, 282–6. [36] *Narrative*, trans. Gladwin, p. 175.
[37] *Fort William – India House Correspondence* (New Delhi, 1949–), I, *1748–56*, ed. K.K. Datta (1958), p. 885.

The revenue system was also maintaining what has been called 'a local gentry, very numerous in some places . . . but quite thin in ranks in others', consisting for the most part of high caste Hindus, often themselves employed in revenue administration, who had acquired small *taluk*s or grants of rent-free land.[38] The system which produced the surpluses that sustained the Nawabs, their captains and their troopers, together with the great hierarchy of those holding revenue rights, ultimately rested on extracting the produce of the land from those who cultivated it.

To provide the revenue, the ryot, or cultivator of the land, was required to surrender a proportion of the value of his crop. In theory those responsible for collecting revenue from him measured the amount of land which he held and ascertained what crops he was growing. He was then assessed at an established rate for each *bigah* (the unit, varying widely from place to place, in which land was measured) according to the crop grown, 'cash' crops usually being assessed at a higher rate than grain. Most payments were made in cash, but, especially in certain parts of Bihar, crops were sometimes physically divided.

So described, the system seems relatively simple. By the middle of the eighteenth century, however, it was arcane to the highest degree. Practice was infinitely varied. Assessments were rarely based on any accurate measurement of the amount of land held or of the types of crop cultivated. The rates at which revenue was demanded from what was deemed to be the holding of the ryot varied enormously. They were usually based on some historic standard to which numerous additions were made and extra surcharges were added, again called *abwab*s, for every sort of pretext. Ryots were charged according to the supposed quality of the land and according to the quality of the person involved. As a general principle, the rich and the well-born paid less than the poor and the low caste. There were rates for the cultivators who had lived for a long period in the village and had acquired some kind of hereditary right to the land they occupied and other rates for the migratory and non-resident cultivators, who had no right to security of tenure, but who paid less. Each village had its own customs, which often varied within the village. To illustrate what he not unreasonably called 'the intricacy and uncertainty of the system', an English Collector described the custom of a particular village, where a

[38] Ray, *Bengal Agrarian Society*, pp. 30–1.

rate per *bigah* existed, but before the ryot knew what he would have to pay, he had to divide the rate by twelve and then multiply it by twenty-seven. Another demand would then be added at a quarter of the rate. Finally, the ryot would have four additional surcharges to pay, which were calculated as proportions of the original demand.[39] In the view of a leading British revenue expert, 'the standard is often so indeterminate', that the ryots could not know 'what they have to pay'.[40] Written records of a ryot's obligations, called *potta*s, were sometimes issued, but at least by the time of the Company's rule it was thought that ryots had little formal protection against increased demands on any grounds at all.

Such safeguards against oppression of ryots as may have operated presumably arose less from the observance of customary rights than from the *zamindar*s' sense of their own self-interest. The ryot's ultimate weapon seems rarely to have been violent resistance; it was usually desertion. Land was abundant in eighteenth-century Bengal and a considerable proportion of the rural population was migratory. Men's capacity to open up land was limited by their poverty,[41] but those who felt themselves oppressed by one *zamindar* could sometimes make terms with another. Abundance of land often meant that although extortionate demands were levied from part of a ryot's holdings, he might also hold land which was not assessed at all.

Their relative scarcity value might have saved the ryots from some degree of extortion, but there seems little doubt that even if the revenue demand did not generally press heavily on the intermediaries, it pressed heavily on most of the ryots. British administrators were to discover that a number of ryots had earned for themselves privileged status and some prosperity,[42] but the mass seem to have been heavily taxed. The theory of Mughal rule was that the revenue demand varied between one-half and one-quarter of the crop.[43] Most British commentators, including some who wrote at the very beginning of the Company's rule,[44] believed that in practice the assessment was usually half the value of the crop.[45] Where there was a physical division, as in Bihar, the peasant was usually left with half, or less than half, of his crop.

[39] IOR, Bengal Board of Revenue, 17 April 1787, Range 70, vol. 26.
[40] J. Shore, Minute of June 1789, *PP*, 1812, VII, 192.   [41] See p. 7.
[42] See pp. 153–4.   [43] Siddiqi, *Land Revenue Administration*, p. 47.
[44] W. Bolts, *Considerations on India Affairs*, (3 vols., 1772–5), I, 148.
[45] E.g. Shore, Minute of June 1789, *PP*, 1812, VII, 180–1.

The revenue system as applied by the late Nawabs ensured a reasonable income for the state, but it evidently also left a large margin in the hands of the revenue intermediaries. Whether this was by design or was the inevitable consequence of military and administrative weakness, it became part of the implied compact on which the rule of the Nawabs rested.

Merchants and bankers were also involved in the compact. They had a most important role in the revenue system. The Nawabs were said to have regarded 'shroffs and merchants as their immediate support as well as a necessary convenience in all their transactions ... The cultivation of the lands has hitherto been carried on by their intervention'.[46] Their purchases enabled peasants to pay their taxes in cash. They encouraged the spread of cash crops on which higher rates of tax were levied. The government received revenue payments in instalments throughout the year. To pay its troops and meet its other expenses, it had to borrow from bankers in advance of receiving the instalments. *Zamindar*s and *faujdar*s also had to borrow to render their payments punctually. Bankers were needed to handle revenue payments in many different species of currency and to arrange for remittances by bills of exchange to the central treasury. Bills could be drawn because of the merchants' needs to transfer funds.

The great house of Jagat Seth, bankers to the government, was virtually a partner with the Nawabs in the management of the Bengal revenues. When the Jagat Seths fled from the Marathas in 1742, the chief *kadi* was sent to persuade them to come back to Murshidabad, 'their presence being as necessary to the government as to merchants'.[47] The house received a large part of the revenue, made payments on behalf of the government and financed the operations of the major *zamindar*s. Part of the imperial tribute was remitted by the Jagat Seths drawing bills on their Delhi agents.

The Jagat Seths were great political figures. In the view of a French observer, they had helped to bring Alivardi Khan to power, had 'conducted almost all his business' and had been 'the main mover in all the revolutions in Bengal'.[48] The Jagat Seths also cultivated support in the imperial court and were said to be able to look after the Nawab's

---

[46] IOR, Bengal Select Committee, 11 Aug. 1769, Range A, vol. 9, p. 430.
[47] Cited in J.H. Little, *The House of Jagatseth*, reprint (Calcutta, 1967), p. 121.
[48] Memoir of J. Law, in S.C. Hill (ed.), *Bengal in 1756–7* (3 vols., 1905), III, 175.

interests there too. For such great services there was a price to be paid. A large commission was presumably deducted from the Bengal revenues. They insisted on control over the Nawab's mint and on a monopoly over the coining of bullion, again for a handsome profit. Their great wealth made the Jagat Seths an obvious target for a predatory Nawab. Superficially they were vulnerable. But if they withdrew their support from one Nawab and committed it to a rival, the consequences could be dire.

The house of Jagat Seth was the largest business concern involved with the Nawabs, and therefore in the politics of Bengal. It was not, however, the only one. For instance, Hindu, Muslim and even Armenian merchants competed for monopoly concessions over certain trades, such as the disposal of saltpetre or the marketing of salt, which was said to be granted on the payment of the equivalent of £200,000.

Merchants were a source of taxable wealth as well as of credit. The government supplemented what it took in land revenue by levying *sayer* duties, that is customs on both internal and external trade. The *sayer* duties were also very extensively collected by the *zamindar*s, who imposed tolls on trade and dues at market places. For at least a part of the revenue which they derived from these sources, the *zamindar*s were accountable to the government. Beyond what they contributed by taxes on trade, it was widely supposed by Europeans that merchants were liable to periodic seizures of their property. Such allegations were an essential part of the Europeans' belief in 'oriental despotism' and should be treated with caution. There can, however, be no doubt that some merchants were subjected to extortionate demands.

Whatever could be taken from merchants by *sayer* or by less regular means was small by comparison with what came from taxing the land. But without the enterprise of merchants, the land could not be effectively taxed. As a recent authority succinctly puts it, merchants were 'indispensable intermediaries in converting agricultural surpluses into disposable state income'.[49]

The supply of silver on which Bengal's currency depended was provided by merchants. Through their enterprise Bengal maintained a favourable balance of commodity trade with areas like the Middle East, the Philippines and above all Europe, which settled their deficits

[49] K.N. Chaudhuri, *Trade and Civilisation in the Indian Ocean* (Cambridge, 1985), p. 11.

in bullion. The European companies were the main importers of silver. Imports by the English East India Company averaged around £200,000 a year in the last years of Alivardi Khan.[50] The Dutch were thought to be even bigger importers of silver, estimates for their Company varying between £300,000[51] and £475,000 a year.[52] Trade with France was seriously disrupted from the mid 1740s, but the French Company still sent two to four ships to Bengal with silver in the years when it was operating effectively.[53] The inflow of bullion to Bengal from Asian sources in other parts of India, the Persian Gulf, the Red Sea, and the Far East is very hard to estimate. It was believed to be large. Nine-tenths of Indian imports into Persia were said to be paid for in specie, so that most of the huge loot taken from Delhi when it was sacked by Nadir Shah was thought to have found its way back to India.[54] As far as Bengal was concerned, the inflow of bullion from Asian sources again demonstrated the importance of Europeans for its economy. In the first half of the eighteenth century the major part of Bengal's seaborne carrying trade with other parts of Asia passed into European hands, above all into the hands of the 'private' Englishmen at Calcutta, individual servants of the Company and others, who were permitted by the Company to operate their own shipping. By 1715 more ships trading round Asia were coming to Calcutta than were recorded as calling at the Nawab's port at Hooghly. In subsequent years the disparity became even more marked.[55] Europeans were becoming well aware of the importance of the role which they played as suppliers of silver. In the 1730s the French chief, Dupleix, believed that the Europeans could impose any terms they wished on the Nawab by blockading his ports and depriving him of silver.[56]

Shipping and silver were only a part of the European contribution to the economy of Bengal. The Europeans were major purchasers of high

---

[50] Listed in the Ninth Report of the Select Committee, 1783, *Reports from Committees of the House of Commons*, (12 vols., 1803–6), IV, 109–10. The major part of British bullion shipments at this time went to the Company's mints at Madras and Bombay in the first instance (K.N. Chaudhuri, *The Trading World of Asia and the English East India Company 1660–1760* (Cambridge, 1978), p. 189).
[51] H. Verelst, *A View of the Rise, Progress and Present State of the English Government in Bengal* (1772), p. 86 fn.    [52] A. Dow, *History of Hindostan* (3 vols., 1768–72), III, p. lxiii.
[53] A. Martineau, *Dupleix et l'Inde française*, 2nd edn (4 vols., Paris, 1929), I, 257–98.
[54] Report by S. Manesty and H. Jones, 15 Aug. 1790, *Selections from State Papers, Bombay, Regarding the East India Company's Connection with the Persian Gulf* (Calcutta, 1908), p. 429.    [55] See P.J. Marshall, *East Indian Fortunes* (Oxford, 1976), chapter 3.
[56] I. Ray, 'Some Aspects of the French Presence in Bengal, 1731–40', *Calcutta Historical Review*, I (1976), 110.

quality textiles and thus either directly or indirectly stimulated commercial agriculture by increasing the demand for mulberries for silk worms and for raw cotton. It has been tentatively suggested that the English and Dutch Companies alone may have created the equivalent of about 100,000 new jobs in textiles by their increased purchases early in the eighteenth century.[57] The trade of both Companies was still running at a high level during the reign of Alivardi Khan. The cost value of the English Company's 'investment' in Bengal goods for the London market was about £400,000 a year.[58] Private English purchases of goods to be used in Asian trade or to be sent clandestinely to Europe are impossible to quantify, but they may have been comparable to the official trade of the Company. In the 1740s the annual average purchases of the Dutch Company for the Netherlands was the equivalent of about £200,000 a year, rising to £250,000 in the 1750s.[59] The French Company's purchases may have been worth about half of these totals.[60]

Commercial operations on this scale meant that the Indian merchant community was deeply involved with the Europeans. Both the Companies and individual Europeans borrowed heavily from Indians. The French Company owed more than it could repay to the Jagat Seths. In the 1750s the Companies began a policy of dealing direct with Indian artisans wherever possible, but until then most purchases of textiles, saltpetre or opium had been made through Indian merchants, and lucrative opportunities for dealing with Europeans continued in spite of the new policies. Within their settlements and in their relative immunity from the Nawabs' customs the Companies enjoyed a privileged status in Bengal. Merchants who dealt with Europeans sought and received a share in these privileges. Some rich men moved their residences into European settlements. A recent study of the English has suggested that they were 'assuming an influence out of all proportion to their number; an influence all the more solid because it was based on the relationship which they had established with Indian commerce and with Indian merchants and artisans'.[61]

[57] Om Prakash, 'Bullion for Goods. International Trade and the Economy of Early Eighteenth-century Bengal', *Indian Economic and Social History Review*, XIII (1976), 173–5.     [58] Annual totals are given in Chaudhuri, *Trading World*, p. 510.
[59] Estimate from the totals in F. Gaastra, 'De V.O.C. en Azie 1680–1795', *Algemene Geschiedenis der Nederlanden*, IX, (Haarlem, 1980), p. 461.
[60] Estimated from Martineau, *Dupleix*, I.
[61] I.B. Watson, *Foundation for Empire: English Private Trade in India 1659–1760* (New Delhi, 1980), p. 285.

Something like an implied compact seems to have evolved between the Europeans and the Nawabs, as it had done between the Nawab and the major *zamindar*s or the wealthiest indigenous merchants and bankers. The Europeans performed functions and they in return extracted privileges. In simple fiscal terms they contributed very little. Their rich settlements were not taxed and as a result of bargains negotiated in the past, in the case of the English directly with the imperial authorities at Delhi, they paid only derisory customs on their huge trade. Periodically the Europeans could be coerced into making extra contributions under threat. In the last resort, in spite of the defence forces they maintained and the power of their ships, their settlements could be plundered, just as the Jagat Seths could be despoiled. Events in 1756 would show that even Calcutta was vulnerable. But could the Nawab afford a total breach with the Europeans? Even if he were willing to pay the price, many of his powerful subjects were not. The European towns provided a large market for agricultural produce. Their trade encouraged manufacturing and commercial crops. Many merchants had invested money with them, did business with them, used their ships and shared their privileges. When a Nawab did force conclusions with a European company, those who delighted in seeing the overbearing Feringhees chastised were matched by those who saw a dynamic part of Bengal's economy put into jeopardy.

Traditional Mughal statecraft was concerned with military matters and with exercising authority over a hierarchy supported by taxation raised from the land. Bengal's vigorous commercial sector meant that the art of ruling it had become rather more complex. The government was in some senses itself a commercial enterprise, dependent on credit and trade. Merchants were formally excluded from power, but in practice the influence of even foreign merchants was considerable.

Europeans liked to portray Islamic regimes in Asia as ruthless despotisms moved by the will of an irresponsible tyrant. Bengal under the Nawabs was often described in this way, but the reality seems to have been different. He who occupied the throne certainly did so because he had the power to seize it and to hold onto it, but his survival depended on more than brute force. A successful claimant had to establish some legitimacy by gaining imperial recognition. He needed the backing of a powerful faction of Muslim aristocrats holding the main offices. Able and experienced Hindu *mutaseddi*s had to be willing to make the financial system work for him. His regime required the support of the major *zamindar*s. The Jagat Seths were the essential props of government finance. Merchants from northern India, Gujarat, Armenia or Europe had important roles in maintaining the prosperity of the three provinces.

All these elements in Bengal's polity had their price. Stability required a proper distribution of rewards and patronage. The major *zamindars*' supposed profits could not be squeezed too hard nor their autonomies infringed. The Jagat Seths had to be allowed to repay themselves for their services. There were limits beyond which it might not be politic to go in restricting the privileges of merchants, especially the European East India Companies. In short, the Nawabs of Bengal were conciliators of interests as well as despots.

Whether the conciliation of interests by the Nawabs of Bengal extended to the conscious conciliation of great masses of their subjects is less clear. It has been suggested that eighteenth-century Indian states were generally moving towards 'cultural syncretism and great tradition eclecticism', and that their rulers were seeking to create 'a mixture of transcendent Mughal and immanent local-regional traditions'.[62] The Bengal Nawabs' total commitment to the Mughal tradition was unswerving. Evidence that they were concerned with a regional tradition is not easy to detect. Persecution of non-Muslims was not enforced by the regime. One of the last of the Mughal grandees gave the British an interesting statement on how Hindus should be treated. They were a subject people and the law to be administered in the province could only be that of 'the true faith'. But Hindus should be left alone to manage their own affairs according to their own customs. They held many offices, they were permitted to endow their own religious charities with rent-free lands and they faced no active discrimination, except for paying customs duties at higher rates.[63] However, toleration did not necessarily lead to cultural ecumenicism.

Such developments at the highest levels may have been more marked in Bihar than in Bengal. At Patna some of the great Hindu office holders became scholars of Persian and Urdu, and presided at Muslim festivals.[64] The Nawabs' capital at Murshidabad had a cultural life of some sophistication. More at present is known about the visual

---

[62] R.B. Barnett, *North India between Empires* (Berkeley, 1980), p. 246.
[63] A.M. Khan, *The Transition in Bengal 1756–75* (Cambridge, 1969), pp. 270–9.
[64] F.L. Lehmann, 'The Eighteenth-century Transition in India. Responses of some Bihar Intellectuals', Unpublished Ph.D. thesis, University of Wisconsin, 1967.

arts and the emergence of a distinct 'Murshidabad style' of Mughal painting than about its literary life.[65] Murshidabad painting seems to have appealed to both Hindus and Muslims, and the Hindu elite had a liking for Persian poetry. Whether the Muslim aristocracy had similarly eclectic tastes is uncertain. The great festivals of the court were those of Shi'ite Islam, above all Muharram, but Holi and Diwali were also observed. At Holi the two hundred or more cisterns in Alivardi Khan's gardens were 'filled with coloured water and on all sides heaps of amber and saffron raised their heads to the sky'.[66] With only fragmentary evidence such as this, it is difficult to make much of a case for a systematic policy of cultural syncretism. Where a 'regional tradition' was developing among Muslims it was among the masses in eastern Bengal, who had been making adjustments to their environment over centuries.[67] The concerns of the Nawabs seem to have been limited to maintaining a decent Mughal order in which the subject communities could be assured of a proper place. If little was done positively to conciliate them, they should not, on the other hand, be driven to active discontent.

This was no doubt another constraint which the Nawabs of Bengal were bound to have recognised. Even a man of formidable capacity and iron will, as Alivardi Khan turned out to be, had to accept many constraints. But if he manoeuvred skilfully within them, he could survive. The survival of the Nawabs of Bengal would ensure that the provinces had at least a serviceable framework of government: one that enabled a very marked commercial expansion and presumably some growth in agricultural output to take place. Cataclysmic interpretations of the fall of Mughal Bengal along the lines of the breakdown of its government or some powerful upsurge of Hindu disaffection do not seem to have much foundation. The regime was not a dynamic one and it had not put down deep roots, but in time it might well have established itself securely. The armies of the Marathas, of adventurers out of northern India and of Colonel Robert Clive did not give the Nawabs much time.

[65] R. Skelton, 'Murshidabad Painting', *Marg*, X (1956), 10–22.
[66] Sarkar, *Bengal Nawabs*, pp. 49–50.
[67] A. Roy, *The Islamic Syncretistic Tradition in Bengal* (Princeton, 1983).

# CHAPTER 3

# THE CRISIS OF EMPIRE, 1740–65

Alivardi Khan's successful usurpation of the throne of Bengal encouraged others to try to establish claims to Bengal's wealth. Most could rely on some degree of endorsement by the Mughal Emperors, who hoped to increase the flow of tribute. The Marathas were the earliest and the most dangerous contenders.

By 1740 a successful northward drive by the Marathas had enabled them to conquer most of central India. In the process the overall control of the Peshwas, or chief ministers, had weakened, allowing various leaders to carve out what amounted to their own independent territories. Beyond their own domains they were pushing their influence further, collecting *chauth*, forced contributions, from areas which they could dominate. The north-eastern arm of the Maratha drive had enabled one of their leaders, Raghuji Bhonsla, to subjugate Berar and to establish his base around Nagpur. From Berar Maratha troops could be sent into either Bihar or Orissa. Fearful that the new Peshwa of the Marathas, Balaji Rao, would try to establish a claim to Bengal first, and given encouragement by the family of Sarfaraz Khan, whom Alivardi Khan had deposed, Raghuji Bhonsla sent his army through Orissa and into western Bengal in 1742. Raiding parties of the Maratha cavalry plundered the area west of the Hooghly up to Murshidabad.

The Nawab's army succeeded in repelling them, but this was only the first of many incursions. In 1743 two Maratha armies invaded. One belonged to Raghuji Bhonsla, the other to Balaji Rao, the Peshwa, whose purposes were ostensibly peaceful. He claimed to be acting in the name of the Emperor, bringing aid against the Berar army. Alivardi Khan was obliged to buy him off, paying him a subsidy, promising *chauth* for the future and persuading him to withdraw. Raghuji Bhonsla was again driven out, but returned in 1744 and 1745, when his forces once again reached Murshidabad. With each wave of attacks the damage became more severe. The Nawab's army could generally win victories and clear territory in western Bengal, but its grip on Orissa was becoming less and less secure. In 1748 the Marathas appeared in

70

Bihar. In 1750 they again raided up to Murshidabad. In 1751 their troops were encamped in western Bengal for some considerable time. But 1751 was to be the last year of active campaigning. An agreement was reached between Alivardi Khan and the Marathas which purchased immunity for Bengal from further incursions at the price of an annual *chauth* of Rs. 1,200,000 and the virtual cession of Orissa. The leading supporter of the deposed Sarfaraz Khan, Mir Habib, who had sided with the Marathas, was to be *Naib* of Orissa and to pay its surplus revenue to Berar.

The Marathas were not the only enemies whom Alivardi Khan had to face. The Wazir of Awadh moved an army into Bihar in 1742 on the pretext of defending it against the Marathas. Bihar itself was ravaged at intervals by Afghan colonists and soldiers settled there. In 1748 12,000 Afghans rebelled and seized Patna, plundering it and extorting Rs. 600,000 from its bankers.[1] They were eventually defeated by the Nawab himself, after a major battle.

By the 1750s Alivardi Khan appeared to have come through his tribulations successfully. Only Orissa had been lost. But nearly a decade of war had placed a very severe strain upon his government. For the time being at least, all restraint in making fiscal demands was abandoned. *Zamindar*s, office holders, bankers, merchants and the European Companies were all harried ruthlessly. The head of the Jagat Seths commented in 1744: ' "At present there is no government; they fear neither God nor the King but seem determined to force money from everybody; I have suffered greatly by them".'[2] The Raja of Burdwan was said to have been forced to yield Rs. 10,000,000.[3] Europeans reported well-authenticated stories of merchants being kidnapped, tortured and robbed by the Nawab's agents.[4] The English East India Company was told to hand over Rs. 2,500,000, which, the Nawab suggested, it might recover from the rich inhabitants of Calcutta. In the end the English escaped with paying only Rs. 350,000.

The fabric of acquiescence on which the Nawabs' government rested

---

[1] *Fort William – India House Correspondence* (New Delhi, 1949–), I, *1748–56*, ed. K.K. Datta (1958), p. 303.

[2] Cited in J.H. Little, *The House of Jagatseth*, reprint (Calcutta, 1967), p. 127.

[3] J.N. Sarkar (ed.), *The Bengal Nawabs* (Calcutta, 1952), p. 152.

[4] K.N. Chaudhuri, *The Trading World of Asia and the English East India Company 1660–1760* (Cambridge, 1978), p. 311; Abstract of Bengal letter, 8 Nov. 1744, IOR, E/4/5, p. 18.

was severely stretched, but, at least so long as Alivardi Khan remained alive, it survived this very rough treatment. Few of the major interests in Bengal can conceivably have thought that it might be to their advantage to change the Nawab for a Maratha or an Afghan overlord. The Marathas did indeed try to establish their rule in western Bengal and to attract the leading zamindars to their side, but they had little success. Their record of atrocities seems to have totally outweighed any appeal from Hindu to Hindu. The contemporary Maharashtra Purana described how one of the Maratha generals organised great sacrifices in honour of Durga, but 'Durga ordered her followers to be gracious to the Muslim Nawab and oppose the Marathas, because the evil-minded ones had killed Brahmans and Vaisnavas'.[5] Robert Orme, who believed that Alivardi Khan was becoming so rapacious that the English must seriously think about swinging 'the old dog', still reflected that the Nawab's exactions had cost the Company no more than the equivalent of £100,000 in all, which was no great price.[6] Yet in the long term, the emergency measures to which Alivardi Khan had resorted probably did seriously weaken the position of the Nawabs. What a ruthless government might be like had been clearly demonstrated and a return to fiscal terrorism was unlikely to be tolerated again.

The invading Marathas never succeeded in crossing the river Hooghly, but they inflicted very severe damage on rich and highly productive areas in western Bengal. The horrors committed by the 'Bargis', as the Maratha raiders were called, left a deep mark on the traditions of the people of Bengal. They were grimly commemorated in poetry. According to the Maharashtra Purana:

They shouted over and over again, 'Give us money', and when they got no money they filled peoples' nostrils with water, and some they seized and drowned in tanks, and many died of suffocation. In this way they did all manner of foul and evil deeds. When they demanded money and it was not given to them, they would put the man to death. Those who had money gave it, those who had none were killed.[7]

[5] The Maharashtra Purana, translated by E. Dimock and P.C. Gupta (Honolulu, 1965), p. 52.
[6] S.C. Hill (ed.), Bengal in 1756–7 (3 vols., 1905), I, p. xxxiii; R. Orme, History of the Military Transactions of the British Nation in Indostan (2 vols., 1763, 1778) II, 46.
[7] Maharashtra Purana, p. 32.

Contemporary European accounts corroborate much of this. The Dutch believed that 400,000 people had been killed.[8] Losses of weavers, silk winders and those who cultivated mulberry were particularly high. Rumours that the Bargis were in the area could prove almost as destructive as actual raids. Orme commented that large numbers of people 'were continually taking flight, even on imaginary alarms, and wandering from their homes . . . Examples of these distresses were frequently seen by the English at Calcutta, to which place the inhabitants of the opposite side of the river often came over in great numbers for refuge, and perished through want.'[9] Local shortages, leading to greatly increased food prices, were reported, but general famine seems only to have come in 1752, after the invasions were over, when the monsoon failed.

Some districts in western Bengal, like Burdwan, appear to have recovered quite quickly. But the Maratha invasions and the Nawab's response had long-term consequences. Poor districts, such as Birbhum, felt the effects over a long period. Shortages and dislocations probably contributed to a very marked price rise which began in western Bengal in the 1740s.[10] Many merchants were permanently crippled by losses and exactions. Both the English and the Dutch Companies found that merchants no longer provided reliable quotas of goods for their trade and increasingly turned to direct dealings with the artisans through the companies' own agents.[11] It has been suggested that this weakening of the links between the Europeans and the merchants may eventually have had important political consequences. Indian merchants had in the past acted as the intermediaries between the companies and the Nawabs' government, mediating when disputes occurred. When a major crisis blew up between the English and the Nawab in 1756, Indian mediation was ineffective.[12]

For all the damage, both immediate and long-term, inflicted by the Marathas, the Nawab survived the war. In 1755 the English reported that 'from the time he made up his dispute with the Morattes and disbanded the greater part of his forces he has undoubtedly laid up every

[8] Chaudhuri, Trading World, p. 253.
[9] Orme, History, II, 44–5.
[10] Chaudhuri, Trading World, p. 102.
[11] Ibid., pp. 310–12.
[12] J.D. Nichol, 'The British in India 1740–63: A Study in Imperial Expansion into Bengal', Unpublished Ph.D. thesis, Cambridge University, 1976, pp. 95–6.

year a large sum and is now esteemed so immensely rich'.[13] One part of his dominions was, however, lost to him.

From 1751 the resources of Orissa were handed over as part of the settlement with the Marathas, although the Nawabs of Bengal continued to nominate the *Naib*s of Orissa until 1760, when the first Maratha *Subedar* was appointed as Governor. In outline the Marathas appear to have preserved the Mughal system. Hill chieftains were permitted to continue paying a tribute, which often had to be extracted from them by force. In the plains the Marathas appointed *amil*s, who dealt with the few existing *zamindar*s and the mass of *talukdar*s and others possessing rights over villages. Surplus revenue was remitted through bankers to Nagpur, the capital of the Bhonslas.[14] The Marathas applied strong economic pressure against the Rajas of Khurda, who wielded powerful influence throughout Orissa as patrons of the Jagannath temple. The Marathas themselves aspired to the temple patronage; they deprived the Rajas of much of their lands and confined them at Cuttack.[15]

An overall assessment of Maratha rule in Orissa, which was to last until the British conquest in 1803, is hard to make. Contemporary Englishmen and the first administrators after 1803 held it in contempt. A traveller in 1766 warned his readers that it would be unnecessary for him to say 'that any place I came to was once considerable, since all the places that were once so, are now depopulated by the Mahrattas'.[16] Such verdicts, and that of the famous nineteenth-century historian of Orissa, Sir William Hunter, that Maratha rule was a fifty year 'nightmare' with endlessly repeated cavalry raids,[17] are likely to be exaggerated. Orissa seems never to have been very central to the interests of the Bhonslas. It did not yield revenue easily and its administration was largely sub-contracted to Maratha commanders or Gosain merchants. Once the Marathas had become established in an area, they did not behave as they had done in western Bengal.

Alivardi Khan died in April 1756. He had made it clearly known that he wished his successor to be his grandson, Siraj-ud-daula. The suc-

[13] *Fort William – India House Correspondence*, I, 885.

[14] B.S. Das, *Studies in the Economic History of Orissa* (Calcutta, 1979); B.C. Ray, *Orissa under the Marathas* (Allahabad, 1961).

[15] H. Kulke, 'Kings without a Kingdom: The Rajas of Khurda and the Jagannath Cult', *South Asia*, IV (1974), 68.

[16] T. Motte, 'Narrative of a Journey to the Diamond Mines', *Asiatic Annual Register*, I (1798–9), 55.    [17] W.W. Hunter, *Orissa* (2 vols., 1872), II, 32–3.

cession was at first a relatively easy one, but in little more than a year Siraj-ud-daula was overthrown. With his defeat the virtual independence of the Nawabs quickly came to an end.

Much of the blame for the failure to establish his rule has been attributed to the personal defects of the new Nawab. Many stories of his cruelty, debauchery and even his insanity were circulated. Such is usually the posthumous reward of the vanquished. Whatever their truth, there is little to suggest that Siraj-ud-daula was an appropriate successor to Alivardi Khan. It would seem that he was extremely ambitious and was not prepared to accept the limitations on the full power of his office that were implied by the privileges which powerful groups within Bengal had been able to establish. This was an understandable point of view; it may well have seemed to him that some limit must be set to the erosion of the Nawabs' authority. But the manner in which Siraj-ud-daula pursued his objectives was imprudent to the highest degree. Instead of tackling potential opponents one by one, within a year he had built up a formidable coalition of enemies, including most of his own high officials, the greatest *zamindar*s, the Jagat Seths and the Europeans. His ultimate achievement was perhaps to make Frenchmen in Bengal hope that the English would defeat him.[18]

The inevitable early challenge to Siraj-ud-daula from more or less plausible rivals among the Muslim aristocracy came from Shaukat Jang, the *faujdar* of the virtually autonomous district of Purnea. He was brought to battle by Siraj-ud-daula and killed in October 1756. The defeat of Shaukat Jang was followed by imperial recognition for Siraj-ud-daula's title. He was thus well placed to consolidate support for his rule, but he appears to have made no effort to do so. Instead, he alienated many of those who were most influential. He remodelled the civilian and military administration, demoting old office holders of Alivardi Khan in favour of men of his own. According to the historian Ghulam Husain Khan, 'the grandees and commanders... now set no bounds to their discontent'.[19] 'The chief officers of the army,... all the ministers of the old court... and nearly all the secretaries, the writers of the Durbar, and even the eunuchs of the harem' were said to have turned against the Nawab.[20] The most distinguished general of

[18] Memoir of J. Law, in Hill, *Bengal in 1756-7*, III, 177.
[19] [Ghulam Husain Khan], *A Translation of the Seir Mutaqherin* (3 vols., Calcutta, 1789), I, 718.    [20] Memoir of J. Law, in Hill, *Bengal in 1756-7*, III, 191.

Alivardi Khan's army, Mir Jafar, and the leading Hindu administrator, Rai Durlabh, were among those alienated. Rai Durlabh was to encourage disaffection among the leading *zamindars* of western Bengal. By 1757 the Hindu *zamindars* of Burdwan and Nadia were joined in their opposition by the Muslim Raja of Birbhum.[21] Merchants and bankers also turned against the Nawab. The head of the house of Jagat Seth was ordered to provide Rs. 30,000,000 for the crushing of Purnea. When he demurred, the Nawab struck him.[22] Thereafter the Seths were implacable in their hostility, evidently believing that they would not be safe until Siraj-ud-daula was deposed.

The European settlements were quickly made aware of the new Nawab's accession. As in the past, money was demanded from them. The Dutch eventually yielded Rs. 450,000 and the French Rs. 350,000. The penalty for the English was much more severe: the Nawab's army stormed and sacked Calcutta. In the aftermath of the catastrophe Englishmen asked one another what Siraj-ud-daula had intended. Few thought that he had aimed at the total destruction of the English Company. Even he recognised the value of its trade. A minority believed that had the Company reacted to the Nawab's demands with some degree of diplomatic skill and avoided needless provocation, they could have bought him off with a reasonable offer, as had the French and Dutch. A majority, however, thought that the Nawab had more serious purposes than the mere extraction of money. They believed that he intended to bring about a major reduction of the privileges of the Europeans, starting with the English. The symbolic issue for him seems to have been the fortifications round Calcutta. 'It has been my design to level the English fortifications raised within my jurisdiction on account of their great strength', he wrote.[23] Without their fortifications the Europeans would once again be like other merchant groups, or even like the Armenians or the Portuguese. Pressure could be applied to them and their settlements with a minimum of difficulty. The settlements would cease to be enclaves of alien power. The authority of the Nawab would have been reasserted over one of the great privileged interests of Bengal.

If the Nawab was indeed determined on a major change in the status of the Europeans in Bengal, it would have been very difficult for the

---

[21] Nichol, 'The British in India', pp. 138–9.
[22] Little, *House of Jagatseth*, p. 165.     [23] Hill, *Bengal in 1756–7*, I, 3.

British to negotiate any settlement with him. The Company's trade and the huge network of private British and Indian interests loosely connected with it were all thought to depend on the privileged position of Calcutta and on other immunities which the Europeans had acquired. A voluntary surrender of them was scarcely conceivable. But the British at Calcutta seem neither to have negotiated seriously with the Nawab nor to have organised any effective defence. Calcutta was captured in June 1756.

The military resources of the East India Company in Bengal had proved to be of little significance, but much more formidable forces were available at Madras, where the Company had been fighting a full-scale war against the French for several years. Thanks to its troops in the south, the Company could recover by force what had been taken from it by force and could introduce an entirely new element into the politics of Bengal, a highly professional European army. This army was not only to recover Calcutta but to intervene with decisive effect in the internal affairs of Bengal, bringing about the deposing of Siraj-ud-daula after the battle of Plassey in July 1757.

An expedition dispatched from Madras with warships, British soldiers and sepoys, under the command of the already famous Colonel Robert Clive, arrived off the coast of Bengal in December 1756. Calcutta was recovered after the Nawab's army had been driven away from it. Siraj-ud-daula agreed in February 1757 to what seemed a generous restoration of the Company's privileges. Over the next few months British aims gradually widened to include the destruction of the French settlements in Bengal, and eventually to encompass the downfall of the Nawab himself. By April it was clear to the British that there was a party of malcontents in Bengal, led by the Jagat Seths, who were prepared to try to use British power to gain their ends. They had fixed on Mir Jafar as their alternative Nawab and were willing to offer the Company both full compensation for its losses and increased privileges. Private individuals were also to be fully reimbursed, and Clive, the Company's servants and all the armed forces could be assured of huge rewards. Over £1,250,000 were eventually distributed to individuals.[24]

A deal was struck on 4 June. The British army then moved up the river towards Murshidabad, attacking the Nawab's forces posted at

[24] P.J. Marshall, *East Indian Fortunes: The British in Bengal in the Eighteenth Century* (Oxford, 1976), pp. 164–5.

Plassey some way down river from the capital. The famous battle of 23 June 1757 was a limited affair of artillery exchanges and a successful British assault on that part of the Nawab's army that was willing to fight. The great body of the army, under Mir Jafar and Rai Durlabh, stood aloof. Siraj-ud-daula escaped from the battle, but was caught in flight and murdered on the orders of Mir Jafar's son. Mir Jafar himself entered Murshidabad and was proclaimed Nawab.

Clive and his friends immediately started to write of the 'revolution' brought about by the battle of Plassey. Within a year or so it was to become apparent that this battle had indeed begun a revolution of very great significance. But at the time the intentions of all members of the winning side were extremely conservative. A return to the conditions presumed to have existed during the reign of Alivardi Khan was the avowed objective. A headstrong, unpredictable, domineering Nawab, who had exalted his own power, was to be replaced by one who would respect the balance of interests under the old order. Muslims of good family would fill the great offices. Experienced Hindu *mutaseddi*s would be employed in the administration. The Jagat Seths would be sure of their privileges. *Zamindar*s would not face extortionate demands. The trading companies would be left to go about their business undisturbed.

Mir Jafar immediately took Alivardi Khan's title of Mahabat Jang. Clive advised him to 'consult Jaggat Seat on all occasions', as Alivardi Khan had done.[25] The Jagat Seths' advice was 'to replace Allyverdi Cawn's officers in their old posts'.[26] The Seths would obtain the essential imperial confirmation from Delhi. For those who had conspired against Siraj-ud-daula with the aid of a foreign army to suppose that they could simply restore the situation that had existed in 1756 seems in retrospect to be highly unrealistic. Was not Mir Jafar being more perceptive when he insisted on being handed onto his throne by Clive in person? Be that as it may, it seems clear that most of the Indian actors in the events of 1757 did not see the extent of what they had done. The Mughal aristocracy in particular do not seem to have found it difficult to assimilate military men of all sorts to their order of things. They gave the English, especially the good soldier Clive,

[25] Hill, *Bengal in 1756–7*, II, 441.     [26] Ibid., II, 438.

Mughal titles and assumed that they would fulfil their appointed role as allies and upholders of the Mughal state.[27]

Even most Englishmen did not appreciate the full significance of what had happened. They too had impeccably conservative motives. They did not see themselves as the agents of an imperial drive which was to dominate the government of Bengal within a very few years. Rather they believed that they too had fought Siraj-ud-daula to restore the status quo and recover what they often called their 'ancient rights and immunities'. They too were being imperceptive when they used such arguments, but they too had reasons for their lack of perception. With the vital exception of Clive's army, there was little that was new about the British presence in Bengal in 1757. The volume of the Company's trade and probably of the trade of individuals remained at levels which it had attained in the 1720s. The major privileges and immunities had been acquired rather earlier. Events were to show that a political revolution in Bengal would lead to a surge forward in both Company trade and private profit, but there is little evidence that men in either Britain or India envisaged such a change at that time. No dynamic direction was coming from London. The Directors of the East India Company were broadly satisfied with the dominant position the Company enjoyed in the trade between Bengal and Europe. They saw no need to change the pattern of trade or of trading methods, and invariably counselled caution in politics and the avoidance of expense. Following the successful intervention of Europeans in southern India, some of the Company's servants seem to have been contemplating the possibility of similar adventures in Bengal. But such bold spirits seem to have been in a minority. Clive himself moved cautiously during the crisis. He was well aware of the possibility that he might have to disengage and return to the south. He did, however, insist on something which Alivardi Khan would never have tolerated, the right to fight the French in Bengal and to capture their settlements. In other respects he worked for the restoration of the Company's position with certain specific improvements in it, not for a revolution.

What Englishmen who spoke of restoring 'ancient rights and immunities' usually ignored was the very serious challenge to the Nawabs which the growth of their trade and settlements had posed over the past thirty or so years. Alivardi Khan appears to have been

---

[27] A.M. Khan, *The Transition in Bengal 1756–75* (Cambridge, 1969), pp. 10–12.

concerned about the wealth that was accumulating beyond his reach in Calcutta and about the very large volume of trade, much of it undoubtedly conducted by his Indian subjects, which escaped his regulations and his customs. Evidently recognising the importance of the European contribution to Bengal's economy, Alivardi Khan had done little to restrict the companies. Siraj-ud-daula made the disastrous error of attacking the British before he had been able to assure himself of the loyalty of the most important among his subjects. But his desire to make an issue of Calcutta's fortifications is an entirely comprehensible one. Since the 1720s a major section of Bengal's economy had passed into European hands. Siraj-ud-daula tried to prevent the Europeans from exercising political power commensurate with their economic importance. The attempt miscarried. When Clive brought his army into Bengal and the conspirators decided to make use of it for their own purposes, the Company was able to take political power on any scale it might wish. However conservative the conscious intentions of most Englishmen might be, this was the Plassey revolution.

The agreement formally concluded between the new Nawab, Mir Jafar, and the East India Company was certainly a conservative one. As one of Clive's agents later put it: 'The general idea at this time entertained by the servants of the Company was, that the battle of Plassey did only restore us to the same situation we were in before the capture of Calcutta: the Subah [Mir Jafar] was conceived to be as independent as ever and the English returned into their commercial character'.[28] The Nawab was to guarantee the old commercial privileges and to add some new ones. For instance, the Jagat Seths' monopoly over the mint was broken; the Company would have their own mint. The Company were also given control over an area to the south of Calcutta, called the Twenty-four Parganas, from which they could collect revenue to defray their military costs. In the future the Company and the new Nawab were to be allies. The assumption on the British side was that the allies would be independent of one another. The Nawab would of course have absolutely no authority over Calcutta or over the Company's trade. On the other hand, it was supposed that the Company would not interfere in the Nawab's government. There would be a Resident at Murshidabad to maintain good relations and the Com-

[28] L. Scrafton, *Observations on Mr Vansittart's Narrative* [1767], p. 2.

pany's troops would be available to fight for the Nawab if required, but Clive seems to have assumed that the Company would largely keep itself aloof from the Nawab. He immediately commissioned the building of a massive fort at Calcutta and asked for a strong garrison of European troops.

Both sides to the agreement of 1757 hoped that there would be a return to the situation as it was under Alivardi Khan and that the old balance of interests in his reign would be restored. This quickly proved to be an illusion. Mir Jafar could not play the role of Alivardi Khan effectively, while the British could not resist pressures to intervene in his affairs. Clive no doubt wished to treat the Nawab as an independent ally, but he felt that too much was at stake for a policy of restraint to be followed too strictly. 'I do not want to aggrandize the Company at the expense of all equity and justice; long may the present Subah enjoy the advantages gained by our arms, if he abides strictly by his treaties', he wrote.[29] On the other hand, however, the British now had a compelling interest in the survival of a stable and well-disposed regime in Bengal. If the Nawab was threatened by internal disaffection or by invasion from outside, British intervention would be inevitable.

Mir Jafar appears to have lacked conviction as a reincarnation of Alivardi Khan. A contemporary Persian historian noted that although there was little overt opposition to the new Nawab, 'every one had thoughts of availing himself in such a time of trouble'.[30] Clive reported that Mir Jafar had alienated many of 'the principal officers' and that the local administration in certain areas was openly resisting him, 'all of which may be attributed to the Nabob's own imprudence'. Mir Jafar must be saved, Clive felt, from the consequences of his imprudence by British interference. Clive was prepared to take sides among the factions in the Nawab's government, keeping in office some whom the Nawab would have dismissed and extending British protection to others who were thought to be in danger, such as Rai Durlabh, one of the leading conspirators of 1757.[31] British intervention was most marked in the government of Bihar. Clive would not let the Nawab dismiss the *Naib*, Ram Narain, and laid down the terms for reconcili-

[29] Letter to L. Sulivan, 30 Dec. 1758, IOR, Home Miscellaneous, vol. 809, pp. 365–8.
[30] *Seir Mutaqherin*, II, 6.
[31] *Fort William – India House Correspondence*, II, *1757–59*, ed. H.N. Sinha, (1957), 257–8.

ation. Thus the British became an active party in Bengal politics. The Resident at Murshidabad and other leading Company servants were courted by contestants for power, even to the extent of large bribes. Non-intervention was replaced by an openly acknowledged policy of balancing the Nawab with 'a party within his own court to be a continual check upon him'.[32]

Within two years of his usurpation, just like Alivardi Khan, Mir Jafar had to face predators from outside Bengal. The main burden of repelling the invaders was, however, born by the Company, not by the Nawab, with the inevitable consequence that the British grip on Bengal grew tighter. In 1759 Bihar was invaded by the Shahzada, the Mughal prince who was shortly to become the Emperor Shah Alam. His army was supported by some of the major *zamindar*s in Bihar, whose loyalty to the Nawab was always tenuous. Patna was successfully defended and the Shahzada was then driven out by Clive's army, which marched right up to the border of Awadh, enforcing submission by the *zamindar*s. Shah Alam was back in Bihar in 1760, this time as the acknowledged Mughal Emperor coming to reclaim Bengal for the empire. The threat to the British and Mir Jafar quickly assumed serious proportions when the Bihar *zamindar*s again rebelled and, as the Emperor broke through the hills into western Bengal, the Raja of Birbhum and some of the other *zamindar*s in west Bengal joined them. Finally, the Marathas invaded western Bengal from Orissa. For a time it seemed likely that the Nawab's government would collapse. The British thought that: 'The whole country seemed quite ripe for an universal revolt.'[33] But after intermittent fighting, which lasted into 1761, the Company's troops won on all fronts: the Emperor was totally defeated, the Marathas were expelled and the *zamindar*s of Bihar and west Bengal were forced to submit. A challenge from an entirely different quarter, specifically aimed at the British, was also beaten off in 1759. This was an attempt by the Dutch East India Company to try to restore some kind of parity among the Europeans in Bengal by bringing a force of European and Indonesian soldiers from Batavia to reinforce their settlements. Clive saw this as entirely unacceptable and prevented the Dutch from landing their troops.

The success of the Company's arms gave Mir Jafar security, but left no doubt of his total dependence on the British. The extent to which

[32] L. Scrafton, *Reflections on the Government of Indostan*, 2nd edn (1770), p. 99.
[33] H. Vansittart, *A Narrative of the Transactions in Bengal* (3 vols., 1766), I, 156.

its troops were used strengthened the hold which the Company was already establishing on the Nawab's financial resources. In the first place, to ensure that the Company's troops were paid, it claimed the right to insist that much of the Nawab's own army, which had proved ineffective, should be disbanded. The Nawab was solely to rely on British troops in the future. But beyond that, as the Company's claims on the Nawab's resources grew ever larger, it was to insist that these must be put under its direct management. To meet the Company's demands, Bengal was dismembered bit by bit until the whole province came under British rule in 1765.

Mir Jafar had begun his reign with huge financial obligations to the British. Sums of the order of Rs. 28,000,000 or, as Clive put it, 'three million sterling',[34] had been pledged as indemnity to the Company and individuals, rewards to the army and personal presents. This staggering sum could not of course be paid at once. The Jagat Seths made themselves responsible for seeing that half was paid quickly and that the rest would be discharged over a three-year period. Clive was not content with mere promises and in 1758 he insisted that the Company must be given assignments of the revenue of specific parts of Bengal. The revenue of three large districts was to be paid directly to the Company. The implications of this arrangement were very significant indeed. Certain areas had become in a sense, if only temporarily, the Company's territory. In November 1758 the Calcutta Council was considering the possibility of making the grants permanent; 'such an opportunity can never again be expected of aggrandizing the Company'.[35]

New obligations were quickly added to the debts which the Nawab had incurred at his accession. He was pledged to pay Rs. 110,000 a month for the use of the Company's troops, who after 1758 were in the field for very long periods. Beyond what it believed that it was entitled to recover from the Nawabs, the Company's interest in the resources of Bengal was being sharpened by its own financial difficulties. The burdens which Bengal was forced to bear in the early phases of British rule over India were being laid on it very early indeed. In the first place, it remained what it had been since early in the eighteenth century, the main centre of the Company's commercial operations. Exports of textiles and saltpetre were now to be increased,

[34] G. Forrest, *The Life of Lord Clive* (2 vols., 1918), II, 36.
[35] *Fort William – India House Correspondence*, II, 327.

financed as far as possible from local resources, not from bullion shipped from Britain. Bengal was also called upon to finance the trade of the other Company settlements in Asia, especially the purchase of tea at Canton in China. Secondly, its own army of sepoys and Europeans was being recruited and was to expand very rapidly, while huge sums were spent on the new fort at Calcutta. Finally, Bengal must support the war effort of the Company's settlements in Bombay and Madras against the French or Indian powers. 'Bengal is in itself an inexhaustible fund of riches,' Clive assured the Governor of Madras, 'and you may depend on being supplied with money and provisions in abundance.'[36] The pressing demands of its own trade, its army and the needs of the other settlements were to throw the finances of British Bengal into repeated crises for many years ahead.

The first of such crises broke in 1760. What the Company was receiving from the Nawab was inadequate for the obligations that it was laying on Bengal. Henry Vansittart, Clive's eventual successor, wrote:

Far from being able to supply the necessities of Fort St George [Madras], we were obliged to put a stop to our own investment, and scarcely could provide for the pay of our own troops, and the other indispensible charges of the settlement. Things could not remain in this state. Means must be sought for procuring for the Company larger and more certain funds, and this could only be done by having countries ceded to them.[37]

Temporary assignments held since 1758 must be turned into permanent additions of British territory. Those specifically demanded were the very rich *zamindari* of Burdwan, one of the areas already assigned to the Company, and the districts of Midnapur on the western frontier and Chittagong in the east.

Mir Jafar would not consent to the amputation of his provinces. He is a somewhat enigmatic figure, but there is every reason to believe that he intensely resented the British dominance over him, which had grown so quickly since 1757. He had engaged in ineffectual manoeuvres against this dominance, even making contacts with other Europeans. This gave the Company a pretext for accusing him of disloyalty. The final crisis came when the Company reached an agreement with Mir Kasim, the Nawab's son-in-law and a man of proven administrative

[36] J. Malcolm, *The Life of Robert, Lord Clive* (3 vols., 1836), I, 370.
[37] *Fort William – India House Correspondence*, III, *1760–3*, ed. R.R. Sethi (1968), p. 290.

ability. Mir Kasim would cede the territory that the British demanded; in return they would force the Nawab to give him virtually all power as *Naib*, or Deputy. A deal was patched up, cemented by large bribes, and was put into effect by Vansittart. When Mir Jafar refused to yield authority to his son-in-law, he was compelled to abdicate by the Governor, backed by a force of the Company's troops, in October 1760.

The deposing of the Company's faithful ally of the Plassey conspiracy aroused much recrimination among the English. Clive and his supporters insisted that it would not have happened if he had remained in India. It is, however, hard to see how a different outcome could have arisen, unless the Company had been willing to renounce interference in the internal politics of the Nawab's court and, above all, had been willing to moderate its demands on the Nawab's resources. Since Mir Jafar could not ensure the flow of funds which the Company required, it had no alternative but to insist that he permanently alienate a sizable part of his revenue.

Mir Jafar would not accept these terms; Mir Kasim would. While the Company established its authority in its three new districts, bringing the Raja of Burdwan to obedience by a military expedition, Mir Kasim took possession of the rest of Bengal and Bihar. His three years as Nawab were in fact to prove to be the most determined effort ever made to establish an independent state in eastern India. Mir Kasim's overall strategy seems to have been that lower Bengal should be abandoned to the British, but that elsewhere their influence must be rigorously restricted. The central axis of the new state was no longer to be along the Hooghly–Bhagirathi with its outlet to the sea, but was to be much higher up the Ganges with links to northern India. A new capital would be established at Monghyr in Bihar, where a British Resident would not be received. The administration would no longer aim for the balance of interests of Alivardi Khan's era. It was to be highly centralised under the direct authority of the Nawab. In putting these plans into effect old office-holders, especially those maintained by British influence, were dismissed. Mir Kasim's greatest triumph was to force Ram Narain out of his office of *Naib* of Bihar, and to have him killed. The army was remodelled. The troops who had served previous Nawabs were disbanded and replaced by new regiments deliberately planned in the European manner.[38] Arms were manufactured at

[38] Vansittart, *Narrative*, II, 185.

Monghyr. Important commands were given to members of the Armenian community, who had not previously been extensively involved in Bengal's politics. The Jagat Seths were required to pay off the Nawab's outstanding obligations to the British. Once this had been done, they were given no part in the new order. They were ordered away from their house in Murshidabad and kept under supervision at Monghyr.

Mir Kasim's ambitions required the highest possible yield of revenue. He was said to have been 'in his heart . . . at all times an enemy to Zemindars'.[39] The revenue which they paid was forced upwards; in some cases the new assessment was spectacularly higher. Much greater use was made of the direct administration of districts by officials. Whereas Alivardi Khan's assessment of Bengal had aimed at a revenue of Rs. 18,684,067, Mir Kasim was said to have tried to collect a further Rs. 3,000,000 in spite of the loss of districts to the East India Company.[40] Mir Kasim was particularly concerned to establish his authority firmly in Bihar, far removed from British interference. He personally campaigned there to force the major zamindars to make an adequate contribution. The British believed that he had 'entirely reduced the province to obedience' and was obtaining a revenue from Bihar comparable to that from Bengal.[41] Later inquiries suggested that a large part of Mir Kasim's revenue assessments remained unpaid, but at the time it was supposed that the Nawab by 'confiscations, as well as by the order and regularity he introduced in every branch of the administration, and especially in the finances, came to be possessed of an immense hoard of ready money'.[42]

In theory the British should have had no objection to the emergence of a powerful, self-contained state which left them in undisputed control of the delta. But it was most unlikely that they would agree to see the influence which they had built up under Mir Jafar disappear from most of Bengal and Bihar, especially as it became increasingly apparent that the districts which they had taken over in 1760 were not going to provide a sufficient revenue for what they deemed to be their indispensable needs. Sooner or later, new cessions of territory would be demanded. Thus the long-term prospects for Mir Kasim were not

[39] Seir Mutaqherin, II, 156.
[40] J. Grant, 'Analysis of the Finances of Bengal', PP, 1812, VII, 304–7.
[41] Memoirs of the Rt. Hon. Warren Hastings, ed. G.R. Gleig (3 vols., 1841), I, 113.
[42] Seir Mutaqherin, II, 185.

encouraging. His bold attempt was, however, wrecked on a quarrel with the British that developed immediately.

The quarrel was over British commercial penetration far into the interior of Bengal. In 1757 Mir Jafar had been compelled to concede total freedom of movement for the Company's trade all over Bengal. But the private trade of individual Europeans remained a grey area. Such private trade had grown extensively in the early eighteenth century; it expanded very rapidly indeed after 1757. Englishmen, together with their Indian agents and followers, moved into parts of the provinces where Europeans had never ventured to trade before and began to deal in commodities which had been reserved as government monopolies. Salt trading by Europeans was a particularly contentious issue. Mir Kasim took strong exception to the extension of private trade which materially diminished his customs revenue and, perhaps most serious of all from his point of view, meant a potent growth of British influence outside the area to which he had hoped to keep it confined. His local officials tried to stop the movement of what they regarded as unauthorised trade.

The British response to the deterioration of relations with the Nawab was divided. Vansittart and those who had been responsible for Mir Kasim's succession hoped to effect an accommodation by agreeing guidelines for private trade. A majority of the Council at Calcutta, however, refused concessions. They believed that the private trade issue was symbolic of wider questions and that the Nawab must be confronted. 'It is, indeed, high time,' wrote one of them, 'to overset the ruinous system Mr Vansittart has so industriously endeavoured to establish' by allowing Mir Kasim 'to be independent and master of his own actions'.[43] They vetoed all agreements with the Nawab, who evidently became convinced that the Company's forces intended to attack him and end the control he had established over much of Bengal and Bihar. Fighting actually broke out in July 1763. The Nawab's new army proved ineffective and Mir Kasim was quickly driven out of Bihar into the territory of the Wazir of Awadh. The following year he, the Wazir and the Emperor Shah Alam came back into Bihar in what was to be the last of the many incursions that had been launched eastward out of northern India. The forces of the Wazir were formidable and the Company's army was for a time hard pressed.

---

[43] Letter of Major Carnac, 26 Feb. 1763, in Malcolm, *Clive*, II, 282-3.

But on 23 October 1764 it won a decisive victory at Buxar that was to give Bengal permanent immunity from invasion.

When fighting broke out, the British declared Mir Kasim deposed and reinstated Mir Jafar for the brief remainder of his life. All concerned on the British side seem to have accepted that the status of the Nawabs of Bengal was now irrevocably diminished. Relations with Mir Kasim had shown that the Company could not coexist with a Nawab who took seriously the assumption that he was the independent ally of the British. That had been the assumption behind the 1757 settlement, but it must now be formally renounced. As Clive wrote at the time, 'either the princes of the country must, in a great measure, be dependent on us, or we totally so on them'.[44] It was made clear to Mir Jafar on his restoration that, even if the Mughal Emperor confirmed his title, he must depend on 'our force to secure his government'.[45] When Mir Jafar died in 1765, the British selected his successor and installed him with a ritual which deliberately played down the Mughal link and stressed the Company as the source of his authority.[46]

With a dependent Nawab there were no obstacles to overt control over appointments in his government. On Mir Jafar's death, the Company chose Muhammad Reza Khan, an experienced administrator, to be the *Naib Subah*, or Deputy, for the new young Nawab.[47] Other administrative appointments were to be subject to British consent; *mutaseddi*s were to be appointed or dismissed only after the Company's approval had been obtained.[48] The government was recast in 1765 when Clive returned to Bengal. Muhammad Reza Khan was confirmed as *Naib*, and other ministers were also of the Company's choice. The Company's Resident, a figure of great influence in court politics in the past, was for the first time vested with formal authority. He was to check the accounts of the Nawab's ministers.[49]

The defeat of Mir Kasim meant that the Company could extract ever larger sums from the revenues of Bengal. The districts ceded in 1760 gave the Company a territorial revenue of some £600,000, but

[44] Malcolm, *Clive*, II, 340.
[45] *Fort William – India House Correspondence*, IV, *1763–6*, ed. C.S. Srinivasachari (1962), 246.  [46] Khan, *Transition in Bengal*, p. 78.
[47] See Khan, *Transition in Bengal*, for a biographical study of Muhammad Reza Khan.  [48] *Fort William – India House Correspondence*, IV, 315.
[49] Khan, *Transition in Bengal*, p. 97.

this was not enough to finance the war in Bihar in 1763–4.[50] The restored Mir Jafar must pay more. He and his successor had to pay Rs. 500,000 a month, while the Company searched for 'further fixed revenue', that is for more territory. When Clive arrived in 1765 he decided to reverse the existing arrangements whereby the Nawab allocated a very large amount to the Company and kept the rest of the revenue for himself, and institute new ones in which the Company would allocate what it thought an appropriate amount to the Nawab and keep the rest for itself.[51] Thus by 1765 an independent government of Bengal had virtually no existence. The Nawabs and their ministers were appointed by the Company. The Company had disbanded much of the Nawab's army, while accepting for itself exclusive responsibility for the defence of the provinces and exercising the right to appropriate the lion's share of the resources of Bengal for its own use. For all practical purposes, power had been transferred to the British.

The formal transfer of power took place at the famous treaty of Allahabad on 12 August 1765, when the Mughal Emperor appointed the East India Company his *Diwan* for the provinces of Bengal, Bihar and Orissa. The *Diwani* of Bengal was a bait which Emperors had dangled in front of many adventurers who aspired to seize control of the provinces. In return for granting their recognition to any prospective conqueror, the Emperors expected a guaranteed tribute. Each time Shah Alam had been worsted by the East India Company in Bihar, he had offered them the *Diwani*. To have accepted it would, however, have contradicted the Company's avowed policy of seeking a lasting and stable settlement with the Nawabs of Bengal. By 1765 this policy had obviously foundered; the Company had systematically destroyed the Nawabs. When he returned to India Clive conceded: 'We must indeed become the Nabobs ourselves.'[52] As he travelled up the Ganges to make a definitive peace with the Emperor and the Wazir of Awadh, Clive had evidently made up his mind that the time had come when it was appropriate for the British to seek what they chose to regard as formal legitimacy for what the Company had in practice taken for itself. He would accept the *Diwani*. The Emperor duly made the offer.

[50] A rough balance sheet for the Company in Bengal was later to be reconstructed in the 3rd Report of the Secret Committee of the House of Commons, 1773, *Reports from Committees of the House of Commons*, (12 vols., 1803–6), IV, 60–1.

[51] Khan, *Transition in Bengal*, p. 100.

[52] Cited in P. Spear, *Master of Bengal: Clive and his India* (1975), p. 146.

The Company was vested with the financial administration of the three provinces of Bengal, Bihar and Orissa. In return the Emperor was guaranteed a tribute of Rs. 2,600,000. The Nawabs of Bengal retained the office of *Nazim* with formal responsibility for defence, law and order and the administration of justice according to Islamic law. As a military power, however, the Nawabs had already been reduced to insignificance. They were granted a fixed allowance for their court expenses and such activities as the *Nazim* tried to undertake. The rest of the revenues of Bengal were at the disposal of the East India Company.

With the grant of the *Diwani*, the provinces of the Nawabs of Bengal came not merely under the dominance of the East India Company, but under full British rule. The Nawabs were not even to survive as British clients, as their neighbours the Wazirs of Awadh and the Nizams of Hyderabad were to do. But the debacle of the Bengal Nawabs is not necessarily evidence of overwhelming weakness on their part. As Chapter 2 tries to show, by 1757 the Nawabs had neither succeeded in creating a strong state machine nor succeeded in forging close links with the mass of their subjects. On the other hand, other entities evolving out of the Mughal Empire, including the longer-lived Awadh and Hyderabad, had not been markedly more successful. It may indeed be the case that the positive achievements of the Nawabs contributed most to their undoing. They had provided the stable framework for a huge growth in European trade, thus providing the base from which British conquest was to be launched. Whereas the revenue system of Awadh has been described as 'brittle, precarious and inpenetrable',[53] the manner in which Murshid Kuli Khan had organised the flow of revenue, mostly from the great *zamindar*s, made Bengal a very tempting target for invaders.

Invaders had indeed come thick and fast, subjecting Bengal to strains much more severe than those faced by other regimes. The Marathas and the Mughals had been followed by the British. The British onslaught was of course decisive in bringing down the old order, but the motives behind it and its timing still remain difficult to explain. Attempts to relate it to the needs of the metropolitan economy have not proved convincing.[54] The economic relationship between Britain and Bengal had changed little since the late seven-

[53] R.B. Barnett, *North India between Empires* (Berkeley, 1980), p. 191.
[54] E.g. A.G. Frank, *World Accumulation 1492–1789* (1978), p. 150.

teenth century. Such direction as came from Britain was cautious in the extreme. Neither the Directors of the East India Company nor the national government gave Englishmen in Bengal any encouragement to seize power. On the other hand, a British presence in Bengal, removed from effective control from home by a sailing time of some six months, had obvious opportunities to develop what is called its own 'sub-imperialism', that is to act on its own initiative. As a number of historians have pointed out, incentives for attempting a coup were not lacking.[55] In the years before the Plassey 'revolution' both the Company's trade and that of British individuals were encountering difficulties, in some cases acute ones. Economic conditions in Bengal in general were deteriorating. In the latter part of Alivardi Khan's reign and at the opening of Siraj-ud-daula's the Nawab's regime had shown itself increasingly unpredictable. A new political order could only be an improvement. But if the incentives for political intervention seem clear in retrospect, study of the behaviour of the British in Bengal in 1756–7 shows a mixture of confusion and caution. Calculated plotting seems to have been absent until the last few weeks before Plassey. The Calcutta Council appears to have blundered into the crisis with Siraj-ud-daula which led to the loss of the settlement. When he came to Bengal, Clive's objectives were very circumscribed. The possibility of achieving a 'revolution' was only slowly revealed to him; even then he intended it to be a very conservative revolution.

Purposeful sub-imperialism may be hard to prove, but the destruction of the Nawabs was brought about by the expansion of Calcutta, not by an assault directed from London. For thirty years or so the relationship between the Nawabs of Bengal and the British had been potentially a highly unstable one. With their privileges and immunities, their huge volume of trade, both private and the Company's, their burgeoning city, and their close alliances with many of the richest men in Bengal, the British were an object of justifiable apprehension for the Nawabs. Some attempt to curb the British was always likely. The British for their part felt that their stake in Bengal was far too important to depend on the whims of a succession of men whom they regarded as bigoted tyrants; some show of force against the Nawabs was always likely. Peace was kept because Alivardi Khan generally left the English alone and because the English lacked the

[55] B. Gupta, *Sirajuddaulah and the East India Company* (Leiden, 1966), pp. 15–26; see also the discussion in Nichol, 'The British in India'.

military resources to attempt a coup. In 1756 and 1757 these re-straints no longer operated. Siraj-ud-daula turned on Calcutta before he had secured his position among his own subjects; at the same time the arrival of Clive's army from Madras enabled the British to exploit the Nawab's weakness and destroy him.

It was official policy both in London and in Calcutta to restore the Nawabs' authority. Once this had been breached, all attempts to do so were in vain. There was no coherent plan for giving the Company full control over the provinces, but the survival of the Nawabs stood in the way of too many advantages that were now clearly seen. Their resources were plundered both by the Company and by individuals and all re-straints on trading were broken down. The Nawabs were swept aside as Calcutta conquered Bengal.

# CHAPTER 4

# THE NEW REGIME

In retrospect the year 1765, when the East India Company became the Emperor's *Diwan*, has come to be seen as the dividing line between Mughal and British Bengal. The establishment of British predominance in eastern India was, however, a gradual and protracted process, beginning before 1757, let alone 1765, and taking a considerable time to become fully effective throughout Bengal and Bihar. Subjugation of Orissa did not begin until the expulsion of the Marathas in 1803.

In theory the settlement of 1765 had not established a British Bengal. It had been no more than a reversion to an earlier division of power characteristic of Mughal provincial government. The *Nazim* and the *Diwan* were again to be separate offices held by separate people, as they had been before the rise of Murshid Kuli Khan. The Nawabs would still be *Nazim*s, holding court at Murshidabad, from where they would direct the defence of the provinces and the ordering of their internal peace and justice. The East India Company, through its Governor and Council at Calcutta, would be *Diwan*s, collecting revenue. Any implication that the two powers were effectively separate was, however, totally without substance after 1765. Events since 1757 had deprived the Nawabs of any capacity to take independent military or political action. The independence of the *Nizamat* was a fiction preserved by the Company for its own convenience, as in its dealings with other Europeans.

The functions of the *Nizamat* were nominally carried out under the direction of the Nawab, but in reality under the direction of a *Naib*, or Deputy, appointed by the British until 1790, when the Company assumed full responsibility for them. These functions were, however, limited, and from the outset the Company insisted on its right to regulate them. The internal order of the provinces depended on the forces of the Company, not on those of the Nawab. Indeed, within a very few years the Nawabs had virtually no forces left. In 1766 many of the Nawab's troops which had survived earlier purges were disbanded. Mughal gentlemen were left to mourn the disappearance of the mounted troopers who had been their pride. 'A horseman is as scarce in Bengal as a phoenix in the world', one of them lamented.[1] In 1770 the *faujdar*s, the agents of the Nawab's government in the districts, were recalled. In 1772 another wave of retrenchments was forced on the Nawab by the Company. Troops, office holders and pensioners were all struck off, and the Nawabs were compelled to live within the very circumscribed allowances which the British *Diwan* allowed them.

The *Nizamat* was, however, permitted to survive for a longer period as an instrument for administering justice. Even here it was subject to British intervention and regulation. What they classified as 'civil' justice, was, the British assumed, the concern of the *Diwan*; so it became their concern after 1765. 'Criminal' justice according to Islamic law they still conceded to be the concern of the Nawab. But from 1772 Europeans began to inspect the Nawabs' courts and the Governor and Council claimed the right to hear appeals from them. European magistrates dispensed criminal justice after 1781. In 1790 the office of *Naib Nazim*, the British-appointed Deputy to the Nawab, and therefore the nominal administrator of criminal law, was abolished. The courts were reorganised under the sole authority of British judges and magistrates. With this final usurpation of the last functions of the *Nizamat*, all traces of the Nawabs' authority in Bengal were obliterated.

The dispersal of the Nawab's army had eliminated the main rival to the Company's military supremacy. Lesser rivals, the forces of the Muslim grandees or of the major *zamindar*s, were also compelled to disband. The troops of the East India Company not only enjoyed a virtually uncontestable monopoly of force but also constituted an instrument of coercion far more formidable than any possessed by previous rulers of Bengal. The nucleus of the Company's army was its European regiments, which were supplemented by ever-growing numbers of sepoy battalions. Immediately after 1757 the Company began to form its own army recruited from the same kind of soldiers from northern India and Bihar as had enlisted under the Nawabs. Twenty-five thousand sepoys were enrolled by 1768. The number had grown to 40,000 by 1784, and by 1814, when the Bengal army's area of responsibility stretched beyond Delhi, 65,000 Indian soldiers were

---

[1] [Ghulam Husain Khan], *A Translation of the Seir Mutaqherin* (3 vols., Calcutta, 1789), II, 410.

divided into 54 regiments of infantry and 8 regiments of cavalry.[2] Regular regiments of the King's army from Britain were increasingly posted to India to serve alongside the Company's forces.

The loyalty of this great military apparatus could never be taken entirely for granted. Both the European soldiers and the sepoys were mercenaries who could not tolerate anything other than the strictest and most punctual observance of what they considered to be due to them. In 1764 many of the sepoys had shown little inclination to fight. European officers in large numbers refused to obey orders in 1766, when their allowances were cut. There was more disaffection among the officers in 1795–6 and mutiny among some sepoys ordered to Burma in 1824. Prompt payment of its troops was, not surprisingly, always the first claim on the Company's resources.

Apart from occasional outbreaks of insubordination among its troops, the Company's control of its provinces was not in serious danger after 1765 from any armed challenge from within. It was never again threatened, as it had been in the 1760s, by a combination of outside incursions, breakdown of relations with the Nawab and *zamindari* resistance in Bihar and western Bengal. Periodic resort to force was, however, needed to maintain full British authority throughout eastern India. The two most formidable insurrections which the Company faced occurred in Bihar and Orissa. In 1781 armed resistance by the autonomous Raja of Benares, a chieftain very similar to the major *zamindar*s in neighbouring Bihar, was followed by a series of rebellions among them. These uprisings appear to have been the last bid by the Bihar *zamindar*s to reassert what they saw as their traditional right to limit the claims which any ruler of Bengal could make upon them.[3] In Orissa in 1817 the Company's control over most of the district of Puri was broken by a revolt led by one of the major office holders under the Rajas of Khurda. Early British rule appears to have caused much dislocation in Orissa, and to have aroused widespread resentment.[4]

Overt armed resistance to the new regime on the plains of eastern India was relatively uncommon, but there were some significant exceptions. In 1783 there was extensive rioting against the high rates

[2] J. Pemble, *The Invasion of Nepal: John Company at War* (Oxford, 1971), p. 91.

[3] L. Prasad, *Opposition to British Supremacy in Bihar 1757–1803* (Patna, 1981), pp. 77–86.

[4] P.K. Pattanaik, *A Forgotten Chapter in Orissan History* (Calcutta, 1979); B.S. Das, *Studies in the Economic History of Orissa* (Calcutta, 1979), pp. 168–83.

of taxation being exacted in the northern Bengal district of Rangpur.

The Company also had very little control over the district of Birbhum in the 1780s in the face of repeated insurrections apparently directed against its revenue assessments.[5] In the late 1820s the grievances of Muslim peasants against Hindu *zamindar*s and European indigo planters in central and eastern Bengal appear to have been articulated by an Islamic millenarian called Titu Mir.[6] In several parts of Bengal early British rule had to contend with the movements of large bodies of mendicants, *sannyasi*s and fakirs, who came from northern India to visit shrines in Bengal. Piety was mixed with trade and money lending, and the ascetics evidently expected to receive support from the countryside through which they passed. A large body of *sannyasi*s on the move was a formidable force. To the British they were plunderers who must be prevented from pillaging Bengal. This seems to have been a serious over-simplification of their complex role, but the Company servants acted on their beliefs, using force to block the passage of the *sannyasi*s and break up their parties. Fierce conflicts resulted, by no means always ending in victory for the Company's troops. Clashes were most frequent in the early 1770s, but *sannyasi* incursions continued to cause the Company concern until about 1802.[7]

Along the frontiers of the Company's provinces, in hilly and wooded areas, where the power of the Nawabs had counted for little,[8] British rule was established and maintained only by a considerable expenditure of force. Campaigns were waged all along the western frontier. At the southern end, in the hilly districts beyond Midnapur, repeated efforts were made to coerce 'jungle' *zamindar*s and settlers with military tenure, the *paik*s or 'chuars', into making what were regarded as adequate revenue payments for the lands they held. Sporadic resistance to the Company's rule continued for a long period, culminating in a serious rising of the 'chuars' in 1799.[9] Further north the Company was consistently opposed by other holders of land on military tenure, the *ghatwal*s. The frontier along the foothills of the Chota Nagpur plateau, in an arc from Birbhum in the east to Palamau in the west,

[5] R.K. Gupta, *The Economic Life of A Bengal District: Birbhum 1770–1856*, (Burdwan, 1984), pp. 43–52.
[6] Muin-ud-Din Ahmad Khan, *History of the Faraidi Movement in Bengal* (Karachi, 1966).   [7] A.M. Chandra, *The Sannyasi Rebellion* (Calcutta, 1977).   [8] See Chapter 1.
[9] B.S. Das, *Civil Rebellion in Frontier Bengal* (Calcutta, 1973).

remained disturbed well into the nineteenth century. On the plateau itself British influence was very tenuous until the 1820s. Even then the area required further 'pacification' after the 'Kol' rising among the tribal peoples in 1831–2.[10] A stable frontier on the eastern side of Bengal was also difficult to establish. In the late eighteenth century there was conflict with the Chakmas to the south and in the Khasi and Jaintia Hills. During the first two decades of the nineteenth century the Company became increasingly preoccupied with the westward advance of the Burmese into Assam and Arakan. In 1824 the British launched an offensive which ended in the expulsion of the Burmese and annexations which carried Bengal's frontier far into the eastern hills.

Except for the different scale of the operations needed to control them (police rather than army), the East India Company's servants made no great distinction between rebellion and frontier wars, and the gang violence they called 'dacoity' in nominally pacified areas. In both cases law must be enforced on the lawless. Predatory peoples in the hills had to be taught to obey the government and to leave their neighbours in peace; supposedly hereditary bandits, or dacoits, had to be persuaded to take up another calling. Modern historians are not generally inclined to accept the traditional picture of colonial rule as the pacifier of an otherwise disorderly society. They too see common features between a disturbed frontier and dacoity. What is said to have united frontier resistance and dacoits is resistance to alien rule and the hardship and dislocation which it had brought in its wake. 'Crime' and deprivation seem to be connected.[11] The evidence that might demonstrate such a connection for Bengal dacoity has yet to be assembled, but a few Englishmen were prepared to concede that the scale of the problem suggested something more significant than recurrences of violence thought to be endemic in pre-colonial society.

Dacoity was usually taken to mean violent robbery by gangs. The extent to which it was prevalent under the Nawabs is impossible to assess. From the beginning of British rule it attracted much attention. Draconian penalties, including execution and the enslavement of the families of those convicted, were enacted in 1772. It was generally

[10] J.C. Jha, *The Kol Insurrection of Chota-Nagpur* (Calcutta, 1964).
[11] R. Guha, *Elementary Aspects of Peasant Insurgency in Colonial India* (Delhi, 1983), pp. 77–108.

believed, however, that the incidence of dacoity continued to increase. Calcutta itself and the major rivers of Bengal were thought to be badly affected. As European magistrates assumed greater powers in the 1790s, dacoity concerned them more and more. By the beginning of the nineteenth century the failure to control dacoity had come to be identified as an outstanding weakness in British rule. In 1809 the Governor General wrote of the dacoits:

It is impossible to imagine without seeing it, the horrid ascendancy they had obtained over the inhabitants at large of the countries that have been the principal scene of their atrocities. They had established a terrorism as perfect as that which was the foundation of the French Republican power, and in truth the *sirdar*s, or captains of the band, were esteemed and even called the *hakim*, or ruling power, while the real government did not possess either authority or influence enough to obtain from the people the smallest aid towards their own protection.[12]

In the years 1803–7 the Company recorded an annual average of some 1,500 dacoit offences a year.[13] The British believed that the great majority of the dacoits' victims were relatively poor. One official writing in 1802 considered that it was 'literally true' that in certain parts of Bengal 'the lives and the property' of ordinary cultivators were at risk.[14] Attacks on the government or on Europeans were not common. The scourge, as the British regarded it, was thought to have passed its peak in about 1807 and to be on the decline throughout the second decade of the nineteenth century.

Whatever interpretation is put on the causes that underlay the phenomenom of dacoity, the failure of the Company to curb it, or, as seems likely, to prevent a major increase, suggests serious limitations on the effectiveness of British rule in Bengal for at least fifty years after 1765.

While its military power could not give the Company total control over its new subjects, it could at least provide a guarantee against internal insurrection or outside invasion, leaving the Company free to pursue its purposes in security. To describe what these purposes were is not a simple task. During the first sixty years of its existence the Company's rule was intended to fulfil a variety of purposes: which was

---

[12] Countess of Minto (ed.), *Lord Minto in India* (1880), p. 188.
[13] *PP*, 1831–2, XII, 202.  [14] Report of H. Strachey, 30 Jan. 1802, *PP*, 1812, VII, 533.

dominant at any particular time depended on how competing claims were resolved within a very complex structure of authority.

Like that of other colonial regimes, the development of the East India Company's rule was of course partially shaped by pressures emanating from the metropolitan society. Such pressures came from different sources in Britain, often with conflicting aims. Throughout the period of this volume formal authority over British India was exercised by the Court of Directors of the East India Company, who were responsible to their shareholders. Yet within a few years of 1765 the East India Company was forced to accept intervention by the national government over the way in which it managed its Indian concerns. The power of the government was eventually defined in famous statutes, notably in Lord North's Regulating Act of 1773 and Pitt's India Act of 1784. After 1784 the government had the legal power to determine the main outlines of Indian policy if it so wished.

Seeing to the commercial success of the Company can in general be assumed to have been the main purpose of the Court of Directors. The Company's commercial viability was also likely to be an objective of the national government. Yet by the end of the eighteenth century the government's support for the Company as a trading body was tempered by its willingness to respond to pressure from other British commercial interests who were opposed to the Company's monopoly and felt that it made too little of the economic possibilities of British dominance in Bengal. Such pressure led to the substantial modification of the Company's monopoly in 1793, its termination in 1813 and the final abandonment of the Company's trade after 1833. The government had other concerns, not narrowly commercial, of which the Company could also be compelled to take account. Both Company and government were of course committed to the effective defence of Bengal against European and Indian threats to it, but governments also expected the Company to allocate resources to defence plans of their own devising. Under pressure from within Parliament or from outside it, governments tended to see themselves as representing a national conscience on Indian questions. The Company could be compelled to pay attention to the views of men like Edmund Burke or William Wilberforce, who criticised apparent abuses in its administration or its failure to propagate Christianity.

Whether they were shaped by the intervention of the government or whether they originated solely from the Directors, orders from

Britain took up to six months to reach Bengal round the Cape. The 'overland' route through the Middle East was potentially quicker, but remained erratic until the effective use of steam ships. Thus orders from home, always liable to be inadequate because of ignorance of the issues, were often seriously out of date. This gave the men in India a degree of freedom to decide their own purposes. There was no lack of strong-willed men willing to take advantage of their autonomy. But in India, as in Britain, purposes were diverse and often in competition.

The apparatus for governing the Company's new provinces grew out of that which had been conducting the Company's trade for many years. It was already a recognisable bureaucracy. Under the overall direction of the Governor and Council a hierarchy of offices was filled by 'servants' sent from Britain. Promotion was strictly by seniority. Elaborate records were kept. In the years after 1765, the functions of a late Mughal provincial state, as the British understood them, were engrafted onto the organisation of a trading company. The Company maintained a large army, tried to preserve the internal peace of its provinces, collected taxes and dispensed justice. Many more servants were appointed and new offices and boards were created, but there was no radical break with the administrative methods of the trading company. The Governor, styled the Governor General after 1773, presided with a more streamlined Council over a service of more than 400 'covenanted' 'civil' servants, who specialised in various branches of the Company's affairs. By the end of the eighteenth century the system had become a highly formalised one. Its working was defined by an elaborate code of public regulations, which reflected such British ideals as the separation of the judiciary and the executive.

For some time after 1765, however, the Company's administration continued to incorporate many characteristics of that of the Nawabs which it had replaced. Indeed, the British element was at first little more than a thin veneer. Virtually all the new regime's contacts with its subjects were through Indian agents. At the highest level the functioning of government no longer depended, as it had done under the Nawabs, on a consensus of powerful Indian interests, but it was still accessible to Indian influence. The Company could not do without the services of the merchants and bankers, of the great zamindars, and even, for a few years, of the Muslim grandees. It also enlisted the help of men who would not have been of much conse-

100

quence under the Nawabs, the so-called 'banians', who attached themselves to individual Europeans and became their personal agents, interpreters and general intermediaries in a world of which they were profoundly ignorant. Ambitious Indians now competed for the favour of the Governor and his senior colleagues, as they had competed for favour at the old court. They quickly learnt how to exploit factional rivalry among the Europeans.

Warren Hastings, Governor, and the first Governor General from 1772 to 1785, embodied the mingling of old practices and new ideals. A highly educated man with scholarly tastes, he did much to devise orderly ways of transacting the intricate business arising from the Company's new responsibilities. At the same time he was not unmindful of private interests, including his own,[15] and often operated in an informal manner through Indian intermediaries. The major *zamindar*s were left in no doubt that he personally determined their fate.

After 1786 the Company's Governor Generals were usually men with British military and political experience but no previous knowledge of India. Men such as Lord Cornwallis, Lord Wellesley, Lord Minto, the Marquess of Hastings and Lord Amherst were completely beyond the reach of Indian aspirants for influence. By contemporary standards the service they headed was a highly professional administrative corps, whose generous salaries attracted well-educated young men of high social standing. Although Indian agency at lower levels was still essential for the running of the government, the ethos of the higher ranks of the service had become firmly British. In time the members of the service, both civil and military, developed a distinctive *esprit de corps*, based on strong feelings about their role and the rights and privileges due to them, which not all contemporaries found admirable. At the end of the period the Governor General was astonished at 'the degree to which this feeling for individual interest domineers over the public'.[16]

A service so confident of itself was not likely to prove very amenable to control by inevitably remote home authorities. Its members tended to exploit to the full the practical autonomy which they enjoyed. But for all their *esprit de corps* there was no uniformity of opinion among the Company's servants as to how Bengal was to be governed. The service

[15] P.J. Marshall, 'The Personal Fortune of Warren Hastings', *Economic History Review*, 2nd ser., XVII (1964–5), 284–300.
[16] J. Rosselli, *Lord William Bentinck* (1974), p. 312.

was divided into separate hierarchies, reflecting the Company's varying functions: the Company was at the same time soldier, general
administrator, tax collector and merchant. These functions were
often in competition with one another. Within the hierarchies there
was much debate about policy and priorities. The Company's copious
records were studded with the 'minutes' through which its servants
delighted to engage in public controversy with each other. In short, if
crucial decisions affecting the government of Bengal were more likely
to be taken in Calcutta than in London, overriding purposes behind
the new regime's rule are no easier to detect in Bengal than in Britain.
Priorities emerged from conflict both between London and Calcutta
and within the home and the Indian administrations.

Like the Directors in London, the Company's administration in
Bengal was subject to pressure from outside. From its early days the
Company had been unable to prevent the establishment of private
interests in India. Private enterprise had in fact built up a tolerated
status allowing it a wide scope by the early eighteenth century. The
Company defended its monopoly of trade with London but permitted
individuals to trade extensively in their own ships with other Asian
ports from Calcutta. Both Company servants acting in their private
capacities and men outside the service, who might or might not
have permission to live in India, became considerable investors in
shipping.

The boundary between public and private interests was thrown into
confusion in the years after the Plassey upheaval. There was a massive
invasion of the internal trade of Bengal by private British enterprise:
men who had suddenly acquired political and military power exploited
it ruthlessly in the interests of their personal trade. A spectacular ran-
sacking of the Nawabs' resources also occurred, including the exac-
tion of well over £2,000,000 in 'presents', and there was much looting
of the Company's first revenue collections. A new division between
the public and private spheres was eventually enforced; it was intended both to safeguard the Company's own interests and to protect
Indians from unauthorised spoliation. The Company's servants,
except those actually employed in the commercial branch, were
eventually excluded altogether from trading. Henceforward they
were supposed to depend entirely on official salaries rather than rely
on private profit.

A substantial area was, however, left for the activities of those who

102

were not in the service. Permission was still formally needed for residence in India, although the unlicensed were rarely evicted, and the right to hold land was restricted to Calcutta. However, participation in internal trade was freely conceded, except in certain commodities which were reserved as Company monopolies. With modifications, especially in 1793, the Company's monopoly of trade to and from Britain remained intact until 1813, but individuals were still free to trade by sea all over Asia. Within these limits there was vigorous growth in the private British sector in Bengal. The number of Englishmen living there outside the service is always hard to estimate: a figure of under 1,000 has been suggested for 1800,[17] while the census of 1837 put the European population of Calcutta at over 3,000.[18] Many of these people were concerned with shipping. The fleet of private merchant ships based at Calcutta was put at 82 vessels, with a tonnage of 36,427 in 1801, rising to 158 vessels, with a tonnage of 60,083 in 1821.[19] Within Bengal by the early nineteenth century private Europeans were involved in producing silk, sugar and above all indigo. Institutions called Houses of Agency played a dominant role in all forms of private enterprise. Their main function was to manage the savings of the European community; they used them to finance shipping and undertakings like indigo factories and private banks. By 1803 twenty-nine Agency Houses were in existence, but a few large ones dwarfed the rest and were to dominate private British enterprise in Bengal until they failed spectacularly between 1830 and 1834.[20]

The private British community in Bengal was essentially a commercial one, ranging from shopkeepers to bankers, but by the end of the eighteenth century they were joined by the first Protestant Christian missionaries. Missionary Christianity, as opposed to the official Christianity of the Company's chaplains, was a form of private enterprise of which the East India Company was inclined to be sceptical, seeing it as a possible threat to the stability of the Company's rule. Missionaries arriving in India, like the great Baptist William Carey, who came to Bengal in 1793, were generally tolerated, but the main influx came only after the relaxation of controls which the Company was forced by Parliament to concede in 1813.

[17] J.C. Ghosh, *The Social Condition of the British Community in Bengal 1757–1800* (Leiden, 1970), p. 60.     [18] P. Sinha, *Calcutta in Urban History* (Calcutta, 1978), p. 43.
[19] J. Phipps, *A Guide to the Commerce of Bengal* (1823), p. 90.
[20] S.B. Singh, *European Agency Houses in Bengal (1783–1833)* (Calcutta, 1966); A. Tripathi, *Trade and Finance in the Bengal Presidency 1793–1833*, 2nd edn (Calcutta, 1979).

In theory the private British community in Bengal existed only on the sufferance of the Company. Individuals who offended could be deported. Effective representative institutions were not permitted, and a surprisingly prolific press was subject to censorship. Yet the relationship between the Company and the private sector was much less unequal than it appeared to be on the surface. As the operations of private interests in Bengal grew more extensive, the Company came to depend on them in certain areas and found that it could not ignore their claims.

The new British regime in Bengal was shaped by the interplay of a wide range of ideals and interests, exerted both in Britain and in Bengal itself. Different groups endowed it with different functions: it was principally to be a hybrid of merchant and ruler, aiming at commercial profit, military security and various concepts of good government. During the first sixty years of the Company's rule a pattern of priorities for these goals slowly emerged.

Whatever new dimensions may have been added to it, most sections of British opinion continued for many years to regard Britain's connection with Bengal as essentially a commercial one. Down to 1833 the East India Company remained a trader and the private British community was largely a community of traders. For most contemporaries the standard by which the success or failure of British rule was judged was the volume of trade between Bengal and Britain.

So long as its monopoly lasted, trade between Bengal and Britain was formally reserved for the East India Company. The Company's Directors felt that it had been drawn into the politics of Bengal to protect its trade, and they intended to exploit the great victories culminating in the grant of the *Diwani* to develop Bengal's trade with Britain to the fullest extent. It was presumed that the *Diwani* had created a much more favourable environment for trade and that the large surplus of taxation which was anticipated could be used to purchase a greatly increased 'investment' of Bengal goods. Such expectations were at first fulfilled, at least in part. The sterling value of the sums laid out for Bengal goods rose from some £400,000 at the time of the granting of the *Diwani* to well over £1,000,000 in the late 1770s.[21] Thereafter growth was to be restricted. In good years, as in

[21] *Reports from Committees of the House of Commons* (12 vols., 1803–6), IV, 60–1, VI, 112.

the early 1780s or for part of the 1790s, exports costing more than £1,000,000 would be dispatched to London on the Company's ships, but for most of the next fifty years investments were at rather lower levels. It was only in the late 1820s, when the Company was about to cease trading altogether that it consistently applied more than £2,000,000 a year to Bengal goods for London.[22]

The Company's failure to develop the Bengal investment on the scale it had anticipated in 1765 can be explained only in part by the difficulties it faced in disposing greatly increased quantities of Bengal goods in a still pre-industrial world. Fluctuations in the volume of the investment seem in fact to have had relatively little to do with fluctuations in world demand. The investment quickly became primarily a channel through which funds were transferred from India to Britain, whatever the level of profit on the goods concerned. For some years after 1765 the Company hoped that its Bengal investment would be the means by which a 'tribute' was to be remitted to Britain. This tribute would consist of the surplus revenue left after the costs of government and defence had been met in Bengal. Events were to show that in many years the Company would find it very difficult to contrive a surplus for the investment because of the very high level of its costs. Nevertheless, the provision of an investment, even if this involved borrowing in Bengal, remained a high priority because of the heavy obligations which the Company was required to meet in Britain. In the early nineteenth century some £3,000,000 a year were needed to pay for stores, pensions, dividends to shareholders and interest on money borrowed in London.[23] The sale of Bengal goods, even at a loss, was the main means by which these charges could be met.

So long as the Company's monopoly survived, the role played by British private traders in Bengal's exports to Britain was a restricted one. But there were opportunities for private consignments on the Company's shipping before 1813, while many of the goods which the Company exported to Britain were obtained from private traders in the first instance. This was also true of goods shipped by foreign European concerns, which flourished under the new British order. The old Dutch and French East India Companies withered away, but in their place, according to the state of international relations in Europe, came American, Danish, Portuguese and private French concerns. These all

[22] *PP*, 1812, VI, 431; 1812–13, VIII, 601–3; 1831–2, X, part i, 108–9.
[23] *PP*, 1831–2, X, part i, p. xxv.

worked closely with the private British traders and to a considerable degree provided them with the access to world trade which the Company's monopoly denied them. Private traders often claimed that their commercial acumen would enable them to develop Bengal's trade in ways that the Company had never attempted to do. Even after 1813, however, their trade, like that of the Company, was to a large extent a means of transferring money to Britain and its volume was determined by the sums available for remittance. Accumulated savings which the British community in Bengal wished to send home were the main source of finance for the private traders. In the early nineteenth century some £1,000,000 a year was said usually to be awaiting remittance to London.[24]

Since the late seventeenth century, the staple item of Bengal's exports to Europe, as well as throughout Asia from a much earlier period, had been cotton piece goods. Contemporaries were well aware of the potential threat posed to Bengal's exports by the rise of a new British cotton industry, but for at least forty years after the grant of the *Diwani*, the threat did little to check the growth of piece good exports to Europe. The East India Company was determined to retain its leading position in this trade. In the years after 1765 it posted its commercial agents wherever it believed that high quality textiles could be developed, and it armed them with powers to control weavers and restrict competition. The volume of sales in London, by far the largest part of them on behalf of the Company, was maintained at a steady level until the end of the eighteenth century. In the ten years 1777–86 on average 550,790 pieces were sold per year; for the ten years 1792–1801 the average was 777,237 pieces.[25] By the turn of the century it was only too apparent that sales of certain Bengal lines, most notably muslins, were suffering from British competition. On the other hand, the Directors still believed that 'a quantity of callicoes far exceeding our most extended order' could find an outlet in 1802.[26]

In the early nineteenth century, however, difficulties multiplied. Between 1802 and 1819 duties on imports of Indian textiles for the British market were increased on nine separate occasions. At the highest point in 1813, the duty on calicoes was 85 per cent.[27] Duties on

[24] G.A. Prinsep, 'Remarks on the External Commerce and Exchanges of Bengal', *The Economic Development of India under the East India Company 1814–58*, ed. K.N. Chaudhuri (Cambridge, 1971), p. 62.   [25] W. Milburne, *Oriental Commerce* (2 vols., 1813), II, 226.
[26] Directors' Commercial letter, 30 June 1802, Add. MS 13399, fo. 29.
[27] Table in H.R.C. Wright, *East Indian Economic Problems* (1966), p. 243.

cloth which was re-exported were much lower, but re-exports to Europe faced constant disruption from war and blockade. After the ending of the European wars in 1815, the competition of British cloth reduced the sale of Bengal cotton goods in London to miniscule proportions. Direct shipments to the Americas or to Portugal remained significant into the 1820s, but by then British exports were effectively eliminating Bengal's outlets throughout the western world and were beginning to invade its Asian markets as well.

The British textile industry had been given virtual protection in its home market while it developed its capacity to cut its costs dramatically and to respond quickly to new export opportunities. Competition between it and the export sector of the Bengal industry was inevitably unequal. Even if the British had not been ruling Bengal its export markets would have been in jeopardy. Yet a case can be made for suggesting that British rule accentuated the problems of the Bengal industry. A recent study has argued that the Company's system of procurement crippled the productive capacity of Bengal. The Company prevented competition and reduced the weavers to becoming its full-time servants at rates of wages which were so low that their employment became unremunerative. Thus the high quality piece goods industry was dying even before it faced significant British competition.[28] The evidence on which this case rests is, however, largely drawn from the old textile centre at Dhaka, whose muslins were particularly vulnerable to British imitations and where the East India Company's coercive power was especially strong. In some other parts of Bengal production was expanded and new lines were developed in response to new, if transitory, export opportunities. Nevertheless, the point that the Company's apparatus of controls may have robbed some part of the Bengal industry of its flexibility to cope with formidable competition may still be a valid one.

Raw silk comprised the second major staple of Bengal's exports. Part of the silk output was woven into cloth, in which the Company did a considerable trade, but the Company's main interest was in supplying the English silk industry with raw silk from Bengal. News of the acquisition of the *Diwani* was followed by orders from London that the

[28] H. Hossain, 'The East India Company and the Textile Producers of Dacca 1750–1813', Unpublished D.Phil. thesis, Oxford University, 1982, and her article, 'Alienation of Weavers ... 1750–1800', *Indian Economic and Social History Review*, XVI (1979).

Company's servants must increase exports of silk and improve the standard of reeling. The major silk districts had suffered severely, first from the Marathas and later from the famine, but the Company was in time able to ensure that a large part of the silk worm harvest came to them and that much silk was reeled by methods introduced from Europe. These methods involved the setting up of what were called 'filatures', depots at which groups of winders were employed reeling silk under close supervision using equipment imported from Italy. Once successfully pioneered by the Company, silk filatures were quickly adopted by private Europeans and by Indians, although what was called 'country-wound' silk continued to be produced in large quantities.

Bengal silk took some time to win a commanding position in the supply of the British market; this was not achieved until the 1790s. Thereafter silk exports encountered none of the difficulties that so beset piece goods; they continued to grow. A considerable part of Bengal's output remained under the control of the Company, in spite of the loss of the monopoly in 1813. Bengal silk sold for the Company in the 1820s rarely showed a profit, but involved smaller losses than other ways of remitting money to London.[29] Right up to 1833 the Company maintained a complement of twelve commercial Residents who managed the purchasing of cocoons from mulberry cultivators and supervised the reeling of silk at over one hundred filatures.[30] Private traders complained that they could not compete effectively.

In the old staples of Bengal's export trade, cotton piece goods and silk, the Company and the private traders were often rivals. In developing new export commodities, the two usually acted together. Indigo was a prime example. Indigo was the principal blue dye used by the world's textile industries. The indigo plant was widely grown in northern and western India, but intensive cultivation of the plant in eastern India was largely the consequence of European enterprise. The stimulus to develop the production of indigo in the new British provinces was provided by the dislocation of major American sources of supply during the wars of the late eighteenth century. Private individuals began to set up factories to process the indigo plants. Most of the early factories of the 1770s and 1780s were near Calcutta. From

[29] W. Simon's evidence, 12 March 1832, *PP*, 1831–2, X, part i, 91–3.
[30] Listed in *PP*, 1831–2, V, 659.

there they spread to Bihar north of the Ganges, which became a major centre of indigo production. In a very rapid proliferation of factories in the early nineteenth century, many were set up in northern districts of Bengal, for example in Dinajpur, and above all in the western half of the delta, where on flooded alluvial land the indigo plant could be sown and harvested annually; Jessore and Nadia were especially favoured districts. It was estimated that by 1830 there were 700 indigo factories in Bengal and Bihar.[31] The plants which the European factories processed were rarely directly cultivated by the factory owners on their own land in the period covered by this volume. The factories relied almost entirely on indigo plants grown for them by Indian peasants. This involved a relationship about which much controversy developed. There is a great deal of evidence which suggests that factories used coercion and intimidation both to persuade peasants to grow indigo and to fix the prices given for the crop.[32]

Unlike the silk filatures, the indigo factories were exclusively owned by private individuals, but the great expansion of production was underpinned by the Company. In its early phases the Company either brought the indigo made by the factories or advanced them money and shipped their dye to London. In the 1820s, when production of indigo entered upon an ambitious if vulnerable phase of expansion, the Company was making very large purchases, based on estimates of its needs for remittances to London. With the end of the monopoly, shipments on private account were also very large. Financed by massive loans from the Houses of Agency, said to amount to Rs. 20,000,000, of which four-fifths came from six great houses,[33] output surged forward. By the end of the decade the London market was proving uncertain, prices were falling and the great Agency Houses were slipping towards disaster.

Both the East India Company and the private traders had an interest in the export of sugar. Bengal had a highly developed sugar industry long before the rise of British power and it was already a considerable exporter of sugar by land and by sea to northern and western India and to the Middle East. Europeans did little more than divert some part of

[31] H.R. Ghosal, *Economic Transition in the Bengal Presidency (1793–1833)*, 2nd edn (Calcutta, 1966), pp. 291–2.
[32] The spread of indigo production is described in B.B. Chowdhury, *The Growth of Commercial Agriculture in Bengal* (Calcutta, 1964–) I, 125–63; B.B. Kling, *Blue Mutiny: The Indigo Disturbances in Bengal 1859–62* (Philadelphia, 1966), pp. 27–41.
[33] Singh, *European Agency Houses*, p. 234.

Bengal's production to new destinations overseas. Like indigo plants, sugar cane in Bengal remained a peasant crop. The few experiments in European sugar plantations were a dismal failure. But unlike indigo, Europeans who traded in sugar rarely had direct dealings with those who cultivated the cane. Cultivators received advances from Indian sugar merchants which they repaid by deliveries of *gur*, or boiled cane juice. The merchants then processed the *gur* to produce various grades of coarse or refined sugar.

Europeans purchased their sugar from the Indian merchants. In some cases the sugar was further refined in factories owned by private individuals, but most of it was exported without processing. The Company began shipping Bengal sugar to London on its own account in the 1790s, hoping to take advantage of interruptions in West Indian supplies. Although Bengal sugar faced heavy duties, the Company maintained a small sugar investment until 1811. After 1813 private merchants bought much Bengal sugar, usually of coarse quality, to be re-exported from Britain.[34]

Indigo was an example of one phase of the partnership between the Company and private interests, with the Company exporting a commodity produced by private factories. Opium was an example of another phase: private merchants exported a commodity produced by the Company.

During the eighteenth century parts of Bihar, especially districts around Patna, became the main source of opium for China and southeast Asia. In the 1760s individual servants of the East India Company had succeeded in displacing the Indian merchants who had dealt in opium and in controlling the production and sale of opium for their own advantage. In 1773 this virtual private monopoly was replaced by a formal public one run by the East India Company. From the outset, however, the aim of the Company was to augment its revenue by the sale of opium to private exporters, rather than to ship opium on its own behalf. The opium put up for sale in Calcutta was distributed throughout the Far East by private British shippers. Sales in China, in spite of official prohibitions, played a very important role in the overall pattern of the Company's trade. The proceeds of private opium sales were handed over to the Company's agents in Canton in

[34] There is a wealth of material on European involvement in Bengal sugar in *Papers Respecting the Culture and Manufacture of Sugar in British India* (published by the East India Company, 1822).

return for bills of exchange on London, and thus contributed to the financing of purchases of Chinese tea for the British market. By the 1820s opium provided 10 per cent of Bengal's revenue.

The opium monopoly in Bihar was operated by a system of tight controls. The Company aimed to regulate production so as to keep up the price and quality. This strategy persisted until competition from cheap opium from western India in the 1820s forced a shift to a policy of allowing output to increase. Regulated output inevitably meant control over the producers. Those who cultivated opium received advance payments from the Company's opium contractors or opium agents and were to a degree tied to the Company's service.[35]

The salt monopoly was by far the largest of the Company's commercial operations conducted for purely fiscal purposes. The Company organised the production of salt throughout the provinces in order to sell it to its subjects, the profit making a substantial contribution to its overall revenue. The Company's salt monopoly, inaugurated in 1772, was built on a monopoly established by the Nawabs and made much more intensive by private British enterprise in the 1760s. The Bengal monopoly was extended to the great salt-producing areas of Orissa following the British conquest in 1803. At first the Company contented itself with receiving and selling salt which was produced for it by a network of sub-contractors or by the *zamindar*s of the coastal districts where salt was manufactured. In the 1780s, however, the Company became directly involved in the production of salt. European agents were appointed to supervise the work of the salt boilers, the *mulangi*s, who became yet another sector of Bengal's labour force tied to the Company's service by the system of payments in advance. Salt made for the Company was put up for auction and then distributed throughout the provinces by Indian salt dealers.

The salt monopoly attracted criticism. In spite of attempts to reform them, the conditions under which the *mulangi*s worked and the level of their rewards often seemed deplorable, while the price at which salt was sold at the Company's sales climbed steadily, the price to the consumer being accentuated, it was alleged, by collusive dealing among Indian merchants. The price of salt was said to be so high that the poorest sections of the population could not afford it. Those who defended the Company's salt policy tended to deny specific alle-

---

[35] Chowdhury, *Commercial Agriculture*, I; D.E. Owen, *British Opium Policy in China and India* (New Haven, 1934).

gations, while pointing out that by selling salt at four times what it cost them to produce it, the Company was by 1827 receiving a revenue of Rs. 15,000,000, double what they had received in 1793.[36] With the yield of the major source of taxation, the land, largely fixed, this was a formidable argument against disbandment of the monopoly or even subjection of it to major reforms.[37]

In the years after 1765 the Company as merchant had been engaged in different kinds of operations. It had tried to make a profit for its shareholders by its trade with Britain, to remit funds to Britain almost regardless of profit and, if its apologists are to be believed, to maintain employment in Britain and in Bengal. It also ran monopolies to raise revenue for the Company as soldier and ruler. At many points the Company and private British enterprise were interlocked. Although they might appear to be rivals, they were in reality partners and it was by no means clear that the Company was the dominant partner. Long before 1813 it was leaving new commercial ventures to private hands, concentrating on the old staples of its export trade and on its revenue-raising monopolies.

In 1813, with the ending of the Company's monopoly of trade with Britain, all obstacles to the success of private trade seemed to have been removed. Rapid growth certainly took place over the next fifteen years, but it was uneven growth and the nature of Britain's economic relationship with Bengal did not undergo the fundamental transformation that had been widely prophesied. The opening of British–India trade to private shipping meant that the Company's investment was immediately eclipsed by large consignments to London on private account. But the early boom in private exports to Britain was not sustained. There was a slump in 1818. When exports to Europe began to grow rapidly again after 1822, a large part was taken up by the Company's shipments of indigo and silk. Between 1813–14 and 1827–8 it was estimated that the Company's exports to Britain doubled in value, while private exports increased by only 14 per cent.[38] The volume of exports still reflected the need to remit money to London as much as the world demand for Bengal goods, which private traders claimed to be able to satisfy more effectively

[36] Report of the Board of Customs, Salt and Opium, 27 Nov. 1827, *Selections of Papers . . . Relative to the Bengal Salt Monopoly* (Calcutta, 1833), pp. 262–8.

[37] For additional material on salt, see N.K. Sinha's Introduction to *Midnapore Salt Papers* (Calcutta, 1954).

[38] H.H. Wilson, *Review of the External Commerce of Bengal from 1813–14 to 1827–8* (Calcutta, 1830), p. 54.

than the Company had ever done. By 1833 private merchants were insisting that they must have more concessions, above all unrestricted access to land and the free migration of European settlers, so that they would no longer have to depend on what they regarded as the deeply ingrained backwardness of Bengal's peasant agriculture and thus could compete successfully with European producers of tropical products in other parts of the world.

Huge sales of British manufactured goods had been another promise of the campaign against the Company's monopoly. This promise had some substance. The years after 1813 saw a boom in the import of British goods into Bengal even more spectacular than the surge in its exports. But again progress was erratic and marked by checks, although the overall growth was greater than the growth in exports to Britain. Between 1813 and 1828 Bengal's imports doubled in value.[39] The achievement here was almost entirely to the credit of the private merchant: the Company ceased importing altogether in 1824.

The price of the new British imports into Bengal tended to fall and they faced duties which were in some cases lower than the rates on the movement on goods within the provinces that were being charged by the Company after 1810.[40] Thus for the first time imports from Europe were beginning to come within the range of some consumers in Bengal. British cotton textiles were in the vanguard of the new imports. In 1817–18 imports of piece goods from Britain exceeded for the first time Bengal's exports of piece goods to Britain.[41] Imported British cotton yarn was beginning to be used at Dhaka in 1824 and was causing a decline in local spinning by 1828.[42] The implications of large British imports for the future of the textile industry in Bengal are obvious. Its internal markets might be threatened as well as its export markets. But the extent to which British imports penetrated beyond a few towns remains unclear. In 1837 a British commentator suggested that at £2,000,000 a year imports of British piece goods might amount to no more than 6 per cent of indigenous production in the British provinces.[43]

[39] Ibid., p. 50.
[40] This is described in the famous *Report on the Inland Customs and Town Duties* of 1834 by C.E. Trevelyan. (For a recent edition, see T. Banerjee (Calcutta, 1976).)
[41] Wilson, *Review of External Commerce*, Tables, pp. 12, 14.
[42] J. Taylor, *A Sketch of the Topography and Statistics of Dacca* (Calcutta, 1840), p. 170.
[43] J. Crawfurd, 'A Sketch of the Commercial Resources ... of British India', *The Economic Development of India under the East India Company*, ed. Chaudhuri, p. 241.

Such estimates are a reminder that the history of British economic activity in Bengal is not necessarily the history of Bengal's economy, although it is often treated as such. Most of Bengal's internal trade as well as its overland trade with other parts of India had been only indirectly affected by the establishment of the new British order. Great changes, had, however, taken place in Bengal's overseas trade. During the first sixty years of British rule the volume of Bengal's overseas trade increased hugely. According to Customs House valuations, exports from Calcutta grew five-fold between 1777 and 1797, when they were worth Rs. 15,000,000.[44] In 1813–14, at Rs. 45,000,000, they were three times higher than in 1797. Fifteen years later they were worth Rs. 60,000,000.[45] The direction of Bengal's trade had also changed. By the 1820s about half of Bengal's trade, both imports and exports, was with Britain. Another 20 per cent was with China.[46] A large part of the Chinese trade was in fact indirect trade with Britain, Bengal goods being used to pay for shipments of Chinese tea to London. Finally, the composition of Bengal's overseas trade had changed as well. Manufactured textiles, the major component of Bengal's exports to both Europe and Asia, had largely been replaced by raw silk, indigo, sugar, opium and grain by the 1820s. Manufactured goods were beginning to be imported on a large scale from Britain.

A simple comparison between the pattern of Bengal's overseas trade before 1765 and that which had come into existence by the 1820s suggests the classical relationship between an industrial and a pre-industrial society. The magnetic power of the British industrial economy appears greatly to have increased the flow of Bengal's trade and radically to have changed its composition. But whatever might lie ahead, to portray the sixty years after the acquisition of the *Diwani* as a period in which Britain's industrial economy progressively tightened its grip on Bengal would be both an exaggeration of the pace of change and a misrepresentation of the modes of operation of the Company and of the private traders.

Old patterns of trade remained intact until well into the first decade of the nineteenth century. Bengal piece goods were exported in grow-

[44] Report by J.T. Brown, IOR, Home Miscellaneous, vol. 68, p. 821.
[45] K.N. Chaudhuri, 'Foreign Trade and Balance of Payments', *Cambridge Economic History of India*, II, *1757–c. 1970*, ed. D. Kumar (2 vols., Cambridge 1983), p. 828.
[46] Wilson, *Review of External Commerce*, pp. 52, 90.

ing quantities, which dwarfed exports of what can be regarded as raw materials.[47] Imports of British manufactured goods remained low. The Company's trade was still to a large extent geared to its traditional objective of re-exporting Asian commodities throughout the world, rather than to supplying new British industries. The concerns of the private traders were very similar. They had few links with industrialising Britain. They raised their finance in a volatile and restricted Calcutta money market. They depended heavily on the Company, which purchased their indigo for its remittances to London and used the proceeds of their opium to buy its Chinese tea. In emergencies the Company lent them money. In its methods of doing business in Bengal the Company can hardly be regarded as the sharp competitive edge of the new industrial society. It relied on well-tried practices from the past, reinforced by the use of its new political powers. It preferred to control labour, fix prices and establish monopolies, rather than trust to its superior efficiency. Private merchants had the same inclinations, as their dealings with the indigo cultivators suggested.[48] Neither Company nor private merchants did much to introduce new technology into India. The Company achieved major changes in methods of winding silk and was experimenting with steam power at the end of the period. Some private entrepreneurs were more adventurous with projects for mines, distilleries, and textile mills driven by steam. These enterprises were, however, carried out on a very small scale. So long as the British economic presence in Bengal was dominated by the Company and the older generation of Agency Houses, it would not be a very dynamic one.

The Company's various roles in Bengal were closely related to one another. The Company as merchant invoked the authority of the Company as ruler in its trading, which was carried on with the resources that the Company as ruler allocated for the provision of the investment. In return the Company as merchant made a contribution to the sum of resources available by the profits it derived from its salt and opium monopolies. For all the Company's enterprises, civil, military and commercial, the level of financial resources was crucial, and this

---

[47] Table in Chaudhuri, 'Foreign Trade', p. 821.
[48] See D.A. Washbrook's comments on the ' "State Mercantilist" form of economy' in 'early colonial India' in 'Law, State and Agrarian Society in Colonial India', *Modern Asian Studies*, XV (1981), 661–70.

overwhelmingly depended on the Company's greatest single asset, taxation of the land.

The Company had been drawn into creating a territorial empire in Bengal by what it regarded as its dire need for more revenue from taxation. Every accession of territory since 1757 had been intended to guarantee funds which would enable the Company to pay its troops and maintain its trade. The acceptance of the *Diwani* was the last stage in this process. After 1765 the first priority for the Company was to maintain a level of revenue adequate for its needs. This priority was inescapable at any period in the Company's rule.

Clive and his colleagues assumed in 1765 that active intervention by the Company in the management of the *Diwani* would be very limited. 'The power of supervising the provinces, though lodged in us', Clive wrote, 'should not, however, in my opinion be exerted.'[49] A British Resident would live at Murshidabad to ensure that the Indian ministers appointed by the Company did their duty. He must not, however, make any appointments or hear complaints.

Yet within three years of the signing of the treaty of Allahabad the Company's servants had become convinced that the Bengal revenue system which they had inherited could not serve their purposes and must be reformed in ways that would introduce direct British involvement. Dissatisfaction had differing causes. On the one hand, there was a simple concern for more money. Although the Indian ministers had in fact maintained a high level of revenue after 1765, the Company's expenditure on its own trade and troops and in aid to the Madras Presidency had been immense, and the Company was going into deficit. The solution seemed to be to make the system provide more funds than the Indian ministers appeared to be willing or able to extract. Other Englishmen, however, took a longer-term view. The Governor, Harry Verelst, and his closest adviser, Richard Becher, believed that Bengal's economy was in serious decline. Too much rather than too little was being taken in taxation. The Company was facing 'a crisis in our affairs', in which 'the present state of the revenues, public and private commerce, manufactures and agriculture are such as to give room for the most serious apprehension'.[50] Painful as it was to admit

---

[49] *Fort William – India House Correspondence* (New Delhi, 1949–), IV, *1764–6*, ed. C.S. Srinivasachari (1962), 337.

[50] H. Verelst, *A View of the Rise, Progress and Present State of the English Government in Bengal* (1772), Appendix, p. 224.

it, 'the fact is undoubted . . . that since the accession to the Dewanee the condition of the people of this country has been worse than it was before'.[51] Reform must be fundamental and must concentrate on improving the productive capacity of Bengal before higher revenue assessments could be imposed.

Debates about the management of the revenue, which began almost immediately after the acquisition of the *Diwani*, reveal that two assumptions of the utmost importance for the future of British rule in Bengal were already firmly established. The first was that Indian officials were deeply suspect. They must be closely checked, if not wholly replaced by Europeans. Secondly, conditions of continuity and security of tenure had to be established throughout the revenue system. Those who paid revenue to the Company must not be transitory plunderers whose only concern was a quick profit. They must have a long-term interest in promoting the prosperity of the areas for which they were responsible. They would thus have an incentive to bring about improvements in agriculture and in the living standards of the cultivators, since they would ultimately benefit.

For many years to come the Company's records were to be filled with copious and often highly polemical dissertations about the kind of European supervision that was appropriate for the revenue or about the categories of people to whom long-term revenue rights were to be granted and the degree of security which they were to enjoy. These controversies have been closely analysed by historians, who have established distinctions of nicety between the various 'schools' within the Bengal service. What united European opinion about the administration of the revenue seems, however, to be more remarkable than what divided it. The principles of European supervision and of security of tenure for revenue payers were not seriously questioned. The history of the evolution of revenue policy is the history of the search for an acceptable format for these two desiderata.

Those who first enunciated the two great maxims of the untrustworthiness of Indian officials and of the efficacy of security of tenure in the years after the acquisition of the *Diwani* usually justified them by the record of the Company's experiments in the territories granted to it in 1760. The administration of Burdwan was repeatedly held up as

[51] Cited in W.K. Firminger, *Historical Introduction to the Bengal Portion of 'The Fifth Report'* (Calcutta, 1917), p. clxxvi.

the model of what could be achieved by European involvement with guarantees to those who paid revenue. If the Company's experience at Burdwan could in fact be used to justify such assumptions, it seems that it merely reinforced what nearly all educated Englishmen believed, whatever the practical lessons of Indian administration might be. That Indian officials would prove worthless could be deduced from a huge body of writing about 'oriental despotism'. Those who served cruel and rapacious 'oriental' regimes must be cruel and rapacious themselves. The superior virtues of Englishmen in such situations was also a matter of faith rather than of demonstration, resting on increasing national and racial self-confidence. Verelst referred to those 'national principles of honour, faith, rectitude and humanity', which he believed to 'characterise the name of an Englishman'.[52] Belief in improvement through continuity of tenure reflected the conviction that individual enterprise was the motor of human progress and that enterprise would only be exerted if there was a reasonable expectation that its fruits would be enjoyed in security. Britain itself was thought to be the prime example of the truth of this maxim. It must also apply to India. The Company's revenue records were filled with statements such as 'The security of private property is the greatest encouragement to industry, on which the wealth of every state depends'.[53]

The initial response of the Company servants to the crisis which they diagnosed in the late 1760s was to increase their own involvement in the revenue system. Individual Europeans were appointed to the head of some of the major units of revenue administration, the large zamindars, or to the jurisdictions of faujdars and amils, with the title of Supervisor. Their powers were at first limited, but from 1770 they were given full authority to levy the revenue, and faujdars and amils were dismissed.[54] From 1772 Supervisors were known as Collectors, a title deemed to be more appropriate for the functions they now performed. At the same time tighter British control was being applied to the central administration of the revenue. What were called Controlling Councils of Revenue were set up at Murshidabad and Patna; they were to assume most of the authority previously left to the

---

[52] *View of the Rise and Progress*, Appendix, p. 238.

[53] Governor and Council to Directors, 3 Nov. 1772, *Reports from Committees*, IV, 301.

[54] These changes are examined in detail in A.M. Khan, *The Transition in Bengal 1756–75* (Cambridge, 1969), pp. 137–264.

Nawab's ministers. The ministers survived only until 1772. Then the newly appointed Warren Hastings carried out the instructions which he had received from London to 'stand forth' as *Diwan*. Muhammad Reza Khan, Clive's choice as *Naib Diwan* in 1765, was dismissed and his office was abolished. The Governor and Council would now directly control the management of the *Diwani*. The *Khalsa*, the Nawab's treasury and revenue secretariat, was transferred to Calcutta and put under the supervision of Company servants. There was to be much devising of new schemes and rearranging of offices over the next twenty years, but the principle that there should be European involvement in the revenue administration at local level and European direction at the centre was irrevocably established by 1772.

For some time European authority over the revenue system was more nominal than real. The experienced *mutaseddis* might be demoted but their services in some form or other were indispensable for inexperienced Europeans. The Collectors were assisted by *diwans* and *sheristadars*, who appear often to have managed the districts in practice, while there can be no doubt that during Warren Hastings's period much of the central administration was under the control of an Indian who enjoyed his confidence to an unusual degree. It was said that Ganga Govind Singh, Hastings's personal choice as head *mutaseddi*, was 'looked upon by the natives as the second person in the government if not the first'.[55]

While Europeans were being placed in key offices, the Company was also moving towards the second of its panaceas for successful revenue administration: the creation of long-term interests in the collection of revenue. The system by which the Nawabs made bargains year by year with the leading revenue payers at the *Punyah* ceremony at Murshidabad[56] was considered to be deeply flawed. The sums agreed appeared to have no relation to actual resources and annual renewals provided no incentive for long-term improvement. Detailed surveys of ability to pay were out of the question, but it was assumed that in competition with one another knowledgeable Indians would offer to undertake to pay the government a realistic revenue in return for a long-term contract. They would have an incentive to improve the area for which they had secured the 'farm' because they were entitled to retain anything they could collect beyond their stipulated revenue.

[55] Cited in P.J. Marshall, 'Indian Officials under the East India Company', *Bengal Past and Present*, LXXXIV (1965), 112.   [56] See p. 59.

The first long-term settlement based on these principles was made in 1772 by Warren Hastings. A 'farmer', was given tenure for five years, a period thought to amount to 'a permanent interest in his lands'.[57]

If farming contracts for a period of years seemed to be the best way of ensuring that the Company got its revenue and the lands were improved, with whom should the contracts be negotiated? In particular, should *zamindars* be allowed to farm the areas over which they had established rights or should they be set aside? Early Company revenue administrators were inclined to be sceptical about the *zamindars*. Becher believed that 'many of them have behaved ill and that they are most of them ruined men'.[58] But Hastings felt in 1772 that *zamindars* should in general be given the preference as farmers, provided that they made realistic offers. He had few doubts about what he called the 'inferior zemindars and talookdars',[59] but was more cautious about those who had inherited the great holdings built up in the early eighteenth century. He believed many of them to be both incompetent and untrustworthy. In the 1772 settlement some great *zamindars*, like the Rajas of Nadia and Vishnupur, were for a time deprived of revenue managements. Most retained their control at the price of increased bids to beat off competitors.

Within a very short time it was generally accepted that the 1772 scheme had achieved neither of its purposes. Many of the farmers were unable to pay the Company the revenue for which they had contracted, while their efforts to realise it were said to involve much extortion from cultivators. Recrimination about the 1772 settlement was relayed to London by members of a new Supreme Council who had been sent from Britain to join Warren Hastings in 1774. As Verelst and Becher had done a few years earlier, they depicted Bengal as being in a crisis of accelerating impoverishment. The 1772 scheme had only made this worse, in their view. The revenue farmers had plundered the countryside and it seemed that they had often been able to do this because of corrupt bargains struck between them and the Company's servants, including Hastings himself.

The new round of the debate on how to manage the Bengal revenues generated much acrimony, but it also produced a new slant

---

[57] Committee of Revenue, 14 May 1772, *Reports from Committees*, IV, 306.
[58] Cited in Firminger, *Historical Introduction*, p. clxxix.
[59] Governor and Council to Directors, 3 Nov. 1772, *Reports from Committees*, IV, 302–3.

on one of the perennial problems: security of tenure for those who paid the revenue. One of the new Councillors, Philip Francis, a man deeply versed in contemporary European social theory, produced a highly doctrinaire solution to the problem of security. The core of his argument was that the Bengal *zamindars* were not simply the possessors of certain revenue rights that had become hereditary, but that they were the outright owners of the lands from which they collected revenue. 'The land is the hereditary property of the Zemindar. He holds it by the law of the country, on the tenure of paying a certain contribution to government.'[60] Only the unequivocal recognition of the property rights of *zamindars* would create that long-term security which all Englishmen believed to be essential for recovery and improvement. Farming was an invasion of property rights which had inevitably led to spoliation. But once the *zamindars*' right to the land was secure, men would buy and sell 'estates'. Hence *zamindars* would do all they could to improve the value of their property. In order to give the *zamindars* complete security, the Company must forgo the search for an increased revenue. It must fix its demand at a reasonable level and pledge itself that this would never in future be raised on any pretext whatsoever. Any threat that improvement would bring the retribution of an increased revenue would kill all incentive for improvement. Francis's writings were to have an influence beyond the immediate circles of the Company's service, but he lost his political battles with Hastings, both in Bengal and in Britain; revenue policy was to be shaped by Hastings until he retired in 1785.

The differences between the two men can be exaggerated; they themselves did so on every possible occasion. Hastings was not prepared to concede that *zamindars* had an absolute property right or to limit the Company's revenue demand to a fixed sum never to be raised. But he too sought to establish 'an *equal*, an *easy*, and a perpetual assessment of the public revenue; to collect it through the medium of zemindars, where they are capable of the charge'.[61] When the five-year farming experiment ran out in 1777, settlements were renewed annually, usually with the *zamindars*, but demands on them rose as the Company faced new financial stringencies.

In as far as opinion in Britain could comprehend Bengal revenue

---

[60] Cited in R. Guha, *A Rule of Property for Bengal* (Paris, 1963), p. 123; see pp. 59–161 for a full analysis of Francis's ideas.
[61] Revenue Consultations, 26 March 1777, *Reports from Committees*, V, 985.

controversies, it seems to have been attracted by the stark simplicity of Francis's ideas that *zamindars* were landowners and that they should be required to pay an unalterable revenue demand. Edmund Burke was convinced by Francis and gave his ideas much publicity in reports from a House of Commons Select Committee in 1782 and 1783. The India Act of 1784 instructed the Directors to redress the grievances of the 'native landholders' and to devise 'permanent rules' to regulate their payments 'upon principles of moderation and justice'.[62] In April 1786 the Directors ordered their servants to make a revenue settlement, which should be 'considered as the permanent and unalterable revenue of our territorial possessions in Bengal'. The settlement should be 'in every practicable instance with the Zemindars'.[63] Their orders were carried out by Lord Cornwallis, the first Governor General appointed from outside the Company's service. He was in some ways as doctrinaire as Francis. He too believed that Bengal was in decline and that security of property rights was the key to its revival. With security 'a spirit of improvement' would be 'diffused throughout the country'.[64]

From the arrival of Cornwallis what has invariably been known as the Permanent Settlement of the Bengal revenues took shape. It was formally enacted in 1793 and was to last at least in name until the end of British rule in 1947. It was based on simple principles. The Company's revenue was to be paid by *zamindars* at a level to be fixed in perpetuity. So long as the *zamindars* paid their revenue punctually, they had total security over the land from which the revenue came. It was their property. If they failed to pay the revenue, the land would be sold to somebody else, whose property it would become.

There was no doubt that the settlement would be with the *zamindars*. Farming to contractors was thought to have been discredited. Later British administrations in other parts of India were to try to deal directly with ryots, who actually cultivated the land, but the Bengal servants of the late eighteenth century were wholly lacking in the expertise for such a venture. Political considerations reinforced administrative necessity. The Company needed allies. 'A regular graduation of ranks . . . is no where more necessary than in this country for promoting order in civil society', wrote Cornwallis.[65] By the 1780s

---

[62] 24 Geo. III, c. 25, sec. xxxix.    [63] *PP*, 1810, V, 156–65.
[64] *Correspondence of Charles, First Marquis Cornwallis*, ed. C. Ross (3 vols., 1859), II, 468.    [65] *Cornwallis Correspondence*, I, 554.

enthusiasm for *zamindari* tenure was not generally buttressed either by deep convictions about *zamindars'* historical rights to be treated as landed proprietors or by any respect for the existing generation of *zamindars*. The aim was clearly to define a tenure called *zamindari*, which would involve effective proprietorship of land in return for payment of revenue for it. Capable and efficient men who acquired these tenures would be able to profit thereby. Incapable men would soon be deprived by their failure to pay the revenue. No excuses for failure would be accepted. 'A sale of the whole of the lands of the defaulter, or such as may be sufficient to make good the arrear, will positively and unvariably take place.'[66] The mechanism of sale would ensure the survival of the fittest. If it led to a wholesale transfer of land away from the present unworthy holders to men more fitted to use it, so much the better. If sale led to the break-up of big *zamindaris*, so much the better too. The framers of the settlement shared the mistrust of the very large *zamindaris* which was deeply rooted in the Company's service. Smaller units were likely to be better managed and their holders to have fewer pretensions to seeing themselves as rivals to the authority of the government. The Company was prepared to deal directly with holders of small revenue rights, called *talukdars*,[67] and to encourage many who had paid revenue through the *zamindars* to make their payments straight to the government and thus to acquire separate 'estates'.[68]

The level of the revenue demand for Bengal and Bihar which was to be fixed for ever more was not determined with any exactitude. A survey of the land and its resources was as impractical as it had always been. Eventually it was decided to make the assessment for the year 1789–90 the standard. The sum aimed at was Rs. 26,800,000 (approximately £3,000,000). The Directors had urged a moderate assessment, professing themselves content with an amount that could be paid punctually and in full rather than a high one on which arrears might accumulate. Whether the 1789–90 assessment was objectively a moderate one in terms of Bengal's resources is a very controversial question; it is examined in Chapter 5.[69] But in terms of what had been collected by the Company in the past it was not moderate; it was aim-

---

[66] Bengal Regulations, 1793, I, sec. vii.

[67] N.K. Sinha, *Economic History of Bengal from Plassey to the Permanent Settlement* (2 vols., Calcutta, 1956, 1962) II, 161–2.

[68] S. Islam, *The Permanent Settlement in Bengal: A Study of its Operation 1790–1819* (Dacca, 1979), pp. 33–40.   [69] See pp. 141–4.

ing at bringing in marginally more than had ever been realised before.

The main principles of the Permanent Settlement aroused little dissent: it should be with *zamindar*s at a fixed rate in perpetuity. But two questions did stimulate debate: how permanent was 'permanent' and should the government reserve for itself any power to regulate relations between the *zamindar*s and their 'tenants'? The assessment of 1789–90 was in the first instance to last for ten years. In what was to become a famous debate with Cornwallis, John Shore, the leading revenue expert within the service, argued that the Company should give itself the chance of correcting errors and making revisions at the end of the ten-year span. Cornwallis believed that anything less than unalterable permanence would undermine confidence and thus defeat the scheme's central purpose: improvement based on security. His view prevailed with the Directors and with government ministers. In March 1793 the Settlement was declared permanent. If the principles of the Settlement were strictly interpreted, the Company should have no concern with relations between *zamindar* and ryot. The land belonged to the *zamindar*s and the ryots were their tenants. Conditions of tenancy should be regulated by supply and demand, not by law. The ryot had nothing to fear since it was so obviously in the *zamindar*'s interest that he should prosper. Even Cornwallis, however, recognised that the Company had in the past, if ineffectually, tried to protect ryots and that it could not abandon its efforts now. A regulation was enacted which laid down that 'rents' paid by ryots to *zamindar*s should be fixed and formally recorded in documents called *potta*s. The ryot could then legally contest unauthorised demands.

In trying to regulate relations between landlord and tenant the Company involved itself in what was to prove one of the most intractable problems throughout the whole period of British rule of Bengal. On the one hand, British administrators felt that the evidence that ryots were often subjected to oppression was overwhelming. On the other hand, intervention to limit demands on ryots was invariably regarded by *zamindar*s as a threat to their capacity to pay the revenue due from them, with the inevitable result that they went into arrears in their payments to the government. The confidence that men like Francis and Cornwallis had felt in the notion of security of property as a means of providing a self-regulating mechanism for ensuring justice between landlord and tenant proved to be illusory. For the next hun-

dred years the Bengal government was to lurch backwards and for-
wards between intervention on the side of the ryot and intervention
on the side of the *zamindar*. Although the *potta* regulation proved to be
largely ineffective[70], in the immediate aftermath of the Permanent
Settlement the Company seemed to have stacked too many cards
against the *zamindar*. His powers to coerce his ryots seemed to have
been unduly restricted. The Company moved to remedy this. Under
the famous Regulation VII (the *heptam*) of 1799 the *zamindar* was
entitled to make an immediate seizure of the ryot's effects as soon as
he fell into arrears. Contemporaries generally believed that the
balance of power had swung back in favour of the *zamindar*s in the early
nineteenth century.

In the last resort social justice was of less concern to the Company
than the security of its revenue. In the early years after 1793, the success of the Permanent Settlement in this respect was in some doubt.
Until 1799 an average of nearly 20 per cent of the revenue demand
remained unpaid at the end of each year. These arrears had to be met
by a large volume of sales, and even then considerable deficiencies
remained.[71] Between 1794 and 1807 land on which some 41 per cent
of Bengal's assessed revenue depended was put up for sale and
changed hands, generally at a relatively low price. From the Company's point of view, things began to improve after 1807; the volume
of sales declined and the price of land rose markedly.[72] In 1813 one of
its senior servants commented that the revenue was now paid with
'unexampled skill and punctuality . . . No remissions, or next to none,
are now necessary.'[73]

Within some twenty years the Company could congratulate itself
that the revenue assessment which it had fixed in 1789–90 was secure.
Since the 1789–90 assessment was the highest realised up to that time,
this was a considerable achievement. Yet if permanence was a
necessary part of that achievement, it was one that looked more and
more dubious as years went by. The Company's costs did not remain
constant at the levels of 1789–90; nor did Englishmen believe that the
resources of Bengal remained constant. But if economic growth was

[70] Islam, *The Permanent Settlement*, pp. 44–7.     [71] Ibid., p. 57.
[72] B.B. Chaudhuri, 'The Land Market in Eastern India 1793–1940', *Indian Economic and
Social History Review*, XII (1975), 18–19.
[73] Minute of H.T. Colebrooke, *Selection of Papers from the Records of East India House* (5
vols., 1820–6), I, 201.

taking place, as was widely believed, the Company had precluded itself from taking a larger share of wealth through taxing the land. Such loopholes as remained were inevitably exploited to the full. Grants of rent-free land seemed to be the most promising one. Under the Nawabs considerable areas had been exempted from rent for various religious or charitable uses or for maintaining those who served the state.[74] It was commonly supposed that such exemptions increased very greatly in the early years of Company rule and that most of the grants were fraudulent devices to evade revenue. Various investigations were attempted and in 1793 the Company asserted the right to cancel bogus alienations. Little, however, was done until the pressure to realise more revenue stimulated offensives against rent-free land in 1819 and 1827.[75]

In theory the Permanent Settlement ran along lines immutably fixed by Regulations which had the force of law. There was therefore little room for executive action. Such executive action as was required would be taken by the European Collector, an office which had grown out of the Supervisorships of 1769 and, after some fluctuations, had become established in the 1780s. Both on the staff of the Collector and in the central administration Indians were to be confined to strictly subordinate roles. The reality was somewhat different. The Indians might lack dignity and formal responsibility, but in the view of Raja Rammohun Roy, who knew what he was talking about from personal experience, the work of the Collectorates was 'chiefly performed by the native officers'.[76] He himself provided an example of how such service could be turned to good account financially.

The Permanent Settlement has attracted a great body of writing. In this it is usually portrayed as a bold piece of social engineering, which had profound effects on Bengal society. Both propositions are in fact questionable. The social consequences of the Permanent Settlement are considered in Chapter 5. Whatever its practical effects may have been, the Settlement did, however, reflect the practical limitations as well as the ideological aspirations of the new British regime. The Permanent Settlement certainly embodied doctrinaire assumptions about improvement through the establishment of secure property.

[74] IOR, Home Miscellaneous, vol. 68, p. 737.
[75] A.M. Waheeduzzaman, 'Land Resumption in Bengal 1819–46', Unpublished Ph.D. thesis, London University, 1969.
[76] S.C. Sarkar (ed.), *Rammohun Roy on the Indian Economy* (Calcutta, 1965), p. 26.

On the other hand, it also revealed pessimism about the extent to which wealth could be extracted from Bengal or improvement could be achieved. Intensive management by Europeans was out of the question. Twenty-five years of trial and error had proved that it was better to accept a fixed sum through the agency of the *zamindars*, for all their faults, than to go on experimenting. The regeneration of Bengal was to be left to the *zamindars*: the Company knew that it could not undertake such a task.

A fixed land revenue made the Company increasingly unyielding about other sources of income. The survival of the salt and opium monopolies was assured and revenue from customs became an important consideration. The history of the administration of the Bengal customs starkly illustrates the conflicts between the objectives which the Company endeavoured to pursue. It was conventional wisdom that internal customs were an obstacle to economic growth which should be eliminated, as they had been in Britain. The Nawabs' customs system was thought to have been excessively oppressive and destructive of trade. By 1788 internal customs levied by the government had been abolished throughout Bengal, and with the Permanent Settlement the various dues on trade which the *zamindars* had exacted were also officially abolished. However, whatever the advantages of a free circulation of trade might be, fiscal needs could not be denied. In the early nineteenth century the government duties were restored, reaching levels which provoked a denunciation by Charles Trevelyan: 'If we were to encourage swamps and accumulate mountains between the differing districts of our country, we could not paralyse their industry so effectually as we are doing by this scheme of finance.'[77] Even those deputed to answer Trevelyan's Philippic, admitted that there were 'real and crying evils' in the system, such as entry of British goods into Calcutta at rates lower than the internal duties on some items, but asked of the customs as a whole, 'can the revenue be dispensed with without causing greater mischiefs?'[78]

Control of the revenue was thought to have brought with it responsibility for what the British considered to be civil justice. It was at first

[77] *A Report upon the Inland Customs and Town Duties of the Bengal Presidency*, ed. T. Banerjee (Calcutta, 1976), p. 96.
[78] [C. D'Oyly and H.M. Parker], *Observations upon the Transit and Town Duty System of the Bengal Presidency* (Calcutta, 1835), pp. 5–6.

assumed that this would involve little more than the supervision of existing courts. Within a few years, however, the Company embarked on a prolonged series of experiments with the aim of devising its own courts and even more prolonged attempts to draft laws to be administered by the courts.

The indefatigable Warren Hastings devised the first of the Company's new civil courts, called *Diwani Adalat*s, over which the Collectors of the revenue presided. After many changes, the system was reshaped by Lord Cornwallis on the premise that revenue collection and justice must be kept entirely separate. The executive arm of government must not itself be the source of justice but must be seen to be distinct. This was an essential reinforcement of the principles of the Permanent Settlement.

No power will then exist in the country by which rights vested in the landholder can be infringed, or the value of landed property affected. Land must in consequence become the most desirable of all property, and the industry of the people will be directed to those improvements in agriculture which are as essential to their own welfare as to the prosperity of the state.[79]

A hierarchy of Company civil courts was created, staffed by servants who specialised in judicial work as judges. The Judge and the Collector were to be quite separate from one another in the districts. Below the European Judges were Indian law officers who disposed of a multitude of cases in which small sums were involved.

There is very little evidence about the standard of justice offered or the volume of business transacted in the early Company courts. The new Cornwallis courts, on the other hand, seem to have been popular with litigants and to have attracted an immense amount of work. In 1795 a single district court was said to have had 30,000 cases awaiting a hearing, while the Indian law officers, having disposed of 328,064 cases between 1795 and 1802, were still left with 131,929 awaiting their attention.[80] In the early nineteenth century, although the courts might dispose of some 200,000 cases a year, it still took some two or three years before a suit reached a European Judge.[81] So great a resort to the law was not regarded by most Company servants as a sign of the success of their rule. They did not believe that Cornwallis's ideal of an

---

[79] Bengal Regulations, 1793, II, preamble.
[80] *5th Report, Select Committee*, 1812, ed. W.K. Firminger (2 vols., Calcutta, 1917), I, 114–15.   [81] See statistics in *PP*, 1831–2, XII, 561.

impartial law that would adjust relations within society was being fulfilled. Instead they accused their subjects of being litigious and of adding resort to the law to the arsenal of weapons with which the strong oppressed the weak. In 1814 the Directors commented on the large sections of the population who 'stand in need of judicial protection, but are either unable or deterred from seeking it'.[82]

The Company prided itself that its courts applied the law to which its subjects were immemorially accustomed. What was regarded as Hindu or Islamic law was used in the Company's courts. In 1812 a parliamentary committee noted how few were 'the rules which the British government has yet found it necessary to prescribe, in amendment to the established laws and usages of the country, upon matters of private contract and inheritance'.[83] This now seems an unreal claim. The Company's courts were offering a law that was wholly alien to those to whom it was applied, not because the substance of the law had been consciously changed, but because of what the Company had selected as the 'established laws and usages of the country' and the manner in which they were interpreted. The Company's courts tended to use translations of classical texts and to apply them indiscriminately with preconceptions which were inevitable in European judges, such as a concern for equality before the law. What emerged was essentially a new form of law with roots in both cultures.[84]

The administration of what the British regarded as the criminal law and the control of the police were matters that were in theory left to the Nawab as *Nazim* after 1765. The maintenance of order throughout the provinces was, however, considered to be a matter of far too great an importance for the Company to leave to what it dismissed as an effete and inefficient regime at Murshidabad. It immediately took steps to invigorate the existing police and courts. Seriously concerned about the prevalence of 'dacoity', Hastings tried to reform the police system in 1774. The effectiveness of this or other early measures to create a police acceptable by European standards seems questionable. It is likely that for some years after 1765 order depended more on the power of the *zamindars* than on any exertion by the government.[85]

In the 1780s the Company servants began to take more direct re-

[82] *PP*, 1819, XIII, 511.     [83] *5th Report*, 1812, ed. Firminger, I, 65.

[84] See the essays of J.D.M. Derrett, reprinted in *Religion, Law and the State in India* (1968).

[85] See for instance J. Westland, *An Account of the District of Jessore*, 2nd edn (Calcutta, 1874), pp. 52–4.

sponsibility as magistrates. As with so many other aspects of the regime, the police system took a shape under Cornwallis that was to last far into the nineteenth century. With the lapsing of the *Nizamat*, police became wholly the responsibility of the Company, in name as well as in substance. The new judges were to be magistrates with a police force acting under them. The magistrates' districts were subdivided into areas called *thana*s, each of which was to have an Indian *darogah* and a posse of constables. The Company insisted that from henceforth it alone had responsibility for law and order. *Zamindar*s were required to disband their forces and were absolved from any policing duties. All establishments of village watchmen or local militia that were not abolished were to pass under the control of the Company's police.

So long as the dacoits appeared to be rampant, that is well into the first decade of the nineteenth century,[86] Company policing was judged to have been an almost unqualified failure. Even when dacoity appeared to have been reduced to manageable proportions, assessments of the state of the police were still pessimistic. Policing was much too thinly spread to be anything like fully effective. Crimes of violence and affrays might be diminishing, but officials freely admitted that the *darogah*s and their men could not prevent burglary on a very large scale or protect property.[87] Obviously suspect statistics seemed to reveal an increase in 'crime' in the 1820s, and it was admitted that many offences were never reported.[88] No element of 'the public' appeared willing to cooperate with the police. Indeed, Englishmen frequently reviled Bengalis for their lack of public spirit or concern for others. But it was recognised that in disbanding *zamindari* guards and village watchmen, the Company may have destroyed institutions with some roots in society while failing to provide any acceptable alternative. The new police hardly merited trust. They were reputed to be corrupt and oppressive. John Beames painted a memorable picture of the older generation of *darogah*s, who were still dominating part of Bihar in the 1850s.

They ruled as little kings in their own jurisdiction and reaped a rich harvest of bribes from all classes. The Darogha of the Purnea Thana was a good specimen

[86] *Lord Minto in India*, p. 188.
[87] Report of Superintendent of Police, 15 May 1816, *PP*, 1819, XII, 679.
[88] G.F.T.S. Barlow Speeds, *The Criminal Statistics of Bengal* (Calcutta, 1847), pp. 71–2.

of the class. He was a tall portly Mahommedan, grey-bearded with a smooth sleek look, crafty as a fox, extremely polished in manner, deferential to his superiors, but haughty and tyrannical to his inferiors . . . Everyone trembled before him . . . The Darogha Sahib could command as many witnesses as he wanted, all of whom would swear to anything he chose to tell them.

The *darogah*'s followers were highly disreputable. They took bribes and extorted money 'by practising a little torture on persons they pretended to suspect'.[89]

The criminal law which the British courts administered purported to be the Islamic law that they had inherited from the Nawabs. But as with the law used by the civil courts, it was subject to much imposing of alien interpretations, and liberties were consciously taken with the substance of the law. The most conspicuous of these concerned punishment. British magistrates had reservations about inflicting mutilation, but they regarded Islamic law as deplorably lenient over matters which should be capital offences, especially in dealing with dacoits. Amendment of the Islamic law by official regulations had gone so far by 1817 that it had in fact produced what has been described as a new law, 'mainly of European origin'.[90]

In collecting taxation, administering justice and maintaining a police force, the East India Company was performing, even if in a radically different manner, the functions of its Mughal predecessors. The Nawabs' government had, however, performed other functions which the Company either largely neglected or allowed to lapse. Like Islamic rulers everywhere, the Nawabs were patrons of religion and learning and protectors of the well-born and other deserving persons. Individuals and institutions were endowed with revenue grants. The Company accepted some of these obligations. It supervised the Gaya shrines and, after the conquest of Orissa, it accepted responsibility for supervising the Jagannath temples too. Otherwise, British inclinations were always to retrench what were regarded as dubious claims on their resources and to confine the Nawabs' generosity by strictly limiting their allowances. All allocations of revenue for charitable purposes were viewed with suspicion.

In time, however, the Company began on a very small scale to sup-

<hr />

[89] *Memoirs of a Bengal Civilian*, new edn (1984), pp. 140–1.
[90] J. Fisch, *Cheap Lives and Dear Limbs: The British Transformation of the Bengal Criminal Law 1769–1817* (Wiesbaden, 1983), p. 85.

port education. In 1781 Warren Hastings endowed a Muslim college, or *madrassa*, in Calcutta. Thirty years later Lord Minto made a plea for the Company to support Sanskrit learning. The Company's duty to promote learning and 'a knowledge of the sciences' in its provinces was given statutory recognition in its new charter of 1813. By then both the Directors in London and the new Governor General, the Marquess of Hastings, were laying stress on the need to try to improve elementary education. In the first distribution of funds under the new charter, the East India Company and private British enterprises again became allies.

Private English schools had been growing up in Calcutta since the 1770s, but by 1813 the main promoters of the schools had become the missionary societies. The Company made its first grants for elementary education to schools founded north of Calcutta by the London Missionary Society. With the easing of access to India for missionaries after 1813, the Baptist Missionary Society and the Church Missionary Society also opened schools to teach elementary subjects in Bengali, while the Baptists founded a College outside Calcutta at Serampore.[91] The Company also in time supported the efforts of philanthropically minded Englishmen and of Indians living in and around Calcutta who were beginning to act as patrons for new schools. To promote elementary schooling, a Calcutta School Book Society and a Calcutta School Society were founded in 1817 and 1818 respectively, with British and Indian membership. Both societies received grants from the government in 1823, the year that the Company set up a Committee of Public Instruction 'for the purpose of ascertaining the state of public education' and suggesting improvements. Some money also went to support colleges, including the new Sanskrit College sponsored by the Company in 1824.

In terms of numbers alone, the efforts of the Company, of the missionaries and of the new patrons of learning cannot as yet have made a significant difference to the overall provision of education in Bengal. Their efforts hardly reached beyond Calcutta and a few areas in western Bengal. Even there, the numbers affected were not very great. The Baptists claimed 10,000 pupils in their schools in 1818.[92] When the Calcutta School Society was founded in 1818, it calculated

[91] For these developments, see M.A. Laird, *Missionaries and Education in Bengal 1793–1837* (Oxford, 1972), pp. 63–176.
[92] E.D. Potts, *British Baptist Missionaries in India* (Cambridge, 1967), p. 119.

that only 4,200 children were receiving education in the city's inner area. It was no doubt justly proud at having doubled that number in fifteen years, but most children in the city must have remained unschooled.[93] Outside Calcutta and areas adjacent to it, where education was being provided, as Adam's inquiries of the 1830s revealed, it depended on the efforts of schools as yet hardly touched by the presence of the British in Bengal.[94]

The Nawabs of Bengal had been patrons of building, poetry and painting. Although Calcutta was in many respects a squalid and philistine city, its European inhabitants supported theatrical and musical performances, commercial printing, a newspaper press, libraries and learned societies, such as the famous Asiatic Society. The East India Company with its press, its observatory and its botanical gardens was not an ungenerous patron. This transplanting of some of the amenities of European urban civilisation to Bengal was to attract the interest of a small but highly articulate section of the Indian community who had settled in Calcutta. They are discussed further in Chapter 5.

This chapter has discussed many different aspects of the British presence in Bengal during the first sixty years of colonial rule. The Company maintained a great army, administered the revenue system, dispensed justice and continued to be a trader. Private British citizens were involved in many different commercial enterprises and pursued vocations as varied as the law and the conversion of the heathen. Yet underlying this apparent diversity were two preoccupations which dominated all the rest: the British were in Bengal as traders and all the functions which they had acquired as rulers of Bengal since 1765 were built around the absolute priority given to the collection of revenue. Experiments in new legal systems or new property relations were all ultimately intended to facilitate the realisation of the revenue. The beginnings of a concern for education might be the first sign of more ambitiously conceived programmes, but in the 1820s the flow of revenue was still the standard by which all else was judged.

If the collection of revenue was the essential task of the Company's Bengal government, the way in which the revenue was allocated /

[93] R. Mitra, 'Unpublished Reports of the Calcutta School Society', *Bengal Past and Present*, XCVI (1977), 151.
[94] W. Adam, *Reports on the State of Education in Bengal*, ed. A. Basu (Calcutta, 1941).

indicated how contemporaries saw the purposes of British rule. In a minute of 1793 Lord Cornwallis defined two 'primary objects' for the Bengal government. It must 'ensure its political safety' and it must 'render the possession of the country as advantageous as possible to the East India Company and the British nation'.[95] He and his contemporaries, like their successors down to 1947, recognised that British India could be 'advantageous' to Britain through its contribution to the power of Britain throughout the world and through its contribution to the British economy. The early phases of British rule in Bengal were to some degree influenced both by Britain's strategic needs and by her economic needs; but in the 1820s British India with its own civil service, its own army and its own commercial 'establishment', the great Agency Houses, was still to a very large extent a world on its own. It was not as yet fully integrated either into Britain's military system or into the working of the British metropolitan economy.

British military resources were dispatched to India, but as yet Indian forces were used on only a small scale for wider imperial purposes, although they had been sent to Manila, to Java and to Egypt. Through the Company's investment and the trade of private merchants Bengal certainly made a contribution to the British economy after 1765, but, as this chapter has tried to indicate, it was as yet a limited one. Although Bengal raw silk and indigo supplied the British textile industry, the volume of exports was to a large extent determined not by what British industry required but by what was needed to enable funds to be transferred to meet the Company's British obligations or to enable individuals to carry their savings home. Until 1813 the flow of British exports to Bengal did not reach significant levels. Even after the spurt that followed the ending of the monopoly, British exports to the whole of Asia still constituted less than 10 per cent of her total.[96] India's role in Britain's overall balance of trade throughout the world, which was to be of considerable importance in the later nineteenth century, was at this time largely confined to her contribution through her favourable balance with China, in which Bengal's opium played a very large part.[97] Studies of 'underdevelopment' lay much stress on the transfer of 'surpluses' from 'periphery' to 'metropole'. Bengal's trade

[95] *PP*, 1810, V, 107.
[96] R. Davis, *The Industrial Revolution and Overseas Trade* (Leicester, 1979), p. 98.
[97] Chaudhuri, 'Foreign Trade', pp. 860–3.

with Britain certainly involved such transfers, to the advantage of many British individuals. Work on capital accumulation in the age of the industrial revolution does not, however, suggest that transfers on this scale were crucial to the British economy as a whole.

While accepting that they had a duty to make Bengal 'advantageous' to Britain, those who managed the Company's affairs in Calcutta concentrated most of their energy on ensuring the 'political safety' of their provinces. They interpreted this to mean that they must maintain a very large army and that they should be prepared to use it against their neighbours. The army had first call on their resources. When the British were establishing their rule in Bengal in the period 1761–2 to 1770–1, figures produced for a parliamentary committee showed that out of a total spending of some £22,000,000, £9,700,000, or 44 per cent, had been spent on the army and fortifications in the provinces, while large sums had also been sent to Madras to sustain wars there.[98] In the six years of Wellesley's administration, 1798–9 to 1803–4, out of a total expenditure of nearly £33,000,000, over £14,000,000, that is 42.5 per cent, was spent on the army.[99] Only at the end of the period, at a time of peace and stringently enforced economy, were military charges reduced to approximately one-third of the total expenditure, the level at which they were generally kept in the later nineteenth and early twentieth centuries.[100]

War and diplomacy, rather than trade and 'improvement' were likely to be what most of the soldiers and would-be politicians sent out to be Governors General in the early nineteenth century felt that they really understood. The 'political safety' of Bengal was their first priority and they interpreted 'safety' as requiring the subjugation of Mysore, the Marathas, the Pindaris, Nepal and the Burmese. Thus there was an apparent continuity between the old Mughal regime and the new British one. The central function of both was to extract revenue from the peasants of eastern India and apply it to military purposes. In theory both the Nawabs and the Governors General were required to apply their resources to serve the needs of great empires; in practice they applied them to purposes largely defined by themselves. In time the Governors General were to lose much of their

---

[98] *Reports from Committees*, IV, 61.

[99] *PP*, 1810, V, 81, supplemented by *PP*, 1812, VI, 431 for commercial expenditure.

[100] Figures for 1827–8 to 1829–30 in *PP*, 1831–2, X, part i, Appendix, p. 346. Estimates for later periods are provided by K.N. Reddy, 'Indian Defence Expenditure 1872–1967', *Indian Economic and Social History Review*, VII (1970), 471.

autonomy and Bengal was to be more fully integrated into Britain's world wide military and economic systems. But that time lies outside the period covered by this volume. The period down to 1828 had seen the creation of a largely autonomous British-Indian state that was rather loosely connected with imperial Britain and pursued its own purposes of 'safety' and consolidation.

# CHAPTER 5

# A NEW SOCIETY?

The regime described in Chapter 4 may not have been a fully effective instrument for transmitting to eastern India the dynamism of late eighteenth- and early nineteenth-century Britain, whether that dynamism be regarded as predatory and destructive or as potentially regenerative. But through their military power, their commercial activities, their tax collecting, their choice of allies and subordinates, their interpretation of justice and even their experiments with education and Christian indoctrination, the British had a considerable capacity to change the societies with which they came into contact. Changes between 1765 and 1828 were manifold. Yet, as Chapter 1 tries to indicate, colonial rule is not in itself a sufficient explanation for change. The new regime was established in societies that were undergoing ecological, cultural, social and economic changes, which had begun long before 1765. Phenomena such as the commercialisation of some parts of agriculture, a brisk circulation of rights to collect revenue, and the stratification of cultivators into rich and poor, which are sometimes attributed to the British, were clearly present in the Bengal of the Nawabs. Realistic assessment of the impact of the new order requires recognition of the limitations on the capacity of the British, as well as awareness of their potential to change society. It seems much more likely that early British rule stimulated, modified or aborted existing patterns of change than that it was able to break long continuities and force eastern India into wholly new directions.

Contemporary British opinion believed that the establishment of a powerful and enduring regime that was capable of imposing order on its subjects was in itself an important agent of change, even if it attempted nothing more positive. The Company was thought to have created an environment of peace and stability, previously unknown in eastern India. The peasant could now till his land and the artisan pursue his craft with a security that was entirely new. With the blessing of security, they could prosper as never before.

Simple comparisons between Indian 'anarchy' and British 'law and order', and the assumption that the one must produce poverty and the other improvement, have very little substance. It is not necessarily the case that a *pax Britannica* had been established by the 1820s that was qualitatively superior to the *pax* of the Nawabs. The three provinces had known much disorder in the 1740s and 1750s, when the Marathas and others had invaded and when the Nawab had virtually looted his richer subjects to raise funds with which to repel invasion. But the contrast between other periods of the Nawabs' rule and the first decade of the nineteenth century, when 'dacoity' was at its height, might not be so flattering to the Company. It hardly needs saying that, even if it can be proved that conditions of greater security existed under the British, a stable but rapacious regime may inflict more damage on its subjects than a weak one. What can, however, be attributed to the new British order without much doubt is that it did in time reduce the use of overt violence within its provinces, and that it did this by establishing a near monopoly of the means of force under its own control. These achievements certainly had important social consequences.

Under the Nawabs military resources had been spread among many hands. The loyalty of the Nawabs' army was often as much to individual commanders as to the ruler himself, while powerful *zamindar*s and even the foreign trading companies had their own troops, and there were military tenures on the frontiers. Under the British nearly all the armed men were in the direct service of the Company. One obvious consequence of this was that existing forces were disbanded and opportunities for further employment were much reduced.

The Company required large numbers of foot soldiers for its new army, which it recruited in Bihar and further west, but it had little use for the mounted troopers, who had been the flower of the old army, and none at all for the Mughal officers. The highest ranks in the Company's army were of course filled by Europeans, while the role of 'native officer' under the Company was not likely to be one that a self-respecting Muslim gentleman would accept. Such people had little alternative to leaving Bengal. Most of those who had received pensions lost them with the cuts in the Nawabs' allowances. In 1773 Warren Hastings reduced the Nawab's military pensions to less than one-fifth of their previous level.[1] The plight of the Muslim military

---

[1] K.M. Mohsin, *A Bengal District in Transition: Murshidabad 1765–93* (Dacca, 1973), p. 180.

gentry was characteristic of the plight of aspiring Muslims in general. There was a sharp decline in civilian employment of any distinction. European Collectors or Magistrates replaced the *faujdars*, while the law officers of the *Nizamat* were demoted to positions below the Company's judges. The soldiers, guards and police of the *zamindars*, who were most commonly known as *paiks*, were also disbanded in large numbers. Land grants made for their maintenance and those of the village watchmen and the *ghatwal* frontier guards were scrutinised and in many cases abolished. From *faujdars* in charge of districts to *chaukidars* or watchmen in the villages, the Company was trying to recover revenue and to eliminate any potential rival to the authority of the new ruler.

Although the Company offered much alternative employment in its new sepoy regiments, its police force and its courts and revenue 'cutcherries', its concentration of the instruments of force in its own hands caused social dislocation. This erupted in revolt by the dispossessed in Orissa in 1817[2] and in prolonged resistance along the western frontier, while many displaced *paiks* and *chaukidars* were thought to have taken to crime.[3]

What historians have called the 'demilitarisation' of Bengal had probably been achieved on the plains by the 1790s, although it took very much longer and was much less complete on the frontier. Unemployment was an obvious consequence of demilitarisation, but it had other less overt but ultimately more important consequences. The position in society of those who had once had the means of coercion was likely to be weakened when it was taken away. The most obvious case was that of the major *zamindars*. Under the Company the *zamindars* passed from being great territorial magnates who effectively enforced their own law to being men who exercised certain rights defined by a law that was both laid down and enforced from above. 'From a public organisation administering the country by customary right, *zamindari* became a private establishment collecting revenue on a permanent contract.'[4] *Zamindars* of small areas could usually make the transition successfully, learning how to manipulate the Company's legal processes to their own advantage or to enlist the service of the Company's police *darogah*, and how to intimidate their tenants. The holders

[2] P.K. Pattanaik, *A Forgotten Chapter in Orissan History* (Calcutta, 1979).
[3] Judicial Letter, 9 Nov. 1814, *PP*, 1819, XIII, 527–8.
[4] R. Ray, *Change in Bengal Agrarian Society c. 1760–1850* (Delhi, 1979), p. 80.

of the largest *zamindari*s, however, seem to have been very seriously weakened by the loss of their coercive powers, which were essential if revenue was to be extracted from a huge and complex system involving many intermediaries.[5] The major *zamindar*s in Bihar, who had only recently carved out their claims by force and relied on force to hold them, proved especially vulnerable when the Company deprived them of the means of force.

By the 1820s many British observers were inclined to be sceptical of the effects of the peace which they had been able to create and to be especially conscious of the defects of their police. The Marquess of Hastings reflected that 'chicanery and litigiousness appear almost universally to have taken the place of violence'.[6] Something had, however, been achieved. Even if late Mughal Bengal was not a conspicuously lawless society, goods and people could probably now circulate with rather more confidence and cultivation may have been extended in some previously disturbed areas. Forces that might rival those of the government had certainly been eliminated. But peace had a price that may not have been anticipated. Gains had been balanced by losses; some of those who had dominated the provinces in the past were now at risk.

Taxation was the central preoccupation of early British rule and the manner in which the Company exercised its powers of taxation had very obvious potential for producing change. The level of revenue which the Company succeeded in extracting was a matter of crucial importance. It seems to be the case that early British tax demands in newly conquered parts of India were generally high ones, inflicting hardship on the societies that were subject to them. For Bengal, Bihar and Orissa, however, comparisons between what the Company collected and the taxes raised by their predecessors are hard to make. British investigations suggested that in 1722 Murshid Kuli Khan had assessed Bengal at Rs. 14,288,186 and that at the time of Alivardi Khan's death in 1756, additional cesses had brought the assessment up to Rs. 18,684,067.[7] In 1760 Mir Kasim had alienated three major districts to the Company, but had made enormous additions to what he

---

[5] J.R. McLane, 'Revenue Farming and the Zamindari System in Eighteenth-century Bengal', *Land Tenure and Peasant in South Asia*, ed. R.E. Frykenberg (New Delhi, 1977), pp. 20–3.    [6] Minute of 2 Oct. 1815, *PP*, 1819, XIII, 620.
[7] *PP*, 1812, VII, 262–4, 282–6.

demanded from the rest of Bengal, estimates of his assessments varying between Rs. 21,500,000 and more than Rs. 24,000,000.[8] The
ministers who operated the *Diwani* for the Company lowered their
sights somewhat after 1765, but still assessed the '*Diwani* lands', that is
Bengal without Bihar and the districts already ceded, at about
Rs. 16,000,000.[9]

After the Company had taken over direct responsibility for the
revenue of its provinces in 1772, it made consolidated assessments for
all the areas under its control. Over the next few years these assessments varied between Rs. 25,000,000 and Rs. 28,000,000.[10] The
assessment which the Company finally declared to be permanent after
1793 was Rs. 26,800,989. Bengal was assessed at nearly Rs. 22,000,000
and Bihar at nearly Rs. 4,000,000.[11] Orissa was not conquered until
1803. During the last twelve years of their rule the Marathas were
thought to have tried to collect an annual average of Rs. 1,350,000. A
Permanent Settlement was not completed in Orissa until 1847, but
the Company was operating an assessment of Rs. 1,600,000 there
by 1822.[12]

Comparisons of paper assessments over long periods of time are
exercises of limited value. Such comparisons do, however, reveal that
the Permanent Settlement assessment was some Rs. 3,300,000, or
about 18.5 per cent, higher than the last assessment of Bengal alone
before 1757. The increase on Orissa was in the region of 20 per cent.
Comparisons for Bihar are impossible to make because the Nawabs
seem to have realised so little from it and they are also complicated by
whether the highly assessed district of Purnea was or was not included
in Bihar. The Rs. 4,000,000 assessment of the Permanent Settlement
was much lower than the Rs. 6,000,000 which Mir Kasim and the first
Company servants posted at Patna had tried to realise. Any judgement
on how severe a burden increases on paper of 20 per cent or 18.5 per
cent might represent in practice depends on knowing something of
changes for the better or for the worse in the provinces' capacity to
pay over several decades. Easy answers to such contentious questions
as whether population and output grew or contracted are hardly possible. But answers can be attempted for some other important ques-

[8] Figures produced by J. Grant and J. Shore, *PP*, 1812, VII, 224–5, 304–7.
[9] A.M. Khan, *The Transition in Bengal 1756–75* (Cambridge, 1969), p. 113.
[10] See table in N.K. Sinha, *Economic History of Bengal from Plassey to the Permanent Settlement* (2 vols., Calcutta, 1956, 1962), II, 105.    [11] Ibid., II, 157, 181.
[12] K.M. Patra, *Orissa Under the East India Company* (Delhi, 1971), pp. 2–3, 41.

tions which have to be considered before comparisons can reasonably be made.

Here →✳ Paper assessments (called the gross *jama*) are likely to have been very different from what was actually collected. Did the Company or did the Nawabs consistently collect a higher proportion of the assessment? Evidence for the Company is clear. Much of the assessment for Bihar remained uncollected for many years. Bengal assessments proved rather easier to realise. Figures for the two provinces between 1772 and 1784 show that considerable 'balances' were often still due at the end of the year, but that the amount not recovered later was usually not much more than 5 per cent.[13] For the first five years of the Permanent Settlement, in spite of the provisions for selling the land of defaulters, about 10 per cent of the revenue had to be 'partly written off as irrecoverable'.[14] In the first decades of the nineteenth century, the Company seems to have collected its revenue practically in full. The situation under the Nawabs is harder to determine. Much of the very high assessments demanded by Mir Kasim seem to have gone uncollected. On the other hand, Alivardi Khan had a reputation for collecting his assessments in full, indeed in times of crisis for collecting very much more than was assessed. One estimate of the outstanding balances at the end of revenue years put them at Rs. 600,000 or Rs. 700,000.[15] Sums of this order would be less than 5 per cent of the total. It therefore seems reasonable to suppose that in normal circumstances the Nawabs and the early Company administrators realised their assessments with something like the same degree of success.

Did the unit of account in which the assessments were made, the Sicca Rupee, vary significantly in its purchasing power over the period? That question should strictly be answered in many different ways for the many different parts of the provinces in which different price levels operated. Bengal did, however, have at least a partially integrated market and some general trends in prices have been detected. From the 1740s prices began to move upwards. In the third quarter of the eighteenth century rises were 'dramatic and wide-ranging'. From the late 1770s prices stabilised and the tendency was for them to drift lower into the early nineteenth century, although

[13] Sinha, *Economic History*, II, 105.
[14] M.S. Islam, *The Permanent Settlement in Bengal: A Study of its Operation 1790–1819* (Dacca, 1979), p. 57.
[15] *The Bengal Nawabs*, ed. J.N. Sarkar (Calcutta, 1952), pp. 154–5.

they never returned to the levels of the 1740s.[16] It may therefore be the case that increased revenue assessments being exacted by the late Nawabs and by the Company in the early years after 1765 were doing little more than keeping up with rising prices. On the other hand, the increases associated with the Permanent Settlement gained added severity from being imposed at a time of stable or falling prices. In Orissa the Company's revenue assessment was made more burdensome by a deteriorating exchange rate for the cowries in which many ryots paid their revenue.

If it can be accepted that the Company did not in general enforce assessments with more rigour than its predecessors had done and that increases in what it demanded were in part at least offset by inflation of prices, generalisations about the crippling new tax burdens imposed by the Company may need modification.[17] It had no real alternative to trying to enforce settlements that were roughly similar to those of the Nawabs. Unlike British administrations in other parts of India at later periods, it felt itself unable to conduct detailed 'scientific' surveys and to make minute inquiries into the capacity of cultivators to pay. Only a few districts, for example Sylhet and Chittagong, were surveyed in this period. The findings of the one major inquiry, the Amini Commission of 1777, were never put to use. Elsewhere, the Company inherited bargains struck by the Nawabs with *zamindars* for the most part. It tried in the early farming experiments to drive the bargains higher, but retreated from the failure of the 1772 scheme.[18] The Company's revenue collections seemed to have reached a level beyond which they could not be pushed, unless the British were prepared to try to break through the crust of *zamindars* and deal directly with the cultivators. Since they were not prepared to attempt this, it seemed better to stop and make a settlement that would be secure and permanent. In the great debate before the enacting of the Permanent Settlement between John Shore and James Grant, it occurred to neither to suggest that the Company might be taking a great deal more than the Nawabs

[16] A.S.M. Akhtar Hussain, 'A Quantitative Study of Price Movements in Bengal during the Eighteenth and Nineteenth Centuries', Unpublished Ph.D. thesis, London University, 1976.

[17] R.C. Dutt's much repeated statement that the Permanent Settlement *jama* was double the *jama* at the time of the acquisition of the *Diwani*, and therefore 'as severe as it could possibly be made' seems to rest on a comparison between the 1765 *jama* for Bengal without Bihar or the districts ceded in 1760 and the 1789–90 *jama* for the full extent of the provinces (*Economic History of India* (2 vols., Delhi, 1960 edn), I, 63).

[18] See p. 120.

had done. Grant insisted that they were taking very much less; Shore replied that they were probably taking somewhat more. The Company's assessment, he wrote, 'will, upon the whole, be found to exceed the receipts of any year' before Mir Kasim and to be 'nearly equal to what it ought to be'.[19]

The increase of approximately 20 per cent in the Company's collections over those before 1757 in Bengal and Orissa, which emerges from a comparison of revenue accounts, may be a rough indicator of what the difference meant in real terms. If that is so, the total increase imposed by the Company may have been less crippling than is sometimes supposed. This is not, however, to deny that serious hardship was caused in particular instances. Orissa seems to have been an obvious case. British officials came to believe that the weight of the increased assessment was much heavier than it might seem, because of the depreciation of cowries and because the Marathas had fallen short of realising their assessments by a wide margin.[20] Whether they greatly exceeded the level of earlier assessments or not, British revenue demands must have been very burdensome indeed in western Bengal after the famine, for which very little allowance was made in enforcing collections. They are likely to have caused hardship also in periods of low agricultural prices, as in the 1790s. Finally, the Company's salt monopoly imposed higher prices on a basic item of consumption for all its subjects.

Nevertheless, on balance it may be that the most important social consequences of the Company's role as tax collector lay less in a general forcing down of living standards through a greatly increased aggregate demand than in the way in which the burden was redistributed. Some gained from the new system; others lost.

In the early years of British rule the most striking shifts in the social contours of Bengal took place in the high hills. Not only did the Muslim notables lose their livelihood, in the ways that have been described, but the great zamindars lost both power and influence and much of the land over which they had exercised control. As late as 1790 twelve families were responsible for over half of the Bengal revenue assessment.[21] Within a few years the Burdwan Raj was the only one of the great holdings that had not disintegrated. The rock on which these great ships broke up was the level of the revenue demand

---

[19] Minute of June 1789, *PP*, 1812, VII, 184.
[20] Patra, *Orissa Under the Company*, p. 2.     [21] Islam, *The Permanent Settlement*, p. 3.

fixed by the Permanent Settlement and backed by the rigid application of the law of sale for defaulters. Some, like the huge Rajshahi zamindari,[22] seem to have been faced with an assessment that was at a penal level. But it seems that others were already drifting in an unseaworthy state before they foundered at the enforcing of the Permanent Settlement. Their problem was not so much that they lacked the resources to meet the Company's demands as that they could not mobilise these resources. Farmers and under-farmers could not be made to fulfil their contracts and pay what they owed to the zamindar, nor could zamindari officials be compelled to account for what they collected. The zamindars' failure was a failure primarily of authority. This had roots that went back long before the Permanent Settlement. Under the late Nawabs zamindars had been forced to accept the intervention of the government's amils in the way they ran their affairs. Under the British they had been compelled to submit to Collectors and Magistrates and many of their retainers had been disbanded. It was the Company's refusal to share its authority with them as much as its insistence on a high revenue which destroyed the great zamindars.[23]

In Bihar the formation of large zamindaris was less advanced than it was in Bengal when the Company established its rule. Ambitious men were still engaged in bringing maliks and other holders of revenue rights under their control and in winning recognition from the Nawabs, by force if need be.[24] Early British rule seems to have pressed hard on such people. They were forced to submit to the Company's troops in the 1760s and those who took up arms again in 1781 were severely chastised. When the settlement of 1789–90 was being made, some British Collectors deliberately set aside the claims of zamindars in order to deal directly with maliks. Nevertheless, large holdings did survive the Permanent Settlement to be consolidated into the famous 'estates' of the nineteenth century.[25] Apart from the hill chieftains, zamindars as the British understood them had not generally developed in Orissa. In the early years of their administration, however, the British treated a number of office and tenure holders as zamindars in

---

[22] Ibid., pp. 81–93.
[23] The failure of the large zamindaris is studied in Ray, *Bengal Agrarian Society* and in S. Taniguchi, 'Structure of Agrarian Society in Northern Bengal', Unpublished Ph.D. thesis, Calcutta University, 1977.  [24] See pp. 57–8.
[25] For an account of one such survival, see J.S. Jha, 'Land Revenue Administration under the Khandvala Rulers of Darbhanga', *Journal of the Bihar Research Society*, LIII (1967), 237–57.

the Bengal sense. Some of those so designated were able to establish themselves as powerful landed magnates, but among the rest there was a very high turnover as they failed to meet the Company's revenue demand and were sold up.

Largely because of the failure of many of the great *zamindars*, a major redistribution of the control of land took place in the early years of British rule. In Bengal between 1794 and 1807 lands on which 41 per cent of the government's revenue depended were put up for sale.[26] Of the 'estates' in Orissa with which the British had concluded revenue settlements 51.6 per cent were sold within fifteen years.[27] Statistical studies concerning Bihar have yet to be made, but it was widely believed that 'many of the old families' had lost their property by sale.[28]

So great a redistribution of control over the land created opportunities in which a new rural elite might have emerged. It would seem that dominant positions throughout the provinces had been forfeited by old established families and were up for sale to anyone who had the money to aspire to them. Traditionally, British rule has been seen as the means by which moneyed men from Calcutta became great landlords. Current interpretations are, however, cautious about the extent to which a new kind of rural leadership did in fact emerge, especially in Bengal itself.[29] Some great new estates were indeed founded in the early years of British rule by families with no previous connections with the land. The most conspicuous examples were estates founded by men who had formed close personal ties with individual Englishmen as their banians, agents or stewards. Krishna Kanta Nandy, for instance, the banian of Warren Hastings, was able to build up a very large and very lucrative holding scattered throughout western and northern Bengal.[30] Such men had tended to begin their operations long before the Permanent Settlement, seizing opportunities to make valuable acquisitions in the early phases of the Company's administration. Among new families who profited from the avalanche of sales

[26] B.B. Chaudhuri, 'The Land Market in Eastern India 1793–1840', *Indian Economic and Social History Review*, XII (1975), 18–19.

[27] B.S. Das, *Studies in the Economic History of Orissa* (Calcutta, 1979), p. 166.

[28] This was the opinion of W.M. Fleming, *PP*, 1831–2, XI, part i, 283.

[29] See the work of Islam, *The Permanent Settlement*; Ray, *Bengal Agrarian Society*; and B.B. Chaudhuri, summarised in 'Agrarian Relations: Eastern India', *Cambridge Economic History of India*, II, c. 1757–c. 1970, ed. D. Kumar (2 vols., Cambridge, 1983), 110–19.

[30] S.C. Nandy, *The Life and Times of Cantoo Baboo* (2 vols., Calcutta, 1978, 1981).

after the Permanent Settlement, the Tagores, whose members were to fill roles of high distinction in the later history of Bengal, were especially prominent. They were one of some thirty 'new' families who rose to prominence through purchases after 1793.[31]

The predominant trend in the disposal of land seems, however, to have been a redistribution among existing landed families rather than the formation of new estates by outsiders. Where major *zamindars* were able to survive, they often became predators on their stricken neighbours. For instance the Rajas of Burdwan incorporated Vishnupur, one of the genuinely ancient territorial powers of Bengal. Many *zamindars* of medium-sized or smaller areas, who could generally manage their affairs more efficiently than could the *zamindars* of large, sprawling estates, amputated pieces from the great estates. Very prominent among the post-1793 purchasers were those who had served in *zamindari* administration. Misappropriation by such men had often been one of the reasons why their employers had failed to meet the Company's assessments. At sales they were able to acquire formal title to land which they had probably been managing for some time for their own benefit.

Although some large new estates were being created, subdivision seems to have been the outcome of most land sales. An ever larger number of people were acquiring rights to collect the revenue. Several tendencies seem to have been at work. *Zamindaris* were being purchased in small parcels. The Company was encouraging previously dependent *talukdars*, that is holders of revenue rights under the overall authority of a *zamindar*, to pay their revenue directly to the government. Finally, *zamindars* were themselves subdividing their holdings. The best known of such devices was for *zamindars* to raise money by selling what were called *patnis*, that is rights to collect revenue independently from a stipulated area. By 1819 the Rajas of Burdwan had created 1,495 *patnis*, and these were in turn beginning to be subdivided.[32] The district of Jessore is an example of the general process of subdivision. In 1793 the Company received revenue from 100 units; payments were being made by 3,444 units in 1809.[33] To amass details of the thousands of small-scale *zamindars*, *talukdars* and *patnidars* who were emerging at the end of the eighteenth century would be a

[31] Islam, *The Permanent Settlement*, p. 189.
[32] Ray, *Bengal Agrarian Society*, p. 103.
[33] J. Westland, *A Report on the District of Jessore* (Calcutta, 1874), p. 105.

formidable task. But indications seem to be that subdivision was not producing very marked changes in the leadership of rural society at the lower levels. It is said to have 'consolidated the position of the high caste local gentry who had filled the middle ranks of the local tribute-collecting hierarchies headed by Rajas and zamindars'.[34] In Dhaka, where the process of subdivision had made especially rapid progress, 'by far the greatest number of auction purchasers came from rural centres of gentry habitation . . . These gentry were mostly Brahmans, Kayasthas, Vaidyas and a sprinkling of respectable Muslims who were small taluqdars in their own right or were employed in the service of the zamindars and the bigger taluqdars.'[35]

The effects of British rule on control of the land in Bihar seem to have been not unlike those in Bengal. Land generally circulated within the existing landed society, with a tendency to subdivision. Well before the Permanent Settlement the British were dealing with many miniscule claimants to revenue rights. Even so, Buchanan, touring the districts around Patna in the early nineteenth century, found 'estates fast frittering into petty portions, so that very few of the proprietors live in the splendour of gentlemen . . . The subdivision of the land has reduced many of the zamindars to the condition of mere peasants'.[36]

In Orissa traditional assumptions about outsiders being able to take advantage of a newly created land market to win control have some substance. Half of those with whom the original British revenue settlements had been made had failed to meet their obligations and had been dispossessed by sale by 1818. Those who took their places included a high proportion of purchasers from outside Orissa, prominent among whom were Bengali underlings of the first British officials. The most conspicuous case was the acquisition by the Bengali *Diwan* of the Collector of Puri of the lands of the leader of the 1817 revolt, the steward of the Raja of Khurda.[37]

At its higher levels agrarian society in eastern India changed significantly in the early years of British rule. Outside Orissa there may not have been major alterations in the social composition of those who controlled land, but property circulated rapidly through sales and there was a strong trend for subdivision. These changes cannot be

[34] Ray, *Bengal Agrarian Society*, p. 253.   [35] Ibid., p. 223.
[36] M. Martin, *History, Antiquities, Topography and Statistics of Eastern India* (3 vols., 1838), I, 309, 312.
[37] P.K. Pattanaik, *A Forgotten Chapter of Orissan History* (Calcutta, 1979), pp. 171–8.

solely attributed to British policies, but there can be no doubt that the Company's rule greatly accelerated them. They were changes which British officials generally welcomed. They hoped that the circulation of property through sales would give efficient new men the chance to remedy the deficiencies of those whose failure to pay the revenue proved them to be incapable, while subdivision seemed to be desirable both on political and on economic grounds. The British were, however, much less complacent about changes in the rest of rural society. To many there was evidence that the status of ryots was deteriorating and that their poverty, so often depicted since 1765, remained as dire as ever. Company policy appeared to have done little for those below the level of revenue payers. Indeed, by strengthening the property rights of *zamindars* and others and by the pressure of its revenue demands it may have added to the hardships of ryots.

In theory British revenue administration was designed to favour the poor against the rich. Any increase in revenue was intended to come from those who could afford it. Superfluous offices were to be abolished, service tenures would be resumed and, above all, land which had been under-assessed or not assessed at all would be taxed effectively. On the other hand, the rates at which ryots paid would not be increased. Since 1772 the Company had been trying to prevent the levying of extra cesses on ryots. Under the Permanent Settlement regulations such cesses would be made illegal and could be disallowed. What ryots owed was to be recorded on a legally binding *potta*.[38]

Within a few years it was generally conceded that the Company's measures aimed at protecting the interests of ryots had been ineffective. Revenue accounts remained as tortuous and inscrutable as ever. *Potta*s, which were intended to be a simple record of obligations, were unpopular with both sides. Those who collected rent obviously had no wish to see any limitation of their power to enforce extra levies. Those who paid rent seem to have seen fixed *potta*s as a limitation of rights which they claimed as customary. The duration of the *potta*s was ten years, which seemed a denial of occupancy rights that ryots regarded as permanent.[39] Others apparently feared that they would be losers in any formal record of rights and obligations. Part of their land might be liable to a high level of impositions, but the *zamindars*' agents might not be aware of the full extent of what they held. To set all down on

---

[38] Islam, *The Permanent Settlement*, p. 16.     [39] Ibid., p. 43.

paper would make all vulnerable. They had more confidence in their own powers of concealment and evasion than in the good intentions of the government and the working of the courts. Especially after the regulation of 1799 had greatly strengthened the power of the *zamindar*s to enforce claims by distraining the goods of ryots, the machinery of the law seemed to be weighted on the side of the *zamindar*. British observers generally felt that the ryots had very little formal protection against arbitrary increases in what they were charged. Particularly bleak accounts came from Rangpur in northern Bengal in 1815. There 'the arbitrary oppression under which the cultivator of the soil groans, has at length attained a height so alarming, as to have become by far the most extensively injurious of all the evils under which the district labours'. Every religious festival and every family celebration of the *zamindar*s produced 'an immediate visitation of calamity upon the ryot', who was charged an extra cess on his revenue to pay for it. The *zamindar* was 'supported in his oppression by the irresistable phalanx' of the police *darogah*s, the Indian law officers, 'distress and sale laws and a long purse'.[40] Holt Mackenzie, one of the most experienced of the Company's revenue administrators, told a committee of the House of Commons in 1832 that ryots enjoyed legal security against increased rent in only a few parts of Bengal.[41]

The government's efforts to hold the ring between *zamindar* and ryot had been a failure. But if the Company had certainly not done the ryots any good, it may not have done them very much harm either. Ultimately it was probably beyond the capacity of any government to regulate relations between ryot and *zamindar* for better or for worse. Such relations depended on custom and custom ultimately derived its sanctions from the balance of advantages between the *zamindar* and the ryot, that is between the ryot's need of land to cultivate and the *zamindar*'s need for hands to cultivate land from which he collected revenue.

All observers agreed that at the beginning of the Company's rule Bengal contained much potentially cultivatable land that was not being used. This seemed to be due to a relatively low level of population, especially after the famine of 1770, and to the poverty of most peasants who lacked the resources to clear 'waste' land. *Zamindar*s who

[40] Report of T. Sissons, 2 Apr. 1815, *Selection of Papers from the Records of East India House* (5 vols., 1820–6), I, 382–91.
[41] Evidence on 18 April 1832, *PP*, 1831–2, XI, part i, 216–17.

wished to attract settlers onto uncultivated land had therefore to offer substantial inducements, usually to headmen able to bring communities of cultivators with them. Loans would be needed for seed and cattle and the level of rent to be demanded would have to be a low one for some years. Warren Hastings commented in 1776 on the large numbers of *paikasht*, that is migratory ryots, who could 'make their own terms with the zemindar' and 'enjoy lands at half price'.[42] Such men could claim no security of tenure, but 'when oppressed easily abandon the lands to which they have no attachment' and in the conditions of post-famine Bengal could expect to find fresh land without difficulty.[43]

By the end of the eighteenth century, however, the balance between land and labour was shifting in favour of those with land to offer and against those who required land. Labour was no longer in short supply. The spread of cultivation was much noted. In 1813 the usually well-informed H. T. Colebrooke commented: 'Increase of agriculture has proceeded with rapidity surpassing expectation and the greatest part of the country has already reached its limit.'[44] A few years later Lower Bengal was said to be 'far too populous to admit of tracts of land remaining uncultivated'.[45] Density of settlement was evident in places: 'Villages of from 100 to 500 inhabitants are astonishingly numerous, and in some parts form a continued chain of many miles along the banks of the rivers.'[46] Even in the east, parts of Tippera were said to be 'cultivated like a garden; there is not a spot of ground where they could feed a bullock on scarcely'.[47] Contemporary estimates of population rest on little foundation, but all who hazarded guesses thought that rapid growth was taking place within the range of 20,000,000 to 30,000,000 people in Bengal and Bihar.[48] An attempt to estimate population in the district of Burdwan, which was based on a count of huts, and was published in 1816, suggested a total population of nearly

[42] Revenue Consultations, 12 Nov. 1776, *Reports from Committees of the House of Commons* (12 vols., 1803–6), V, 949.
[43] Report of the Amini Commission, 1778, cited in R.B. Ramsbotham, *Studies in the Land Revenue History of Bengal 1769–87* (1926), p. 106.
[44] *Selection of Papers from East India House*, I, 201.
[45] N. Alexander, 'On the Cultivation of Indigo', *Transactions of the Agricultural and Horticultural Society of India*, II (1836), 35.
[46] W. Hamilton, *The East-India Gazetteer* (2 vols., 1828), I, 191.
[47] Evidence of G. Harris, 21 May 1830, *PP*, 1830, VI, 307.
[48] Discussed in B.B. Chaudhuri, 'Agricultural Growth in Bengal and Bihar 1770–1860', *Bengal Past and Present*, XCV (1976), 324–30.

1,500,000 with a density of 600 people per square mile, which exceeded that of the most densely populated English county.[49]

In times of increasing pressure of people upon land, those who controlled land were likely to prosper. Those Bengal *zamindars* who had been able to keep afloat in the boulder-strewn rapids of the Company's early revenue experiments and the Permanent Settlement entered into calmer waters in the early nineteenth century. For many running a *zamindari* was becoming a very profitable business. It is commonly held against the Bengal *zamindars* that they sought profit by forcing up rents rather than by making any investment in improvements or by encouraging agricultural innovation. Such accusations may have an element of exaggeration. *Zamindars* invested extensively in promoting the cultivation of new lands and they were much involved in the spread of indigo. Nevertheless, *zamindari* fortunes seem for the most part to have been built on increased rents. 'Everywhere in general landlords virtually doubled their collections as population rose and cultivation was extended', is a recent verdict.[50] The Company obtained irrefutable evidence about the profitability of *zamindaris* when they temporarily took over the management of certain estates through the Court of Wards. The Permanent Settlement was based on the assumption that a *zamindar*'s profit on what he collected would be 10 per cent, the rest going to the government. The profits realised by the Court of Wards were often higher than the revenue payable to the government.[51] In the early nineteenth century the estates acquired by Krishna Kanta Nandy and his heirs produced an income from rent of Rs. 1,664,560, of which only Rs. 245,000 was due to the government in revenue.[52]

Wealth on this scale meant that the major *zamindars* could maintain impressive establishments. Even if they did not rule the countryside as their predecessors had done under the Nawabs, they still exerted a very powerful local leadership. Even newly founded dynasties became patrons of learning and religion. Some of the richest *zamindars* acquired great houses in Calcutta, where they spent a certain part of the year. There too they became leaders of society.

[49] W.B. Bayley, 'Statistical View of the Population of Burdwan', *Asiatick Researches*, XII (1816), 551.

[50] C. Palit, *Tensions in Bengal Rural Society: Landlords, Planters and Colonial Rule* (Calcutta, 1975), p. 12.

[51] H. Mackenzie's evidence, 28 Apr. 1832, *PP*, 1831–2, XI, part i, 255.

[52] Information kindly supplied by Dr S.C. Nandy.

Even though there is general agreement that most *zamindar*s did well in the early nineteenth century, historians are increasingly reluctant to accept without reservation contemporary verdicts, like that expressed by the Marquess of Hastings when he wrote in 1815: 'If it were the intention of our regulations to deprive every class, but the large proprietors who engage with government, of any share in the profits of the land, that effect has been fully accomplished in Bengal.'[53] Any suggestion that *zamindar*s were able to trample on all sections of rural society has been considerably revised. Much attention has been given to a minority of substantial ryots who, it is argued, were well able to resist the *zamindar*s and indeed to join them in oppressing the mass of their fellow ryots. British revenue records of the late eighteenth century contain many accounts of the extent to which rich peasants, whom they commonly called *mandal*s (headmen), had extracted concessions from the *zamindar*s. They frequently acted as mediators for their villages in fixing revenue assessments,[54] sometimes undertaking to collect revenue themselves. In return they were reputed to assess themselves lightly and to allocate to themselves much land that paid no rent at all. In 1788 the Collector of Rajshahi reported that 'the head munduls are become the real masters of the land'.[55] If the *zamindar*s, even with the support of British Collectors, tried to impose assessments that threatened their privileged status, the *mandal*s and other rich peasants obstructed them, even to the point of armed resistance. A recent study of northern Bengal concludes: 'The agrarian disturbances of the late eighteenth century were, without exception, led by small local leaders, especially the wealthy ryots, mainly for the purpose of protecting or increasing their own economic interests at the cost of both the *zamindar* and the inferior ryots.'[56] Such people were the leaders of the rising in Rangpur in 1783. In the 1780s they organised insurrections to defeat increased assessments in Birbhum.[57]

As the Company's police extended their influence and with the Company's courts supporting the *zamindar*s' powers against their tenants, open resistance must have been a less and less attractive option. The extent to which *zamindar*s in the more favourable climate

[53] Minute of 21 Sept. 1815, *Selection of Papers from East India House*, I, 427.
[54] Amini Report, 1778. Ramsbotham, *Studies*, p. 108.
[55] Cited by J. Shore, Minute of June 1789, *PP*, 1812, VII, 193.
[56] Taniguchi, 'Agrarian Society', p. 263.
[57] R.K. Gupta, *The Economic Life of a Bengal District: Birbhum 1770–1856* (Burdwan, 1984), pp. 48–9.

of the early nineteenth century could restrict the gains of *mandal*s and others like them is, however, unclear. Buchanan's surveys of districts in northern Bengal leave no doubt of the continuing importance of such men. In Dinajpur he found a small group, approximately one-sixteenth of the cultivating population, who were men who 'have in general large capitals, advance money or grain, both to those who cultivate for a share, and to their other necessitous neighbours, to enable them to live while the cultivation is going forward. It may indeed be said that their stock carries on at least one half of the whole cultivation of the country.'[58] In Rangpur he found 'great farmers', who were 'well behaved men, supperior by much both in manner and education to the generality of their masters, and many of them live much better than landlords of the first families and largest estates in the district'.[59] An alert and vigorous *zamindar* could no doubt protect his interests and enhance his profits, but any weakness in his management was likely to be exploited by what has been called 'the trinity of the village', the *mandal*, the local money lender and the *zamindar*'s agent; this trinity could 'do with the *raiyat*s as it pleased'.[60]

Informed comment about the state of the rural population of Bengal in the early nineteenth century usually acknowledged the existence of a thin stratum of relatively affluent ryots below the *zamindar*s. But comment, both informed and lay, generally assessed the condition of the rest in pessimistic terms. Holt Mackenzie's verdict was: 'I do not think that any inference can be drawn that the condition of the people has improved, but that cultivation has much extended.'[61] Some British officials who served in east Bengal, where the pressure of people on land was often less marked and where the rivers constantly re-fertilised the land, were more optimistic. For a number of districts 'a moderate degree of subsistence' was said to be enjoyed 'by the very lowest classes' in 1820.[62] An observer of early nineteenth-century Sylhet had 'no where seen a population among whom the ordinary wants of nature were so easily and cheaply supplied'.[63] In western Bengal, especially near Calcutta, the crowding of people was unmistakable. Buchanan left stark statistical estimates

[58] Martin, *Eastern India*, II, 904–5.
[59] Survey of 'Ranggopur', IOL, MS. Eur. D. 75, book IV, p. 103.
[60] N. Mukherjee, *A Bengal Zamindar: Jaykrishna Mukherjee of Uttarpara and his Times* (Calcutta, 1975), p. 94.   [61] Evidence, 28 June 1832, *PP*, 1831–2, XI, part i, 256.
[62] Judicial Letter, 3 Nov. 1820, *Selection of Papers from East India House*, IV, 6.
[63] Captain Fisher, 'Memoir of Sylhet, Kachar and the Adjacent Districts', *Journal of the Asiatic Society of Bengal*, IX (1840), 821.

showing that in the northern districts which he visited almost half of those who cultivated the land did so on holdings which were insufficient to afford them a subsistence and that there were substantial numbers of landless labourers.[64] Although, like some other commentators, Buchanan believed that the demand for labour was increasing and causing higher wages to be paid, he provided specific details of the deprivation of the labouring poor, who lived with their families in a single hut, subsisting on coarse grains and pulses. Buchanan believed that most of the poorer members of the population were in debt from which they would never escape. Holt Mackenzie estimated that between three-quarters and seven-eighths of Bengal's cultivators were in debt.[65]

Bihar after the Permanent Settlement showed some of the same features as Bengal.[66] The number of people grew and more land went under the plough. This was especially marked north of the Ganges. The spread of cultivation in the districts there in the early nineteenth century drew many comments from Englishmen. It was widely believed that, in spite of the increasing pressure of people upon the land, the ryots of Bihar had been able to resist extortion by the *zamindar*s and even to improve their standard of living. Such generalisations seem, however, to have applied in the main to the numerous high-caste Hindu or well-born Muslim ryots. Such people often enjoyed privileged tenures which gave them permanent occupation at low rates. They were likely to be extremely truculent, and, as Buchanan found 'not much afraid of their landlords'.[67] But below the privileged ryots were a mass of small cultivators, sharecroppers and under-tenants, usually marked off from the privileged by caste. Throughout Bihar, both north and south of the Ganges, the rural poor were reduced to labouring and were as hard pressed by debt as those in any Bengal district. For instance, an article on Purnea commented that: 'The mass of its labouring agriculturalists are miserably poor and needy.'[68]

Early British administration of the Orissa revenues resulted in an increased aggregate demand, which presumably pressed on all sections of the community. The extent to which those who had entered

[64] Martin, *Eastern India*, III, 482.
[65] Evidence, 23 Feb. 1832, *PP*, 1831–2, X, part i, 16.
[66] R.M. Sinha, *Bihar Tenantry (1783–1833)* (Bombay, 1968).
[67] Martin, *Eastern India*, I, 303–4.
[68] C.U. Blake, 'An Agricultural Memoir of the Poornea District', *Transactions of the Agricultural and Horticultural Society of India,* I (1829), 155.

into revenue agreements with the Company could extract rent from the ryots must in some degree have been limited by a shortage of cultivators and the abundance of land.[69] But in some districts British officials came to believe that 'dreadful misery and distress' had been caused by 'enormous overassessment'.[70]

By the 1820s, after sixty years of British rule, a generalised picture of rural society in eastern India suggests sharp contours. At the top were a number of great *zamindari* estates. Some of those in Bihar and one or two in Bengal were survivors from previous eras; most in Bengal and Orissa were new. Below the great estates were very numerous smaller *zamindari*s, together with *taluk*s, *patni*s and other tenures with revenue-collecting rights. Some of these were also survivors; most were new. The number of minor *zamindar*s and *malik*s increased under the British in Bihar. There was an equally wide range among those who were technically ryots, paying rather than receiving rent. At the top were some who actually did receive rent from under-tenants, probably cultivated considerable areas on their own behalf and also employed their poorer neighbours as sharecroppers or labourers in return for loans. Terms like *mandal*, *jotedar* or *gantidar*, varying in different parts of Bengal, were applied to them. They were especially numerous in northern districts. In Bihar there were many high-caste cultivators enjoying privileged tenures. Throughout the three provinces there were also considerable numbers of less affluent but still self-sufficient peasant cultivators. Far more numerous than these, especially in the congested areas of northern and western Bengal and in the populous districts of Bihar, were the cultivators who were not self-sufficient, but who had to work for other cultivators or labour in other ways. Most would be in debt, some to the extent of becoming virtually the wage servants of their creditors. Finally, there were a number of wholly landless labourers.

It is relatively easy to indicate the extent of change in the higher ranks of rural society in the first sixty years of colonial rule and plausible suggestions can be offered as to the new regime's role in bringing about change. The process of subdivision of the large *zamindari*s seems to have begun with the Nawabs' search for higher revenue yields. But there seems little doubt that subdivision was greatly accelerated by the British. The great *zamindar*s' power to coerce was taken from them

[69] W.W. Hunter, *Orissa* (2 vols., 1872), I, 55.
[70] Cited in Pattanaik, *Forgotten Chapter*, pp. 165–6.

precisely at the time when they most needed it to keep tough British assessments at bay and thus avoid the penalty of sale by default. *Zamindars* with smaller holdings could organise their collections more efficiently and learn how to use the courts and police as allies.

But if changes at the top of rural society can be identified with some certainty and can to a considerable degree be attributed to the British presence, it is by no means clear either how the mass of rural society changed nor what impact the new regime had on it. It seems likely that contemporary concern about the poverty of the mass of the rural population was well founded. By increasing the aggregate revenue demand, the British had no doubt added to the burdens of the poor. But the relationship between the government's revenue assessments and what the ryots were required to pay remains obscure. There is much evidence which shows that exactions from ryots increased under the nominally fixed assessment of the Permanent Settlement. In earlier years British officials believed that it was 'not infrequent' for an actual reduction in the government demand to be 'immediately followed by new taxes and new impositions' by *zamindars* on their ryots.[71] The effect of colonial rule on the rates of interest charged on loans to cultivators or on the severity with which their terms were enforced is also unclear. High rates were certainly established before British rule. An Englishman who worked in one of the districts ceded to the Company in 1760 reported that cultivators had to borrow at 40 per cent for seed, cattle and irrigation work.[72]

The minority of richer peasants noted by the British may well have increased in numbers under the Company's rule. But again neither the extent of such an increase nor the role of British revenue policies in promoting it are easy to discern. Any weakening of the authority of the *zamindars* was presumably to the advantage of the more substantial ryots who could defy their demands. Such people often seem to have enjoyed privileged tenure of their lands, which no doubt enabled them to deflect increased demands onto those less fortunate than themselves.

On balance the probability seems to be that the great mass of the rural population were beyond the reach of the government's revenue activities. Developments below the level of *zamindar* or other tenure holders with whom the government did have direct dealings, such as

[71] Amini Report, 1778. Ramsbotham, *Studies*, p. 118.
[72] W. Bolts, *Considerations on India Affairs* (3 vols., 1772–5), I, 150.

the unrelieved poverty of the mass or the emergence of an affluent minority, are likely to have had causes which went deeper than fluctuations in British revenue policy. In the absence of major famines or cataclysmic floods, the population began to increase. With larger numbers, the bargaining power of the mass declined. Those who controlled land, labour and money could hold their own.

Even if British revenue policy had only oblique effects on those below the level of *zamindar*, the same may not have been true of British commercial activities. With much agricultural production already geared to the needs of a market economy, changes in the level of demand for the products of the land could affect the lives of many. The enormous increase in the volume of Bengal's exports by sea, described in Chapter 4, suggests that early British rule powerfully stimulated the demands for the products of eastern India. Allowance must, however, be made for the fact that a considerable proportion of Calcutta's exports did not originate in the three provinces, but came down the Ganges from Awadh or overland from central India. A recent estimate is that between 1815–16 and 1828–9 goods from northern India contributed between 41 per cent and 49 per cent to Bengal's inland customs receipts.[73]

The effect of seaborne exports in stimulating the demand for Bengal goods is obvious; the impact of overland trade during the first sixty years after the *Diwani* is hard to determine. In the first half of the eighteenth century very large quantities of Bengal silk and cotton goods went to northern India, their sale providing the mechanism by which a considerable part of the Bengal tribute to the Mughal Emperor was realised at Delhi.

A variety of merchants of different nations and religions, such as Cashmeerians, Multanys, Patans, Sheikhs, Sunniasis, Poggyahs, Betteeahs, and many others used to come to Bengal annually in Caffeelahs, or large parties of many thousands (together with troops of oxen for the transport of goods) from different parts of Hindostan.[74]

Bengal also exported cloth and salt eastwards to Assam. Before 1803 Orissa's trade, consisting of salt and some piece goods, was largely directed inland to Maratha territory.

During the early years of British rule Bengal's exports to northern

---

[73] T.G. Kessinger, 'Rural Economy (1757–1857): Northern India', *Cambridge Economic History*, II, 255.  [74] Bolts, *Considerations*, I, 200.

India fell to a low level as markets were disrupted. They revived again in the 1780s, although by then the reverse flow of imports was much greater. Even if in somewhat smaller quantities than in the days of the Nawabs, Bengal silk and high quality piece goods still sold well in northern India in the early nineteenth century.[75] Most of Orissa's overland trade must have been lost after 1803 as its salt production was included in the British monopoly, but trade from Bengal to Assam continued.

Between 1765 and the 1820s exports from eastern India overland were probably at considerably lower levels than before the establishment of British rule. Nevertheless, allowing for this and the fact that a sizable part of the seaborne exports originated outside the provinces, the net gain to the region from the growth of Calcutta's trade was still very great indeed. Early British rule meant that many more artisans and cultivators were working for external markets.

British rule also produced major changes in the internal market of the provinces: some centres of consumption declined, while one grew prodigiously. The major urban concentrations of late Mughal Bengal and Bihar had been the centres of government and trade: Murshidabad, Patna and Dhaka, together with the ports along the Hooghly river. Places of pilgrimage and the courts of the major zamindars had also become considerable towns. One of the Hooghly ports, Calcutta, was growing into a metropolis well before 1757. British rule greatly accelerated that process. It has been estimated that even in 1750 Calcutta's population was 120,000.[76] The great increase in British trade was attracting to the settlement not only those directly employed by the Company and its European servants, but also Indian merchants and their followers. A large garrison was stationed at the new Fort William after 1757. After 1772 government offices moved to Calcutta from Murshidabad, attracting ever more people who wished to serve the government or who had to do business with the government, such as the zamindars' agents and, later, some zamindars in person. As servants, porters or labourers in the docks or on the new buildings, the poor also moved to Calcutta for shorter or longer periods, setting up their huts or sleeping in the open.[77] By 1780

---

[75] C.A. Bayly, *Rulers, Townsmen and Bazaars* (Cambridge, 1983), pp. 150–1.

[76] A.K. Ray, 'A Short History of Calcutta', *Census of India 1901*, VII (Calcutta, 1902), 59–62.

[77] W. Ward, *Account of the Religion and Manners of the Hindoos* (4 vols., Serampore, 1811), I, 126.

Calcutta could already be described as 'that scattered and confused chaos of houses, huts, sheds, streets and lanes, alleys, windings, gutters, sinks and tanks, which jumbled into an undistinguished mass of corruption, equally offensive to human sense and health'.[78] In 1822 Calcutta was thought to have 200,000 residents, with another 100,000 who came into the city every day for work from the surrounding neighbourhood.[79] The spread of Calcutta's suburbs was as remarkable as the growth of the city itself. In 1834 Charles Trevelyan wrote of a continuous chain of villages stretching nearly fifty miles along the right bank of the Hooghly.[80]

Murshidabad would seem to have been the victim of the rise of Calcutta. The spending power of the Nawabs declined catastrophically, their troops were disbanded, most of the government offices closed and the great banking businesses contracted. Yet Murshidabad gained a Company garrison nearby at Berhampore and it kept much of its trade. Its population was still estimated at 165,000 in 1815 and 146,176 in 1829, although the city had apparently lost most of its grandeur, being called 'probably the meanest capital in Hindustan'.[81] The decline of Dhaka in the early nineteenth century drew much comment. As late as 1801 200,000 people were still thought to be living there.[82] But of all the textile centres, Dhaka was the most vulnerable to the collapse of European exports. The number of houses assessed for tax fell by a half between 1814 and 1830. A person who knew the city well wrote that 'poverty has increased in a far greater ratio than population has decreased'; the mass of the poor were in 'a very destitute condition'.[83] In contrast, the population of Patna appears to have grown or at least to have held its own in the early nineteenth century. Buchanan estimated that there were 312,000 people living there.[84] Heber, who saw it in 1824, thought it 'much exceeds Dacca'. He noted 'Corinthian superstructures among the houses of the rich natives'.[85]

[78] Cited in A. Mitra, 'Calcutta City', *Census of India, 1951*, VI, part iii (Calcutta, 1954), 8.    [79] Ibid., pp. 11–12.

[80] *Report on Inland Customs and Town Duties in the Bengal Presidency* ed. T. Banerjee (Calcutta, 1976), p. 123.

[81] L.S.S. O'Malley, *Bengal District Gazetteers: Murshidabad* (Calcutta, 1914), p. 208.

[82] A. Karim, 'An Account of the District of Dacca', *Journal of the Asiatic Society of Pakistan*, VII (1962), 340.

[83] J. Taylor, *Sketch of the Topography and Statistics of Dacca* (Calcutta, 1840), pp. 366–7.

[84] Martin, *Eastern India*, I, 39.

[85] R. Heber, *Narrative of a Journey through the Upper Provinces of India* (2 vols., 1849 edn), I, 139–40.

The quality of life in the major cities of the Nawabs' Bengal probably deteriorated sharply after they came under British rule. The Muslim aristocracy could no longer afford to embellish the cities and nobody else had much inclination to do so as yet. But in terms of sheer numbers there was probably no significant decline until well into the nineteenth century, and even then Patna was exempt. The situation of the smaller towns is less clear. In 1795 a British observer wrote: 'It is a notorious fact, that the cities and towns of Bengal are universally reduced to an excessive degree; and they continue to decline.'[86] Examples to support this are not difficult to suggest. Malda, once a prosperous textile town specialising in cloth for export, was full of 'ruinous houses, which are overgrown with weeds, and shelter dirt of every kind', giving it 'an uncommonly miserable appearance'.[87] The towns of ruined *zamindars*, like Krishnanagar in Nadia or Vishnupur, must have suffered severely. On the other hand, places of pilgrimage, like Gaya and Puri, flourished under British rule. Major new market centres developed at places like Narayanganj and Sirajganj.

It would be difficult to sustain a case that eastern India in general was undergoing a process of 'de-urbanisation'. Nearly all the growth in major urban centres was concentrated in Calcutta, but of the three older cities, only Dhaka was in precipitous decline. In the small towns, gains and losses may have been roughly in balance.

Well before the establishment of British rule, the needs of the towns had stimulated the production of surpluses in the countryside. As Calcutta grew, its own consumption as well as the demands of its export trade affected an ever wider area. Its dependence on rice from eastern Bengal was well established by the middle of the eighteenth century.[88] By the 1790s Jessore was thought to send half of its rice, one-third of its tobacco and half of its sugar to Calcutta.[89] The Calcutta market was also a powerful force in districts in western Bengal, such as Burdwan: 'Since Calcutta has been the seat of government, its inhabitants are considerably increased, and this province supplying it with provisions as well as with a vast variety of articles of merchandise, the lands from which they are produced are consequently increased in value.'[90] At the same time Europeans noted that districts in northern

---

[86] [H.T. Colebrooke and A. Lambert], *Remarks on the Present State of the Husbandry and Commerce of Bengal* (Calcutta, 1795), p. 130.    [87] Martin, *Eastern India*, II, 657.
[88] *Fort William – India House Correspondence* (New Delhi, 1949–), I, *1748–56*, ed. K.K. Datta, p. 736.    [89] Westland, *Report on Jessore*, pp. 135–7.
[90] D.L. Curley, 'Rulers and Merchants in late Eighteenth-century Bengal', Unpublished Ph.D. thesis, Chicago University, 1980, pp. 50–4.

Bengal and eastern Bihar were suffering from a slackening of Murshidabad's demand. By the end of the century, however, Calcutta was attracting food grains and other crops from precisely these areas. In 1797–8 it was estimated that there were nearly 10,000 'native' shopkeepers in Calcutta, and that, excluding 'provisions and other necessaries sold in the different buzars and markets', their annual turnover 'for the consumption of the natives' was over Rs. 1,000,000.[91]

There can be no doubt that colonial rule, by stimulating exports and by encouraging the massing of people and wealth in a single urban centre, had created an increased demand for cloth, silk, indigo, opium, oilseeds and grain of all sorts over a wide area of eastern India. A very considerable increase must have taken place in the number of people who produced for distant markets. Yet how great this number was remains unclear. Some scholars argue that early in the nineteenth century 'Bengal's system of production was now completely geared to the needs of industrialized Britain, and her economy prospered or decayed according to the fluctuations of the London market'.[92] There are, however, grounds for arguing that Bengal's economy probably still responded as much to the fluctuations in mortality, the chance of the seasons and the movement of the rivers as to the doings of foreign traders or to the appetite of Calcutta. Large sections of the economy of the three provinces were still effectively immune from the various pulls emanating from Calcutta. The rivers were the great arteries of trade, but steam power had as yet done little to speed traffic, which was usually confined to certain seasons. The Company had scarcely attempted to improve roads. In 1823 it could still be said that on no roads in Bengal could all-the-year round carriage be guaranteed for more than twenty miles.[93] Most trade must therefore have remained localised, conducted over short hauls. Most cultivated land was used for food grains for family or for very local consumption. Most artisans also worked for a very restricted local market. The history of Bengal's textile production has inevitably been written largely from records of the Company's dealings in cloth for export. But the unchronicled internal market, much of it narrowly localised, was very large indeed.

[91] IOR, Bengal Commercial Reports, 1797–8, Range 174, vol. 13.

[92] A. Tripathi, *Trade and Finance in the Bengal Presidency 1793–1833*, 2nd edn (Calcutta, 1979), p. 155.

[93] Cited in J. Crawfurd, 'A Sketch of the Commercial Resources and Monetary and Mercantile System of British India', *The Economic Development of India under the East India Company 1814–58*, ed. K.N. Chaudhuri (Cambridge, 1971), p. 236.

One estimate of it for 1795 put its value at Rs. 60,000,000,[94] which would have been ten times the value of the Company's investment in piece goods. Weavers and spinners producing cloth, usually of coarser quality, for consumption within the provinces were subjected to few of the fluctuations that affected the great export centres like Dhaka.

To portray Bengal's economy as completely under the domination of international trade may be to exaggerate. Nevertheless, the influence of overseas trade was much more marked over a much wider area of eastern India in the early nineteenth century than would have been the case in any other, comparable part of the sub-continent; and Calcutta was unique for its time, as a great port and as a great centre of consumption largely of European creation. Recent studies of northern India west of Bihar in the same period have stressed what has been called the lack of 'economic integration' and the weakness of British commercial penetration.[95] Outside Calcutta Europeans were very thin on the ground in Bengal and Bihar, but nowhere else in India was there so elaborate a network of the Company's commercial residencies or private indigo factories. It was no doubt to be expected that deltaic Bengal should become the hinterland of Calcutta, but by 1818 striking estimates were being offered of the amount of trade of a district as remote as Tirhut in northern Bihar. Two-thirds of its grain and most of its oil seeds were said to be exported from the district, Calcutta being the main destination.[96] Even the tribal peoples were being drawn out of their western hills to work in the indigo factories.[97]

Growing crops for the market or working for wages paid by foreign employers were obvious ways in which those who lived at a great distance from the sea could be tied to Calcutta and the world beyond it. They might well feel the full effects of the fluctuations of the London market, especially if they had anything to do with that highly volatile commodity, indigo. Very many others could be affected in less direct ways by the influence, as yet not fully understood, that foreign trade exerted on the general level of prices and therefore of economic activity, at least in Bengal. In the decade or so before the battle of

[97] [Colebrooke and Lambert], *Remarks on Bengal*, p. 130.
[95] Kessinger, 'Rural Economy', pp. 248–9; Bayly, *Rulers, Townsmen and Bazaars*, Chapter 6.
[96] H.R. Ghosal, 'Tirhut at the End of the 18th Century and the Beginning of the 19th Century', *Journal of the Bihar Research Society*, XXXIX (1953), 369.
[97] Evidence of G. Harris, 21 May 1830, *PP*, 1830, VI, 305.

Plassey prices were rising with a high level of European purchases financed by imports of silver. Perhaps surprisingly, the price rise accelerated in the 1760s, precisely when the British shifted from shipping silver in to shipping it out. From the 1770s into the early nineteenth century prices were stable or slightly falling, but at least maintained a level which proved conducive to an expansion of agricultural output, largely by taking in new land.[98]

The consequences that followed from extensive foreign penetration, if not absolute domination, of the economy of eastern India aroused controversy among contemporaries and has continued to do so down to the present time. Warren Hastings believed that 'the produce of the land in common years, so much exceeds the quantity required for the consumption of the people or for the purposes of exportation', that if new land was brought into cultivation, 'the Company would derive no advantage from it, nor the labourers receive any compensation for their toil'.[99] A few years later, another Company servant, Thomas Law, agreed with him. He was fearful of 'exertion ceasing from want of consumption'. Grain was so cheap that it 'scarce repaid the expence of tillage, sowing, etc.'.[100] Greatly increased exports and the growth of Calcutta did much to stimulate consumption. In 1837 John Crawfurd was in no doubt that 'the people of India have benefited' from a wider market for their exports.[101] 'To deny that the improvement of trade between 1793 and 1833, mainly with Britain, benefited Bengal is to fly in the face of facts' is an authoritative current assessment.[102]

Many, however, have denied and continue to deny this. Company servants like Harry Verelst and Philip Francis expressed concern about some of the effects of an increased East India Company investment in Bengal. Their concern was given wide publicity by Burke, and it seemed well founded to a number of writers in the late nineteenth and early twentieth centuries, who were formulating an indictment of what they saw as the impoverishing effects of British rule. Such argu-

---

[98] See discussions in K.N. Chaudhuri, *Trading World of Asia and the English East India Company 1660–1760* (Cambridge, 1978), pp. 100–8; A. Siddiqi, 'Money and Prices in the Earlier Stages of Empire: India and Britain 1760–1840', *Indian Economic and Social History Review*, XVIII (1981); Akhtar Hussain, 'Study of Price Movements'.

[99] 'Memoirs Relative to the State of India', *Selections from the State Papers of the Governors General of India: Warren Hastings*, ed. G.W. Forrest (2 vols., Oxford, 1910), II, 79.

[100] *A Sketch of the Late Arrangements, and a View of the Rising Resources in Bengal* (1792), Preface.     [101] Answers to Queries, *PP*, 1831–2, X, part ii, 513.

[102] Tripathi, *Trade and Finance*, p. 208.

ments have been further refined in recent work on the historical origins of Indian 'underdevelopment'. The potential benefits of increased trade were either all but nullified or actually turned into a cause of poverty by the colonial framework within which it took place. The economic difficulties of eastern India, by comparison with some other regions, have been traced back to the early domination of Bengal by British trade. [103]

Assertions that increased trade after 1765 had a damaging effect on the economy of eastern India usually rest on analyses of the general effect of trade under British rule and of its social consequences in particular instances. For a long period, both before and after 1765, Bengal exported very much more than she imported. Under the Nawabs, it is held, her favourable balance of trade was mostly settled by consignments of bullion from her trading partners; under the British it was largely settled out of Bengal's own resources, as the Company paid for its investment from the taxes it collected, while much foreign European and private British trade was financed by the wealth accumulated in Bengal by British subjects. Hence eastern India was 'drained'. Any assessment of the effect of such a 'drain' requires in the first place a definition of the term, and secondly some attempt to relate the sum said to have been 'drained' to an estimate of the total income of the area. Many definitions of 'drain' and many estimates of income are in contention. Current assessments of the 'drain' and its effects vary between a very damaging '5 to 6 per cent of resources of the ruled land' [104] to the suggestion that 'a unilateral transfer of funds' did not act as 'a net depressor on the Indian economy'. [105]

Underlying any concept of 'drain' is the fact that part of Bengal's exports were financed by taxation rather than by imports of goods or bullion. The Company used its revenue to purchase its own investment, while the Company, foreign Europeans and private traders borrowed the savings of individuals which they had made from the salaries that had been paid out of revenue in the first place. As is discussed in Chapter 4, the need for the Company and for private individuals to transfer money to Europe both increased the volume of

[103] A.K. Bagchi, 'Reflections on Patterns of Regional Growth in India During the Period of British Rule', *Bengal Past and Present*, XCV (1976), 248–50.
[104] A.K. Bagchi, *The Political Economy of Underdevelopment* (Cambridge, 1982), p. 81.
[105] K.N. Chaudhuri, 'India's International Economy in the Nineteenth Century', *Modern Asian Studies*, II (1968), 47.

exports and to a considerable extent determined its pattern. A very different pattern emerged from that which might have existed in Bengal without colonial rule. If it is true that the Company's restrictive policies seriously damaged the production of higher quality cotton piece goods,[106] then it is possible that without British rule exports might have held their own in the face of British competition for a little longer. On the other hand, raw silk and opium exports would have been very much smaller and exports of indigo would hardly have existed at all.

Thus the Company gave back to artisans and to those who grew certain crops part of what it extracted in taxation. It is, however, often argued that any benefits that may have accrued from increased employment generated by government-financed exports were nullified by the conditions imposed by colonial rule on those who worked in the export sectors. Existing methods of exploiting labour were, it is said, intensified to realise greater surpluses. Artisans and cultivators were forced to work for very meagre returns; the main pickings went to Englishmen and to small groups of Indians, either the 'compradors' associated with the British or the money lenders.

Pessimistic assessments of the effects of increased overseas trade under colonial rule stress the fact that the European-dominated sectors of the economy grew at the expense of opportunities for 'native' merchants. There certainly was a marked tendency for the Company to eliminate intermediaries between it and the producers. The Company's textiles, which had once been bought through Indian *dadni* merchants, were directly procured by its own commercial residents and their Indian employees. Salt and opium became state monopolies managed by European agents. Although Indian bankers remained very important to the Company in enabling it to realise its revenue locally, no single house could aspire to anything remotely resembling the position which the Jagat Seths had attained as controllers of the treasury and the mint under the Nawabs. The Company made efforts to encourage European banking, in order to spread the use of paper currency and strengthen the credit system. In 1809 it gave a charter to a new Bank of Bengal. The growth of European private trade inevitably meant a dominant position for European merchants. Vir-

---

[106] H. Hossain, 'Alienation of Weavers ... 1750–1800', *Indian Economic and Social History Review*, XVI (1979), 323–45.

tually all of the ships which handled Calcutta's greatly increased exports were owned by Europeans. The Houses of Agency made further inroads into the areas where Indian banking had once been supreme. Although there was considerable Indian participation in the indigo industry, the greater part of it was owned by Europeans and financed by the Houses of Agency.

On the other hand, opportunities had also been created. The growth of Calcutta had greatly stimulated trade in food stuffs of all kinds, especially grain. This was almost entirely in Indian hands. So too was the distribution and retailing of the vast quantities of salt put up for sale by the Company. In areas where Europeans were active, anything that could be formally described as partnerships between them and Indian businessmen hardly existed until the appearance of firms like Carr, Tagore in the 1830s; but the enterprises of the European merchants opened up a number of fields for Indian investment. In 1802 'the formerly timid Hindoo' was said to be investing in shipping, insurance and indigo factories.[107] When an Indian was actively involved in European business, it was still customary to refer to him as a 'banian'. By the early nineteenth century, though, banians were no longer the commanding figures they had been at the time of the conquest, when they stood discreetly at the elbow of the great Company servants, enriching their masters and themselves at the same time. However, their commercial importance in doing business for Europeans and raising finance for them remained considerable. Some were great entrepreneurs in their own right, for example Ramdulal Dey, who specialised in providing cargoes for American ships. It was thought that very few Europeans in Calcutta could match his fortune, put at £300,000 to £400,000.[108] If no Indian banker could now be compared to the Jagat Seths, outside Calcutta banking remained almost entirely in Indian hands and within the city Indian banking underpinned the Agency Houses. In 1827 John Palmer, of the famous Palmer Company, wrote of the dependence of 'the great mercantile houses' on 'the native money dealers'. Behind 'the money lenders in Calcutta' were the 'great upcountry shroffs and other capitalists'.[109]

It can hardly be disputed that the East India Company and the

[107] Cited in N.K. Sinha, *The Economic History of Bengal from 1793–1848* (Calcutta, 1970), p. 110.   [108] Evidence of T. Bracken, *PP*, 1831–2, X, part i, 160.
[109] Cited in S. Bhattacharya, 'Inequality and Free Trade', *Indian History Congress*, 34th session (1973), II, 96.

private British merchants were able to secure for themselves a very large proportion of the commercial profits arising from the growth of eastern India's overseas trade. But if there were losses of opportunity for some, Indian commercial enterprise was far from being annihilated; and as private British merchants acquired an ever bigger stake, they evoked Indian responses. One recent account describes 'the ceaseless pursuit of wealth by Bengal's residents in Calcutta and the neighbouring European settlements in the first half of the nineteenth century'.[110] Another has seen signs of a 'small-scale industrial revolution', which rested on an 'inter-racial' coalition that was only to founder in the middle of the century.[111]

Increased exports and increased consumption in Calcutta were made possible by those who spun the thread and wove the higher quality cloth, who were employed in the silk filatures or in growing mulberry trees and rearing silk worms, or who grew sugar cane, poppies, indigo plants and the higher grades of rice that were consumed in the towns. Artisanal employment and the acreage under cash crops must have grown considerably. What benefit this conferred on those involved is hard to estimate. As Chapter 4 shows, those drawn into the employment of the East India Company usually had to submit to some degree of control. Weavers, silk winders, those who boiled salt or saltpetre and the cultivators of poppies did not have full freedom to work for others apart from the Company, and they often received fixed payment for work done or for commodities delivered. There is a considerable amount of evidence to suggest that these rates were lower than those offered by other merchants. On some occasions weavers of the Company's cloth even received less than the cost of their raw materials.[112] Opium poppies at the rate the Company paid for them were said to produce a low return for the cultivator in view of the intense labour required and the unpredictable yield of the crop from year to year.[113] In the great silk manufacturing district around Murshidabad cultivating mulberry trees for the Company's silk was

---

[110] Sinha, *Economic History*, p. 105.

[111] B.B. Kling, *Partner in Empire: Dwarkanath Tagore and the Age of Enterprise in Eastern India* (Berkeley, 1976), p. 4.

[112] D.B. Mitra, *The Cotton Weavers of Bengal* (Calcutta, 1979), p. 113; there is much material on the Company's weavers in H. Hossain, 'The East India Company and the Textile Producers of Bengal 1750–1813', Unpublished D.Phil. thesis, Oxford University, 1982.

[113] [Colebrooke and Lambert], *Remarks on Bengal*, p. 80.

thought to produce a lower return that would have been obtained from cultivating rice on the same land.[114]

Private merchants lacked the coercive power of the Company. Accordingly they were believed to pay higher prices than it did. For cotton cloth the difference could amount to 15 per cent to 40 per cent.[115] In the prices which they gave for indigo private British merchants affected a large section of the rural population. In the 1820s some 700 factories were spending up to Rs. 20,000,000 a year. The opponents of the indigo planters accused them of compelling peasants to cultivate an unreliable crop at a rate which offered only a low reward even for a good harvest. Only coercion, they believed, could account for the spread of a form of agriculture which was so unpromising. Coercion was said to be applied through the system of advance payments. Once a cultivator had taken payment from a factory, he, was tied to that factory until he had discharged his debt by delivering the stipulated quantity of indigo plants. If he failed to do this, which was often the case, the debt was carried over to the next year and into succeeding years, as he continued to grow indigo for the factory. Observers who were detached and uncommitted, like Buchanan, recognised that the crop was often an unpopular one but also believed that it could confer benefits. These were stressed too by Rammohun Roy, who found

the natives residing in the neighbourhood of indigo plantations evidently better clothed and better conditioned than those that lived at a distance from such stations. There may be some partial injury done by the indigo planters; but on the whole they have performed more good to the generality of the natives of the country than any other class of Europeans, whether in or out of the [Company's] service.[116]

For many of the commodities that were ultimately intended for export or for supplying Calcutta, artisans and cultivators had no direct dealings with the Europeans, disposing of their goods to Indian merchants. Outright coercion in theory played no part in such dealings, but this does not necessarily mean that buyer and seller were in any sense equal. The producer was often the debtor of the merchant.

[114] G. Bhadra, 'Some Socio-Economic Aspects of the Town of Murshidabad, 1765–93', Unpublished M.Phil. thesis, J. Nehru University, 1971–2, pp. 151–2.
[115] Mitra, *Cotton Weavers*, p. 149.
[116] *English Works of Raja Rammohun Roy*, ed. K. Nag and D. Burman (4 vols., Calcutta, 1947), IV, 83.

Sugar cane, for instance, was a very expensive crop, requiring large advances from sugar merchants, on which the interest could be as high as 75 per cent a year.[117] Much of the grain sent from the countryside to meet the demand from the towns was handed over to merchants in settlement of old debts for money advanced for seed or cattle. The extent of their indebtedness tended, in the view of many British observers, seriously to restrict any benefit that cultivators derived from an expanding market. If prices rose, they could take little advantage of that. The terms of their loans usually required that they should deliver the crop immediately after the harvest and therefore receive the low prices then current. Debts would accumulate and the cultivator would become virtually a wage labourer for the merchant–money lender, who alone reaped the benefits of an expanding demand in Calcutta and beyond.

The balance of advantages or disadvantages in the cultivation of 'cash' crops was a complex matter, in which relative levels of expected profit might not necessarily be the determining consideration.[118] The rate of revenue assessment on land used for different crops was an important element. Crops like sugar or mulberry paid more than grain, but the rates might be based on traditional divisions of the land which did not bear any relation to the actual use of the land. The ability to raise money in advance on a crop was another consideration. Advances were often used not for the process of cultivation but to pay revenue. Here the Company offered real advantages. It might be a stingy paymaster, but its advances did not come loaded with a crushing burden of interest. It was also likely that the Company and the indigo factory would look after their own and protect them from excessive zeal by the revenue officials. Most cash crops involved greater inputs of labour, irrigation and manure and occupied the ground for longer than did food grains. The success of the harvest was also less predictable. Nevertheless, for all the imponderables, informed contemporaries believed that the cultivation of cash crops was generally advantageous. It was on 'the culture of some more valuable produce' that 'the peasant depends for profit, or even for comfortable maintenance'.[119]

Some of the benefits from increased cultivation of cash crops went

---

[117] [J. Prinsep], *Bengal Sugar* (1794), pp. 54–5.
[118] See the discussion in Bayly, *Rulers, Townsmen and Bazaars*, p. 245.
[119] [Colebrooke and Lambert], *Remarks on Bengal*, p. 75.

to the very poorest who worked for wages. Buchanan thought that wages had risen by a half in Rangpur over ten years, largely due to the opening of indigo factories.[120] Between 1803 and 1837 the 'price of agricultural and common labour' in the Dhaka district more than doubled, owing, in part, to the spread of cash crops.[121] Rewards for those who actually cultivated the crops must have largely depended on the scale of their operations. Cultivators with small holdings presumably could not afford to divert land from food grown for their own consumption. If they ventured into cash crops, they were likely to incur a heavy burden of debt that nullified any advantages. The more substantial the cultivator, the more land and labour could be spared for 'valuable' crops and the better were the chances that equitable deals could be made with the Company or with European planters or with money lenders. Thus it may well be the case that British commercial penetration, by encouraging the spread of cash crops, contributed more significantly than British revenue policy had done to increasing the differentiation among the rural population. Most gains seem to have gone to those who controlled large holdings and those who lent money rather than borrowed it, and were able to command the labour of others.

British management of the revenues of their new provinces and British commercial operations in eastern India faced very similar problems. In neither case had the British been able to bring about radical changes by the 1820s. They could not change either the methods by which revenue was extracted or the methods by which goods were produced. At the most they could make existing systems work for them, but not perhaps to the extent that they hoped. A substantial revenue was realised, but not one which matched some British ambitions; commodities were shipped to Europe and China, but their quality and abundance was not such as to give Bengal a commanding position in world trade.

The resilience of established systems limited the extent of the social changes that followed British conquest. Changes were most marked at the top, both among the *zamindar*s and among the richest merchants and bankers. The mass of those who cultivated land or worked as artisans experienced much less disruption. Artisans were potentially the most vulnerable in the new order. Some who worked for Euro-

---

[120] Survey of 'Ranggopur', IOL, MS Eur.D.75, book iv, p. 112.
[121] Taylor, *Topography and Statistics*, pp. 305–6.

peans, especially the employees of the Company, became more like wage labourers than independent craftsmen. The spinners and weavers working on the high quality piece goods for export lost their jobs.[122] But neither the conditions under which they worked nor the technology they used changed much for the great mass of potters, carpenters, smiths or weavers of coarse cloth.

Agriculture over much of eastern India had been 'commercial' long before 1765, in the sense that a proportion of its output was sold for cash, some crops were specifically grown for export, and credit had an important role. All these tendencies were intensified under the British, but neither the techniques nor the structure of agrarian society underwent fundamental change. Although differentiation between the prosperous few and the more or less impoverished mass may have become more marked, the scale of agricultural operations remained much the same. Great plantations employing large forces of labour did not develop. Even large farms, though they were noted by Buchanan and others, were relatively uncommon. Rich ryots seem to have been less inclined to acquire large holdings of land for direct cultivation than to secure the labour of their poorer neighbours, who rendered them a large proportion of their crops to pay off loans. Both in its manufacturing and in its agriculture, eastern India, often to the exasperation of its conquerors, remained a land of very small producers whose way of life had changed very little.

If fiscal and commercial pressure, which were potentially powerful agents of change, had done relatively little to reshape the lives of the vast mass of the population during sixty years of foreign rule, the capacity of the new rulers to communicate new ideas to its subjects is not likely to have been significant. This was certainly true throughout eastern India as a whole, but by the early nineteenth century may not have held for the 200,000 or so who were living in Calcutta, in an environment largely of British creation. Even in Calcutta, however, the great majority must have been immune to foreign influences. They were migratory workers, living in rudimentary conditions with members of their own communities for short periods. But Calcutta also had its permanently resident Indian population living in what Europeans called the Black Town.

---

[122] Mitra, *Cotton Weavers*, pp. 198–203, summarises material in the Company's records about loss of jobs.

By the early nineteenth century certain features of the Black Town were clearly marked. It contained many substantial brick-built houses, some of which were very large and fitted out with elaborate furnishings and displays of glass in the European manner. These were the homes of the richest bankers, of merchants, of owners of *zamindari* property, or of men who had made particularly successful careers in the service of the Company or of individual Englishmen. Nearly all of these people were Hindus, but of varied castes: many were Brahmins and Kayasthas, but others were from artisan, commercial and even agricultural castes. Contemporaries appear to have categorised families in the Black Town more by their wealth and their manner of life than by their caste standing. The very richest were called *abhijat*s. As well as the *abhijat* grandees, the Black Town contained many *grihastha*s, respectable people of good caste, who were making their careers through their literacy and their intelligence in the Company's courts, Collectorates and offices, or in the offices of the Houses of Agency, private banks and insurance businesses. They depended largely on their salaries, but many also drew some income from investment in small revenue-collecting tenures.[123]

The affluence of the leaders of the Black Town Hindu community enabled them to turn Calcutta into a considerable centre of cultural and intellectual patronage. For the most part, their aspirations show little trace of foreign influence. The Black Town and the European White Town preferred to keep one another at arm's length with only a few individuals crossing the divide. Rich Hindus in Calcutta used their wealth in ways that rich Hindus used it anywhere else. They acquired venerated images for their families, often building elaborate *thakurbari*s in which to house them, employed famous priests and pandits, and marked solemn occasions, such as *sradh*s for the deceased, with enormous displays. They sought to gain recognition for their aspirations for improved status for their families or sub-castes by generous patronage of the Brahmins, who could confer such recognition.[124] At a time when the capacity of some of the great *zamindari* families to reward sanctity and learning was diminishing, the munificence of the rich of Calcutta must have been very welcome to pandits. The great festivals of Bengali Hinduism, especially of

---

[123] R.K. Ray, 'Differential Modernization in a Colonial Society: Bengal under the Lieutenant Governors', *Indian Historical Review*, II (1975–6), 98–9.
[124] A process described in H. Sanyal, *Social Mobility in Bengal* (Calcutta, 1981).

Saktaism, became domiciled in Calcutta. During the Durga Puja business came to a halt, and there was a mass exodus to native villages.
Calcutta's claims to cultural leadership appear to have won some
acceptance in other parts of Bengal. Bengali as spoken by educated
men along the Hooghly came to be regarded as standard. 'Men of rank
at Dhaka' were said to be trying to learn to speak like 'the Babus'
of Calcutta. [125]

Although for the most part Black Town and White Town went their
own ways, some contact did take place. Those with ambitions who
lived in the Black Town found it increasingly necessary to learn
English for themselves, and especially to encourage their children to
qualify themselves for employment by learning it too. A number of
private academies for teaching English were established in Calcutta in
the late eighteenth century. In 1817 the desire felt by leading members of Calcutta's Indian community for a college to impart
knowledge of English and of European learning led to the founding of
Hindu College. It received a government subsidy and by the 1820s had
developed into a formidable institution at which English was the
medium of instruction and English literature, western political and
social thought and physics and chemistry were taught. By the end of
the decade, Hindu College graduates, especially those who had been
influenced by the brilliant and mercurial Henry Derozio, were adopting uncompromisingly 'modern', not to say heterodox, ideas. In all
'upwards of three thousand native youths' were reported to be learning English in Calcutta by 1833. [126] Some had gone far beyond the mere
acquisition of a qualification for a job. In 1801 Rammohun Roy had
entered the service of one of the Company's Collectors, already able to
speak English. Five years later, he could write English well and 'was
also in the constant habit of reading the English newspapers, of which
the continental politics chiefly interested him'. [127] English became for
Rammohun Roy a medium which he used with ease and distinction.
He acquired a stock of western learning appropriate to a European
intellectual of some standing and could deploy it in English tracts and
pamphlets of great cogency.

Some movement also took place from the White Town towards the

[125] Martin, *Eastern India*, II, 102.
[126] R. Mitra, 'Unpublished Reports of the Calcutta School Society', *Bengal Past and
Present*, XCVI (1977), 151.
[127] S.D. Collet, *The Life and Letters of Raja Rammohun Roy*, ed. D.K. Biswas and P.C.
Ganguli (Calcutta, 1962), p. 24.

Black. The initial impetus for this was not curiosity about the way of life and culture of modern Bengal, a subject which nearly all Europeans thought to be unworthy of study, but the study of the Hindu past, which was regarded as a legitimate field for scholarship. In 1784 an Asiatic Society was set up under the direct patronage of Warren Hastings. Translations from Sanskrit and essays on the history and literature of ancient India comprised the most distinguished work of the Society's members. In pursuing their studies, the members of the Society, including Hastings himself, employed pandits to teach them Sanskrit and to interpret texts for them. The extent to which a living tradition of Sanskrit learning was accessible in eastern India to be drawn upon by men like Rammohun Roy is unclear. A case has, however, been strenuously argued for the importance of the British 'Orientalists'' patronage of pandits and the collection of texts, not only because of the knowledge it gave to the West, but also because of the help it gave to the Indian intelligentsia of Calcutta to engraft their aspirations onto a Hindu tradition. [128] From whatever sources it was drawn, Hindu tradition was very extensively used in debates in Calcutta about contemporary issues, especially the great controversy about the rights and wrongs of *sati*, widow burning. [129]

European scholarship about India in its early phases was largely concerned with the remote past. But the servants of the new regime also had to learn how to communicate with the Company's new subjects. For the most part, this involved some Englishmen in the learning of Persian, which remained the language of diplomacy and administration. Those who became proficient in Persian acquired some acquaintance not only with the culture of learned Muslims in Bengal, but also with that of some Hindus. What was called 'Moors' (Hindustani) was learnt in order to communicate with up-country sepoys. Bengali was less frequently studied, but a handful of Europeans went beyond learning to speak to learning to write the language, and eventually to setting it up in print. The first attempt at the latter appeared in a grammar produced by Nathaniel Halhed in 1778. Christian missionaries had an obvious interest in communicating in written Bengali. William Carey, the first of the Baptists and a superb

[128] D. Kopf, *British Orientalism and the Bengal Renaissance* (Calcutta, 1969).
[129] Rammohun Roy's use of Hindu concepts is examined in D.H. Killingley, 'Vedanta and Modernity', *Indian Society and the Beginning of Modernization, 1830–50*, ed. C.H. Philips and D.M. Wainwright (1976), pp. 127–40.

linguist, began to prepare a Bengali version of the New Testament, which was printed in 1801 at the press which the Baptists had established at Serampore. A Bengali version of the Old Testament followed, and in 1818 the missionaries published the first magazine in Bengali, followed shortly afterwards by the first Bengali newspaper. In 1800 Carey was invited to teach languages in Calcutta at the new Fort William College, where young Company servants were being trained for their future duties. There he was able to employ pandits and to commission books as aids for teaching, including a number in Bengali. In 1817 the Calcutta School Book Society began to issue numerous text books in Bengali. The effect of printing on the development of Bengali prose was profound. But scholars' assessments of its importance appear to vary according to differing viewpoints. Some see the missionaries in particular as 'having raised the language from its debased condition of an unsettled dialect to the character of a regular and permanent form of speech';[130] some believe that printing helped to standardise an already established prose language.[131]

The Hindu elite in Calcutta had a strong tendency to form groups and associations. Such groupings may have originated on a caste basis, but by the early nineteenth century, in the view of the scholar who has studied them most closely, their membership was beginning to transcend caste and to bring together a variety of people under the leadership of a dominant individual.[132] Some associations were created for specific purposes, sometimes in cooperation with Europeans, as were the Calcutta School Book Society and the School Society. Others appear to have identified themselves with certain social and moral attitudes. By the 1820s major debates were taking place, if within a very restricted section of society, about social and religious reform. European secular ideas, some Christian concepts and varying versions of Hinduism were put into contention. In retrospect historians have been able to classify positions taken in this debate as being conservative or radical. Some appear to have resisted change. Others justified change in terms of a return to a purer Hindu tradition from which later deviations should be removed. Yet others accepted

[130] S.K. De, *Bengali Literature in the Nineteenth Century*, 2nd edn (Calcutta, 1962), p. 141.

[131] P. Bhattacharya, 'Rammohun Roy and Bengali Prose', *Rammohun Roy and the Process of Modernization*, ed. V.G. Joshi (Delhi, 1975), pp. 195–7.

[132] S.N. Mukherjee, 'Class, Caste and Politics in Calcutta', *Calcutta: Myths and History* (Calcutta, 1977).

some adaption to western ideals. A very few emerge as would-be re-formers who were prepared to apply outside criteria rigorously to what they condemned as decadent and outmoded custom. [133] The first of the reforming societies, the Atmiya Samaj, was formed in 1815. The most famous, with the longest life ahead of it, the Brahmo Samaj, was set up by Rammohun Roy in 1828. It seems to have embodied both his yearning for a simple theism, accessible to all, which had made Islam and Unitarian Christianity attractive to him, and his desire to remain within the Hindu fold, at least as interpreted through his expounding of what he called the *Vedanta*.

Any radicalism among the Calcutta intellectuals rarely extended to challenging foreign rule overtly. Most of the intellectuals owed their position in society to the British and many were still in their service. When tempted to make public pronouncements of a political nature, they invariably acknowledged the beneficence of the new regime in the past and anticipated further benefits, even if they ventured to make specific criticisms, sometimes quite pointed ones. Virtually no Hindu of any consequence was converted to Christianity, but public controversy with missionaries was still relatively muted. Yet, within limits, a more assertive note can be detected. In 1826 a petition was devised for the British House of Commons, protesting at the 'political degradation' being inflicted on the 'better classes of the natives of India' by their exclusion from 'employments of trust, dignity and emolument' and urging the Company to accept that 'a race of native gentry' now lived in Calcutta, who ought 'to rank in the eyes of government as an equal with merchants of Calcutta or the civil servants of the Honourable Company'. [134]

By the late 1820s the intellectual life of the Indian elite of Calcutta was entering a phase that was to attract widespread attention outside India and has become the subject of a huge historical literature. Throughout the world Rammohun Roy was winning the reputation of being the first 'modern' Indian, which, in spite of some scholarly reser-vations, has adhered to him ever since. The intellectual stature of other individuals, such as Radhakanta Deb and Dwarkanath Tagore, was also gaining recognition. The Brahmo Samaj was to have a very

[133] See A.F.S. Ahmed, *Social Ideas and Social Change in Bengal 1818–35*, (2nd edn, Calcutta, 1975).
[134] Cited in J.K. Majumdar (ed.) *Raja Rammohun Roy and the Progressive Movement in India* (Calcutta, 1941), pp. 363–5.

long life ahead of it and to gain a fame that excelled that of all the other Calcutta associations. With the arrival of Lord William Bentinck as Governor General in 1828 there seemed to be a western intellectual in authority who was willing to engage in dialogue with the more accessible intellectuals among his subjects. The case for and against the abolition of *sati* seemed to epitomise the issues in contention. Its abolition in 1829 has been depicted as the first triumph of 'modernity'. All this is often taken as evidence of the flowering of a Bengal Renaissance, which was eventually to be taken up in other parts of India.

Such interpretations of the intellectual ferment of the 1820s now have their critics. The isolation of the Calcutta intellectuals from their own society, their dependence on the British, and the inevitably insignificant role of an intelligentsia influenced by an alien culture in a deeply conservative society, are all stressed.[135] It is possible to admire the extraordinary vitality of the Calcutta groups' intellectual endeavours while also accepting that too much has probably been claimed for them. Their isolation, even within their own city, is obvious. The vast majority of the population of Calcutta was entirely unaffected by them. Beyond the city and its immediate neighbourhood they can have had virtually no influence.

Such intellectual influence as Europe had been able to exert on eastern India during this period was effectively confined to Calcutta. Elsewhere, Europeans were thin on the ground and their interests were almost entirely limited to trade or military or administrative duty. Beyond the environs of Calcutta and neighbouring districts in western Bengal, there was only a handful of missionary schools in places like Dhaka. At Puri in 1822 two missionaries began to wage what was to be a rather unequal contest with 'idolatry'.

If eastern India was still effectively insulated from intellectual contact with Europeans or with the Black Town of Calcutta, this does not necessarily imply either stagnation or decay. Major regional centres of patronage, such as Nadia or Khurda for Hindus or Dhaka or Murshidabad for Muslims, had been disrupted. But Sanskrit learning was still the concern of 'hundreds of scholars, most of whom remained obscure throughout their life, who tried to preserve and to sustain and

---

[135] See for instance, S. Sarkar, 'Rammohun Roy and the Break with the Past', *Rammohun Roy and Modernization*, ed. Joshi, pp. 46–68.

to transmit the ancient learning from one generation to th
New movements within Hinduism were emerging, su
Kartabhajars among the cultivators of Nadia.[137] Learned M
studied Persian and served as *kadi*s, while cults of saints and
proliferated. In 1830 a Christian missionary at Puri noted that the
great Jagannath festival was being attended by 'learned and respectable' people from Calcutta, who had been educated in 'the colleges
and institutions of European literature'.[138] Dismayed as he was by this
seeming perversity, he was in fact a witness to the strength of a culture
that could absorb the alien into the powerful flow of its own
traditions.

[136] S.K. Das, *Sahibs and Munshis* (Delhi, 1978), p. 20.
[137] J.H.E. Garrett, *Bengal District Gazetteers: Nadia* (Calcutta, 1910), pp. 47–50.
[138] Cited in K.M. Patra, *Orissa under the East India Company* (Delhi, 1971), p. 250.

# CHAPTER 6

# CONCLUSION

The intellectual ferment in early nineteenth-century Calcutta described at the end of Chapter 5 was one of the changes most obviously attributable to colonial rule. The 'new' intellectuals were of course rooted in a tradition that had often shown itself to be adaptable in the past, but they were living in an environment that was largely new and mastering new techniques and institutions, the printing press, the newspaper and the college, as well as absorbing new ideas.

Colonial rule also brought fundamental change in the way in which the provinces were ruled. The installing of European administrators only represents a part of the break with the past. The new regime, like the old, depended on the services of a huge number of its own subjects: soldiers, police, office staffs and a multitude of revenue payers. But the service was to be on new terms. The Company's authority was to be supreme, and those from whom the Nawabs had been unable to wrest power or to whom they had chosen to delegate it were to lose it now. *Naib*s, *faujdar*s, great chieftains in Bihar and the major Bengal *zamindar*s were all brought to heel. The new system of courts and police were evidence that the new rulers believed that their subjects should render obedience to them directly. The rulers' wishes in this respect might be very imperfectly fulfilled, but a state apparatus had been created which was much more powerful than any previous one.

A new city and a new structure of authority were direct consequences of British rule. Other changes owed much less to the new order. Eastern Bengal was prospering more than the west. The eastward thrust of the Ganges was largely responsible for this, but the rise of the Calcutta market, easily supplied by water from the east, contributed to the spread of new cultivation. Cultivation spread in other areas as well, notably in Bihar north of the Ganges and in the marshes and jungles of the Sundarbans, responding to an increase in population, for which climatic regularity rather than colonial rule must presumably take the main credit. Along the fringes of the three provinces the peoples of the hills and the plains were becoming more closely

180

integrated through trade and migration. This was a process that seems to have proceeded largely independently of the British efforts to bring about a greater degree of political integration.

Between changes in the political and administrative order, which the British had undoubtedly brought about, and long-term social and ecological developments, to which their contribution was small, lies a debatable area. The human actions which had most effect on the condition of the mass of the population were the demands for taxation imposed on them and the price they received for selling their labour or their crops. Both as tax collectors and as traders, the British had some capacity to cause improvement, deterioration or some sort of redistribution. There were, however, severe limitations on this capacity, as has frequently been stressed. The British did not try to reconstruct the system of revenue collection. At first hand their dealings were largely limited to a layer of *zamindar*s and other revenue payers. Here they undoubtedly accelerated certain processes of change: subdivision increased very markedly and there were major changes in the personnel, if not in the social composition, of the leading groups in rural society.[1] Below the level of revenue payers, British influence was much less. They were quite unable to limit the rent demands made on the ryots, but the extent to which they were responsible for increases or for a more marked differentiation between richer and poorer is very hard to determine.

The British as traders could do very little to change either the way production was organised or the techniques used in manufacturing or in agriculture. They could stimulate the demand for some of the products of artisans and for crops like mulberry, poppies, sugar cane and indigo, but with a very large part of what was produced in the provinces they had no direct concern. British trade presumably created some new employment opportunities and offered potentially more profitable uses for some land. On the other hand, evidence of wage fixing and price fixing in the Company's investment or in the cultivation of indigo is clear. While employment may have been created in some areas, by the end of the period the first wave of British imports was beginning to threaten the livelihood of the most vulnerable artisans, those who spun and wove the higher quality cotton cloth. It is by no means easy to strike an overall balance of the advantages and disadvantages brought by increased British commercial penetration.

[1] See pp. 144–9.

In making their own balances for the first sixty years of their rule, few informed British contemporaries believed that they had succeeded in bringing to eastern India a full measure of the 'improvement' which they believed they were now capable of spreading round the world. The debates about the renewal of the East India Company's charter in 1833 were in some ways an inquest on why so little had been achieved and on why India did not contribute more to Britain in the process. Less was being said in the 1820s about dislocation and decline, but very pessimistic assessments of the effects of early British rule had been current in the late eighteenth century and a note of disquiet was never wholly to be displaced by the robust self-confidence of the early nineteenth century. By the end of the nineteenth century the views of the doubters and the critics were generally elevated to what has become an enduring orthodoxy.

Expectations that British rule would bring about spectacular improvement were based on a quite unreal degree of self-confidence in the capacity of the new regime. But at least some of both the contemporary and the later pessimism seems to have been based on a different sort of unreality, an unreal view of the past, when peasant, merchant and *zamindar* were thought to have flourished under what some Englishmen depicted as 'the ancient constitution' of the Mughal Empire, and a golden Bengal had poured out her wealth to the world. In fact, the past that the British inherited largely shaped what they were able to achieve. The Bengal of the Nawabs yielded considerable sums in taxation and exported part of what its artisans made and of what its peasants grew. The new rulers could divert cash away from the coffers of the Nawab or from Delhi and could increase the flow of commodities to London and China. To achieve more would require major changes in the social and economic base on which both regimes rested. Under the Company's monopoly and even under free trade, at least up to 1828, inputs of skilled manpower, capital and technology had been inadequate to achieve such changes. Establishing an empire in eastern India proved to be relatively easy; introducing more than superficial change into eastern India was another matter.

# BIBLIOGRAPHICAL ESSAY

## GENERAL SURVEYS

Valuable studies which enable the history of parts of the region to be seen in the context of its ecology are: R. Mukerjee, *The Changing Face of Bengal: a Study in Riverine Economy* (Calcutta, 1938) and N. Ahmad, *An Economic Geography of East Pakistan* (2nd edn, 1968). Two volumes of a collective history of Bengal cover the period with which this book is concerned: J.N. Sarkar (ed.), *The History of Bengal: Muslim Period 1200–1757* (new edn, Patna, 1973) and N.K. Sinha (ed.), *The History of Bengal 1757–1905* (Calcutta, 1969). *The Cambridge Economic History of India*, vol. II *c. 1757–c. 1970*, ed. D. Kumar (2 vols., Cambridge, 1983) contains much material on eastern India during the period.

## EASTERN INDIA UNDER THE NAWABS 1740–65

Some of the major contemporary histories and chronicles have been translated from Persian into English. The most famous is a translation of the *Seir Mutaqherin* of Ghulam Husain Khan, which first appeared in Calcutta in three volumes in 1789 and has been much reprinted. Other translations are: *Riyaz us Salatin* (trans. A. Salam, Calcutta, 1904); *Tarikh-i-Bangala-i-Mahabatjangi* (trans. A. Subhan, Calcutta, 1982); and the selection in *Bengal Nawabs* (trans. J.N. Sarkar, Calcutta, 1952). K.K. Datta has written a study of Alivardi Khan, *Alivardi and his Times* (Calcutta, 1939). The political balance in Bengal is analysed in P. Calkins, 'The Formation of a Regionally Oriented Ruling Group in Bengal 1700–40', *Journal of Asian Studies*, XXIX (1970), 799–806. For Bengal's relations with the Mughal centre, see Z. Malik, *Reign of Muhammad Shah 1719–48* (Delhi, 1977). J.H. Little's study, *The House of Jagatseth* (new edn, Calcutta, 1967) reveals much about both politics and economics. Other economic studies tend to be focussed on the European companies. O. Prakash's work is especially valuable in this respect, notably his 'Bullion for Goods: International Trade in the Economy of Early Eighteenth-century Bengal', *Indian Economic and Social History Review*, XIII (1976), 159–87. K.N. Chaudhuri's *The Trading World of Asia and the English East India Company 1660–1760* (Cambridge, 1978) is essential for an understanding of the impact of world trade on the region. Suggestive ideas on the pre-colonial economy can be found in F. Perlin, 'Proto-Industrialisation and Pre-Colonial South Asia', *Past and Present*, XCVIII (1983), 30–95.

Documentary material on the capture of Calcutta and the battle of Plassey is presented in the three volumes of S.C. Hill, *Bengal in 1756–7* (1905). Much British material about the events between 1757 and 1765 was published at the time. H. Vansittart's three volumes entitled *A Narrative of the Transactions in Bengal* (1766) is the fullest version. A.M. Khan, *The Transition in Bengal 1756–1775: A Study of Saiyid Muhammad Reza Khan* (Cambridge, 1969) is the best modern account.

Pre-British Bihar is treated in S.G. Mishra, *History of Bihar 1740–72* (Delhi, 1970) and Orissa in B.C. Ray, *Orissa Under the Marathas 1751–1803* (Allahabad, 1960).

## EASTERN INDIA UNDER THE BRITISH 1765–1828

### Published primary material

Very large selections of the immense corpus of records kept by the East India Company were printed for the use of the British Parliament. The major collections ordered to be printed before 1801 are reproduced in *Reports from Committees of the House of Commons* (12 vols., 1803–6), vols. III–VI. After 1801, papers relating to India were extensively printed in virtually every year's *Parliamentary Papers*. Parts of the Company's records left in India have been published. In the early twentieth century some volumes of *Bengal District Records* (Calcutta, 1914–28) and proceedings of the Company's early Revenue authorities were issued by the Government of Bengal. In the 1950s the Government of West Bengal revived the *Bengal District Records* project. A number of volumes of *West Bengal District Records* (Calcutta, 1954–) have appeared. Volumes of *Bangladesh District Records* (Dhaka, 1981–) have now begun to appear. The National Archives of India is publishing its holdings of the correspondence between the Company's authorities in London and Calcutta as the *Fort William–India House Correspondence* (New Delhi, 1949–). Beginning with letters in 1748, this series has now reached 1800.

### The new regime

The standard accounts of the Company's organisation in Britain are L.S. Sutherland, *The East India Company in Eighteenth-century Politics* (Oxford, 1952) and C.H. Philips, *The East India Company 1784–1834* (2nd edn, Manchester, 1961). The Company's organisation in Bengal is outlined in B.B. Misra, *The Central Administration of the East India Company 1773–1834* (Manchester, 1959). Revenue administration is dealt with in the next section. The administration of justice can be studied in a number of books, such as B.B. Misra, *The Judicial Administration of the East India Company in Bengal 1765–82* (Delhi, 1961) and N. Majumdar, *Justice and Police in Bengal 1765–93: a Study of the Nizamat in Decline* (Calcutta, 1960). British perceptions of Indian law are interestingly explored in some of the essays in J.D.M. Derrett, *Religion, Law and the State in India* (1968) and in J. Fisch, *Cheap Lives and Dear Limbs: The British Transformation of the Bengal Criminal Law 1769–1817* (Wiesbaden, 1983). B. Chatterji, 'The Darogah and the Countryside: Imposition of Police Control in Bengal and its Impact (1793–1857)', *Indian Economic and Social History Review*, XVIII (1981), 19–42, is an attempt at examining judicial administration in action.

Biographies of the famous Governors, Clive and Warren Hastings, appear regularly. P. Spear, *Master of Bengal: Clive and his India* (1975) and K. Feiling, *Warren Hastings* (1954) are the most authoritative. Cornwallis's varied career, including the Indian Governorship, is described in F. and M. Wickwire, *Cornwallis* (2 vols., London and Chapel Hill, North Carolina, 1971, 1980). P.J. Marshall tries to analyse the 'unofficial' side of British activities in Bengal in *East Indian Fortunes: The British in Bengal in the Eighteenth Century* (Oxford, 1976) and the role of the essential partners in these activities in 'Masters and Banians in Eighteenth-century Calcutta', *The Age of Partnership: Europeans in Asia before Dominion*, ed. B.B. Kling and M.N. Pearson (Honolulu, 1979).

## Revenue and agriculture

Revenue administration was the central preoccupation of British rule in India until well into the twentieth century. Contemporary revenue records are abundant and there was a vigorous tradition of historical inquiry among later revenue officials. Consequently the history of revenue assessment and collection has had a dominant role in British–Indian historiography. The Company's early revenue experiments, the enacting of the Permanent Settlement and assessments of its consequences have provoked a huge literature. W.K. Firminger, *Historical Introduction to the Bengal Portion of the 'Fifth Report'* (Calcutta, 1917) is an example of earlier traditions of writing which is still highly informative. Authoritative recent studies of revenue administration are N.K. Sinha, *The Economic History of Bengal from Plassey to the Permanent Settlement* (2 vols., Calcutta, 1956, 1962), vol. II; S. Islam, *The Permanent Settlement in Bengal: A Study of its Operation 1790–1819* (Dacca, 1979); and J.R. McLane, 'Revenue Farming and the Zamindari System in Eighteenth-century Bengal', *Land Tenure and Peasant in South Asia*, ed. R.E. Frykenberg (New Delhi, 1977). The ideology of British revenue policy is explored in R. Guha, *A Rule of Property for Bengal* (Paris, 1963).

Older studies of revenue history tended to give little attention to the agriculture that made revenue-paying possible or to social structures below the level of *zamindar*. The work of two scholars, Professor B.B. Chaudhuri and the late Dr Ratna Ray, probes the social and economic basis of the revenue system. Professor Chaudhuri's conclusions for the period covered in this book can be found in his contributions to the *Cambridge Economic History of India*, vol. II, *c. 1757–c. 1970*, ed. D. Kumar (2 vols., Cambridge, 1983) pp. 86–177, 295–332 and in his articles 'Land Market in Eastern India 1793–1940', 2 parts, *Indian Economic and Social History Review*, XII (1975), 1–42, 132–68 'Agricultural Growth in Bengal and Bihar 1770–1860', *Bengal Past and Present*, XCV (1976), 290–340. Dr Ray wrote *Changes in Bengal Agrarian Society c. 1760–1850* (Delhi, 1979) together with 'Land Transfer and Social Change under the Permanent Settlement', *Indian Economic and Social History Review*, XI (1974) 1–45, 'The Bengal Zamindars: Local Magnates and the State before the Permanent Settlement', ibid., XII (1975), 263–92 and (with Rajat Ray) 'Zamindars and Jotedars: a Study of Rural Politics in Bengal', *Modern Asian Studies*, IX (1975),

81–102. C. Palit, *Tensions in Bengal Rural Society: Landlords, Planters and Colonial Rule 1830–60* (Calcutta, 1975) studies agrarian society at the end of the period.

Revenue administration in Bihar is discussed in R.M. Sinha, *Bihar Tenantry (1783–1833)* (Bombay, 1968) and in Orissa in B.S. Das, *Studies in the Economic History of Orissa* (Calcutta, 1978); K.M. Patra, *Orissa under the East India Company* (Delhi, 1971); and P.K. Pattanaik, *A Forgotten Chapter of Orissan History* (Calcutta, 1979).

## Trade, cash crops and manufactures

The abundance of the East India Company's records have heavily slanted studies towards the Company's operations and has tended to lead to assumptions that these constituted the economic life of the region. N.K. Sinha, *Economic History of Bengal from Plassey to the Permanent Settlement* (2 vols., Calcutta, 1956, 1962) vol. I is a survey. The production of cotton cloth is described in D.B. Mitra, *The Cotton Weavers of Bengal* (Calcutta, 1979) and H. Hossain, 'Alienation of Weavers ... 1750–1800', *Indian Economic and Social History Review*, XVI (1979), 323–45. S. Bhattacharya discusses a wide range of manufacturing in his contribution to *The Cambridge Economic History of India*, vol. II, *c. 1757–c. 1970*, ed. D. Kumar (2 vols., Cambridge, 1983) pp. 270–95. The abundant material on the opium monopoly and European cultivation of indigo is brought together by B.B. Chowdhury in *The Growth of Commercial Agriculture in Bengal 1757–1900* (Calcutta, 1964), vol. I. An interesting discussion of the trade in grain is to be found in D.L. Curley, 'Fair Grain Markets and Mughal Famine Policy in late Eighteenth-century Bengal', *Calcutta Historical Review*, II (1977), 1–26.

The increasing complexity of eastern India's overseas trade, especially its commercial relations with Britain, are analysed in H. Furber, *John Company at Work* (Cambridge, Massachusetts, 1951); A. Tripathi, *Trade and Finance in the Bengal Presidency 1793–1833* (2nd edn, Calcutta, 1979); and in the material presented by K.N. Chaudhuri in *The Economic Development of India under the East India Company 1814–58* (Cambridge, 1971). The growth of private British enterprise is charted in S.B. Singh, *European Agency Houses in Bengal* (Calcutta, 1966). N.K. Sinha, *The Economic History of Bengal 1793–1848* (Calcutta, 1970) discusses various aspects of the early nineteenth century.

## Social and intellectual life

Studies of what was new and associated with the British are very much more plentiful than studies of evolving 'traditions'. Missions and western education have attracted much attention: M.A. Laird, *Missionaries and Education in Bengal 1793–1837* (Oxford, 1972) and E.D. Potts, *Baptist Missionaries in India 1793–1837* (Cambridge, 1967) are authoritative recent contributions. The reverberations of western 'Orientalist' scholarship are the theme of D. Kopf, *British Orientalism and the Bengal Renaissance: the Dynamics of Indian Modernization 1773–*

*1835* (Calcutta, 1969) and the more reserved S.K. Das, *Sahibs and Munshis* (Calcutta, 1978). Calcutta, the setting for the cultural interchanges, is described in books which bring together important writings by P. Sinha, *Calcutta in Urban History* (Calcutta, 1978) and by S.N. Mukherjee, *Calcutta: Myths and History* (Calcutta, 1977). Overall assessments of social and cultural change, including consideration of the concept of a Renaissance have been very numerous indeed. Good modern discussions are: A.F.S. Ahmed, *Social Ideas and Social Change in Bengal 1818–35* (2nd edn, Calcutta, 1976) and A. Mukherjee, *Reform and Regeneration in Bengal 1774–1823* (Calcutta, 1968). A collection containing some cogent reservations about the Renaissance is edited by V.G. Joshi as *Rammohun Roy and the Process of Modernization* (Delhi, 1975).

Those who seek information about the 'traditional' culture of the region appear to be less well served. T. Raychaudhuri, *Bengal under Akbar and Jahangir* (2nd edn, Delhi, 1969) is a helpful starting point. B.G. Ray, *Religious Movements in Modern Bengal* (Santiniketan, 1965) describes some aspects of Hinduism. The culture of Orissa is illuminated by A. Eschmann, H. Kulke and G.C. Tripathi, *The Cult of Jagannath and the Regional Tradition of Orissa* (Delhi, 1978). Temples are described by D. McCutchion, *Late Medieval Temples of Bengal* (Calcutta, 1970) and H. Sanyal, 'Temple-Building in Bengal from the Fifteenth to the Nineteenth Century', *Perspectives in Social Sciences* (Calcutta, 1977–), I, ed. B. De (1977), pp. 120–77. A.R. Mallick, *British Policy and the Muslims of Bengal* (Dacca, 1961) is an outline survey. Much new material is presented in A. Roy, *The Islamic Syncretistic Tradition in Bengal* (Princeton, 1983).

There are few studies concerning towns other than Calcutta, but there is valuable information in G. Bhadra, 'Social Groups and Relations in the Town of Murshidabad 1765–93', *Indian Historical Review*, II (1975–6), 312–38 and in A. Karim, *Dacca the Mughal Capital* (Dacca, 1964). 'Traditional' education was surveyed in the 1830s by William Adam, whose *Reports on the State of Education in Bengal* are available in a modern edition, ed. A. Basu (Calcutta, 1941). A very detailed study of an individual who moved between 'old' and 'new' has been provided by S.C. Nandy, *The Life and Times of Cantoo Baboo* (2 vols., Calcutta, 1978, 1981).

*Local studies*

A superb series of local surveys was undertaken by a most gifted contemporary observer, Francis Buchanan (later Buchanan-Hamilton). From 1807 to 1814 Buchanan moved across northern Bengal and through parts of Bihar. He was evidently a true polymath who wrote exhaustively on things physical and human. His reports are in manuscript form in the India Office Library. Publications varying in fullness and accuracy have been produced from time to time. The most scholarly versions are those for some districts in Bihar, published in 1925. The most accessible edition, although far from complete, was that made by M. Martin, *History, Antiquities, Topography and Statistics of Eastern India* (3 vols., 1838). A relatively short manuscript account of a journey into east Bengal by Buchanan is in the British Library, Add. MS 19286. Another very interesting contemporary account is that of the village of Sibpur, across the Hooghly from Calcutta, by Robert Kyd (India Office Library, MS Eur. F.95).

Other local studies that remain very valuable include J. Taylor, *A Sketch of the Topography and Statistics of Dacca* (Calcutta, 1840) and J. Westland, *A Report on the District of Jessore: its Antiquities, its History and its Commerce* (2nd edn, Calcutta, 1874). In the late nineteenth and early twentieth centuries British officials produced *District Gazetteers,* containing much historical information. In both India and Bangladesh *District Gazetteers* are being revised. Recent historical research is also focussing on the district level. Two interesting studies are: K.M. Moshin, *A Bengal District in Transition: Murshidabad 1765–93* (Dacca, 1973), and R.K. Gupta, *The Economic Life of a Bengal District: Birbhum 1770–1856* (Burdwan, 1984).

# INDEX

189

# THE NEW CAMBRIDGE HISTORY OF INDIA